INTERNATIONAL COURTS AND TRIBUNALS SERIES

General Editors: RUTH MACKENZIE, CESARE P.R. ROMANO, AND PHILIPPE SANDS

Selecting International Judges: Principle, Process, and Politics

INTERNATIONAL COURTS AND TRIBUNALS SERIES

A distinctive feature of modern international society is the increase in the number of international judicial bodies and dispute settlement and implementation control bodies; in their case loads; and in the range and importance of the issues that they are called upon to address. These factors reflect a new state in the delivery of international justice. The International Courts and Tribunals series has been established to encourage the publication of independent and scholarly works which address, in critical and analytical fashion, the legal and policy aspects of the functioning of international courts and tribunals, including the institutional, substantive, and procedural aspects.

Selecting International Judges: Principle, Process, and Politics

RUTH MACKENZIE, KATE MALLESON,
PENNY MARTIN, AND
PHILIPPE SANDS

OXFORD
UNIVERSITY PRESS

OXFORD
UNIVERSITY PRESS

Great Clarendon Street, Oxford, OX2 6DP,
United Kingdom

Oxford University Press is a department of the University of Oxford.
It furthers the University's objective of excellence in research, scholarship,
and education by publishing worldwide. Oxford is a registered trade mark of
Oxford University Press in the UK and in certain other countries

First published 2010

Published in the United States of America by Oxford University Press
198 Madison Avenue, New York, NY 10016, United States of America

British Library Cataloguing in Publication Data
Data available

ISBN 978–0–19–958056–9

Cover illustration: ©UN Photo/Evan Schneider

Contents

Foreword

I regard it as being extraordinary that so little attention has been given to the issues that arise from the manner in which the judges of international courts and tribunals are appointed. The task is obviously more complex and difficult than appointing judges to domestic courts.

Just as the state of the rule of law is of critical importance to the wellbeing of a nation, so in the world today is the health of the international rule of law critical to the wellbeing of the global society in which we live. Both nationally and internationally the quality of the rule of law is in turn dependent upon the quality of the judiciary who have the responsibility of upholding the rule of law. Yet very little attention has been given by academics or others as to how international judges are nominated and appointed, though this obviously would have an immense influence on the quality of the decisions of the courts and tribunals to which they are appointed.

Before my retirement as Lord Chief Justice, I had been intimately involved with the appointment system in England and Wales for over 10 years and had been a party to the negotiations which resulted in the new appointment system for that jurisdiction which was enacted in the Constitutional Reform Act of 2005. This experience gave me a shrewd idea of how difficult it must be to devise a system for appointments to an international court. But I have had no direct experience of a process of that nature. I was, however, aware that the process could be highly political and even demeaning to those applying for an appointment. Wanting to learn more about the process, I was naturally delighted when Professor Philippe Sands, QC and Professor Kate Malleson approached me to chair an Advisory Committee they were setting up in conjunction with the research project into the 'Process and Legitimacy in the Nomination, Election and Appointment of International Judges'. The project is now complete and has resulted in the work to which this Foreword relates. I have no doubt the project has produced results which are of very great value and I congratulate the Arts and Humanities Research Council on having the insight to recognize that the project deserved the funding which they provided, without which the project could not have gone ahead.

While not ignoring the general picture, Professor Malleson and Professor Sands, with Ruth Mackenzie and Penny Martin, have wisely concentrated on two of the most significant international courts, the International Court of Justice (ICJ) and the International Criminal Court (ICC). This enabled the research to provide a detailed account of the manner in which appointments are made to what are probably the two most important international courts. The examination of the process in relation to these two courts demonstrates that the process of nomination and appointment leaves ample scope for reform and improvement. Even where the judge appointed is of the required calibre, the process by which the appointment takes place can undermine the credibility of the appointment and the authority and integrity of the tribunal.

What is true of the ICJ and ICC is almost certainly true of most, if not all, other international judicial bodies. Wisely, this highly authoritative team have not sought to produce a blueprint as to the nature of the reforms which are needed. They acknowledge that this is not a situation where one size fits all. However, what they have done is to provide the information which is needed to enable the process of reform to take place. Their description of this process makes apparent shortcomings which can only be described as obvious.

Attention has to be given to the problems that inevitably occur because of the need to ensure adequate representation of the widely different interests that properly have to be reflected in the judiciary appointed to an international court. Merit alone cannot be the sole criteria for appointment. Allowances have to be made for the widely different character of the countries that are subject to the jurisdiction of the international courts. However, in making those allowances a proper balance must be maintained between the need to accommodate the different characteristics of the countries subject to the jurisdiction and the need to create an appointment process and a judiciary which will command respect among those that are subject to the jurisdiction of the international court. The legitimacy of the court will be damaged or even destroyed if it is perceived that the court's membership is largely the product of political bargaining between the states which are subject to the jurisdiction of the court.

I hope their report will therefore be a catalyst for reform and that it will provide a base for further research. The report, together with its helpful appendices needs to be carefully considered by anyone involved or interested in justice at the international level. I very much hope that the past neglect of the subject will be alleviated by the report's clear account of the situation. The team will earn the gratitude of all those who read its report. It is non-doctrinaire, practical and realistic. It is all the more powerful because of its moderation.

The Rt Hon the Lord Woolf

17 December 2009

Series Editor's Preface

In contrast to the extensive literature about national judicial selection processes, particularly in North America and Europe, the selection and nomination of international judges has received minimal attention beyond the narrow group of legal scholars, officials, and judges who are directly involved in those processes. This is surprising, given the growing role that international courts play in international law and relations, and considering the impact of international decisions on domestic legal practice. The fact is that our international judiciary remains the least studied or understood branch of international governance.[1]

This book fills an important gap in the literature, taking the reader to the very heart of the decision-making processes, at all stages. Insiders will find much material that is familiar and some which is controversial. Outsiders will find it instructive, illuminating and often surprising. The preparation of this book has been a massive undertaking, involving large numbers of people over several years. Its findings are based on more than 100 interviews with a wide range of players and key actors in the system. It is their voice, more than that of the authors, that comes through.

This rich and sensitive material is treated in a sober and balanced way. To gain depth, the authors have privileged a narrow focus, addressing two major international courts: the International Court of Justice (ICJ) and the International Criminal Court (ICC). Yet, the research has not unearthed the obvious. While on a number of issues there is a degree of consensus amongst those interviewed, in other areas, there are sharp divergences, both in terms of factual understandings about the way judicial selection processes currently work and the manner in which they ought to work. Such divergences indicate a troubling lack of transparency and the absence of common or minimum standards in the process. This is the crux of the matter.

The authors are careful not to overstate the dangers of political influences on the international judicial selection process. Indeed, few are more overtly political than the process of nomination of the judges of the US Supreme Court, and yet, no one can dispute that it has produced many excellent justices. It is not the presence of politics per se in the international judicial process that is a cause of concern. Rather, it is the endemic and almost total absence of public scrutiny or political accountability that raises alarm bells. The combination of politics and lack of public scrutiny is a toxic mix that threatens the long-term stability,

[1] For a previous study in this series of the international judiciary, see D. Terris, C.P.R. Romano, and L. Swigart, *The International Judge: An Introduction to the Men and Women who Decide the World's Cases*, International Courts and Tribunals Series (Oxford University Press, 2007) in the US University Press of New England, 2007.

effectiveness, and credibility of international courts. It dims prospects for selecting the very best judges for the international courts. That in turn threatens to undermine legitimacy.

Normatively, the authors are careful not to advocate a one-size-fits-all approach to judicial selection. There is considerable scope for a diversity of models at the international level as much as there is between national systems or, as in the case of the US, within a nation itself. The systems for selecting judges of the ICJ and ICC are the product of the particular time and context in which the two courts were created. Also, while certain international courts, like the ICJ, have proven impervious to significant reform, it is the newest courts where changes are most likely. Far from advocating unlikely radical reform, the authors seek greater transparency as a means to tempering overt or crude politicization of the process. They lament the fact that the election systems for two key international courts, the ICJ and ICC, have become part of the broader landscape of international elections, without due regard to the special, judicial nature of the vacancies they need to fill.

The fact that judicial elections are part of the wider international governance structure should not mean that selection, nomination and election processes have to be shrouded in mystery, or applied in a way that results in talented outsiders having no realistic prospect of being nominated. If international courts are to become permanent and meaningful fixtures of the international governance structure, international judges must be able to command widespread respect and authority, including before their peers in national courts. Getting the selection process right should be a central objective of international decision-making.

Cesare P.R. Romano

January 2010,
Santa Monica, CA

Preface and Acknowledgements

This book records the findings of a three-year project entitled 'Process and Legitimacy in the Nomination, Election and Appointment of International Judges', funded by the Arts and Humanities Research Council, to whom we express our gratitude for their support. The aim of the project was to identify the processes that states use to nominate and elect international judges, and the formal criteria and other considerations that play a role in the nomination and election process. Our aims in producing this book are modest—we seek to set out the formal rules for the appointment of judges to the International Court of Justice and the International Criminal Court and to explore how those rules are actually applied in practice, both at national and international levels. Although some anecdotal material has been available, the lack of properly researched and published material on national processes for the nomination of candidates to international judicial office justified the effort to focus our research on this important issue. To this end, we undertook a series of 'case studies' through which we sought to examine in depth the nomination process in nine countries. Most of the information that was of interest to us was not on public record, and thus our research has been based on more than one hundred interviews, conducted over an eighteen-month period between 2006 and 2008.

Many individuals have assisted us in the course of our research. Our thanks go foremost to Lord Woolf who chaired the advisory committee that was established at the outset of the project, and to the members of the advisory committee, including Florentino Feliciano, Gilbert Guillaume, Kamal Hossain, Djamchid Momtaz, Beverley McLachlin, Sir Shridath Surendranath Ramphal, P. S. Rao, Peter Russell, Tuiloma Neroni Slade, William Taft IV, Eduardo Valencia-Ospina, and Elizabeth Wilmshurst. The committee members acted in their personal capacity. We sought advice from them on various aspects of our work at the beginning of the project and several members gave us further input as the work progressed. We are deeply indebted to them for their advice, but stress that the material in this book is solely the responsibility of the authors.

As part of the project, in September 2008, we co-organized a seminar held at New York University to present and discuss our interim findings. We are extremely grateful to the Institute for International Law and Justice at NYU, particularly to Benedict Kingsbury and Richard Stewart, for collaborating in and hosting this seminar, and to all the seminar participants who gave us much food for thought as we sought to finalize our work.

A number of students on the UCL LL.M and related programmes provided invaluable research assistance over the course of the project and we thank Sa'adetu Yahaya, Ijeamaka Elizabeth Nnaji, Sarah Steele, Osvaldo Andres Urrutia Silva,

Gauthier Vannieuwenhuyse, Audrey Bourlon, Fiaz Hussain, Sabina Appelt, Michael Freitas Mohallem, Pasquale Annicchino, and Remi Reichold. We are also grateful to Jo Braithwaite who assisted with the analysis of the interview materials. The project could not have been completed without Kate Barber, administrator of the Centre for International Courts and Tribunals (CICT) until January 2009, who provided a huge amount of assistance throughout the design and implementation of the project and her successor, Kimberlee Moran, who has done a great job in helping us to finalize the text. We also express our gratitude to Jane Robertson, who copy-edited the lengthy and sometimes tangled text that we originally made available to her.

Thanks are due, as always, to our colleagues in the Project on International Courts and Tribunals, especially Thordis Ingadottir, Cesare Romano, and Yuval Shany for their support for this and other work. At Oxford University Press, John Louth and Merel Alstein have been wonderfully supportive.

Given that we have sought to avoid identifying individuals for the most part in this book, we must of necessity refrain from mentioning by name many of those who have assisted most in our research. Numerous individuals—judges, candidates, legal advisers, diplomats, academics, civil servants—gave us advice and assistance as we sought to identify and contact potential interviewees around the globe. Without them this book would not have been written. Finally, of course, we must thank the many individuals who agreed to take part in interviews, for giving us their time and insight, and for entrusting us with the responsibility of drawing our own conclusions from their comments.

Ruth Mackenzie
Kate Malleson
Penny Martin
Philippe Sands

London
1 December 2009

List of Abbreviations

AAA	American Arbitration Association
ABA	American Bar Association
ACHPR	African Court on Human and Peoples' Rights
ACJHR	African Court of Justice and Human Rights
ASIL	American Society of International Law
ASP	Assembly of States Parties (International Criminal Court)
AU	African Union
CANZ	Canada, Australia and New Zealand
CARICOM	Caribbean Community
CCJ	Caribbean Court of Justice
CFI	Court of First Instance (European Union)
CICC	Coalition for the International Criminal Court
CST	Civil Service Tribunal (European Union)
DSB	Dispute Settlement Body (World Trade Organization)
EC	European Community
ECHR	European Convention on Human Rights
ECJ	European Court of Justice
ECtHR	European Court of Human Rights
EU	European Union
GA	General Assembly (United Nations)
GRULAC	Group of Latin American and Caribbean States
IACHR	Inter-American Court on Human Rights
IAWJ	International Association of Women Judges
ICC	International Criminal Court
ICJ	International Court of Justice
ICTR	International Criminal Tribunal for Rwanda
ICTY	International Criminal Tribunal for the former Yugoslavia
ILA	International Law Association
ILC	International Law Commission
ITLOS	International Tribunal for the Law of the Sea
NG	National Group
NGO	Non-governmental Organization
P5	Permanent Members of the UN Security Council
PCA	Permanent Court of Arbitration
PCIJ	Permanent Court of International Justice
RJLSC	Regional Judicial and Legal Services Commission (Caribbean Court of Justice)
TRIPS	Agreement on Trade-Related Aspects of Intellectual Property Rights

UN	United Nations
UNAT	United Nations Appeals Tribunal
UNCLOS	United Nations Convention on the Law of the Sea
UNDT	United Nations Dispute Tribunal
UNITAR	United Nations Institute for Training and Research
WEOG	Group of Western European and other States
WIGJ	Women's Initiatives for Gender Justice
WTO	World Trade Organization
WTO AB	World Trade Organization Appellate Body

Introduction

The international judiciary is probably the least well-known branch of international governance. International courts and tribunals are required to decide upon an increasingly wide range of issues of global importance—from the environment to human rights, from trade and other economic obligations to national border disputes—yet public knowledge of these judicial decision-makers is limited. Even less familiar is the process by which international judges are appointed.[1] This lack of public awareness of international judicial selection processes is mirrored by an almost complete absence of academic research on the subject. In contrast to the extensive literature in many national jurisdictions, particularly in North America and Europe, the international selection and appointment processes have attracted almost no attention outside a narrow circle of lawyers, officials and judges who are directly involved,[2] raising profound issues as to the legitimacy and likely effectiveness of the international courts.

Given the expansion in the number and role of the international courts and tribunals, this widespread lack of knowledge should be of concern to anyone interested in the future of international law and rules-based global dispute resolution. Without meaningful public awareness of, and involvement in, the framing and assessment of the qualities of the men and women who sit on these courts, doubts are more likely to arise as to whether we are selecting the best judges for this increasingly important work. Moreover, even if the judges selected are unimpeachable in terms of their personal qualities, the legitimacy of the international courts is inevitably undermined if there is no minimum level of public knowledge of the process of selection. The importance of the relationship between the processes of judicial selection and the success of the international courts has been highlighted by the human rights group, Interights:

> The process for appointment of judges to these judicial bodies ensuring judicial independence and diverse representation by candidates of the highest merit will be instrumental in determining the future success and legitimacy of these important institutions.[3]

[1] D. Terris, C. P. R. Romano, and L. Swigart, *The International Judge: An Introduction to the Men and Women Who Decide the World's Cases*, International Courts and Tribunals Series (Oxford: Oxford University Press, 2007).

[2] M. Wood, 'The Selection of Candidates for International Judicial Office: Recent Practice' in T. M. Ndiaye and R. Wolfrum (eds), *Law of the Sea, Environmental Law and Settlement of Disputes: Liber Amicorum Judge Thomas A. Mensah* (The Hague: Martinus Nijhoff Publishers, 2007) 358; D. Terris, C. P. R. Romano, and L. Swigart, *The International Judge: An Introduction to the Men and Women Who Decide the World's Cases*, op. cit.

[3] J. Limbach et al, *Judicial Independence: Law and Practice of Appointments to the European Court of Human Rights* (London: INTERIGHTS, May 2003) 7.

The process by which judges are chosen for the international courts generally comprises two distinct phases: (1) the nomination of candidates by states (or in the case of the International Court of Justice, by a state's Permanent Court of Arbitration national group); and (2) the election of judges by intergovernmental political bodies from amongst the candidates nominated. Governing instruments of international courts typically establish criteria to be fulfilled by individual judges, as well as criteria regarding the composition of the bench as a whole (eg geographic representation). However, it is not clear how these criteria are monitored or applied in practice, at either the nomination or election stage. While some mechanisms to review international judicial nominations against objective criteria have been envisaged (such as the Advisory Committee provided for in the Rome Statute of the International Criminal Court), they have rarely been used in practice. Similarly, the use of newer judicial selection models, such as appointments commissions, is rare in the context of international courts, although such a development has occurred in relation to the Caribbean Court of Justice.

The limited, largely anecdotal evidence that exists about the way judges are appointed to international courts rarely raises serious concerns about the integrity and ability of the judges who are appointed. What is less clear is whether able and independent judges have been appointed because of, or in spite of, the selection processes through which the appointments take place. Research by Erik Voeten on the decision-making of national governments in relation to international judicial appointments has identified a range of motivations for the selection of different candidates: 'Governments are neither simply picking the best qualified candidate nor are they singularly obsessed with limiting sovereignty costs, although both motivations are sometimes important.'[4] Voeten's research highlights the importance of other factors, such as the desire on the part of states to signal a credible commitment to the international legal order and the role of political patronage. Similarly, Karen J. Alter's work in the 1990s on the European Court of Justice found that national nominations to the Court were governed by a variety of political considerations 'including party affiliation and political connections'.[5] It is this political element in the system which has more recently attracted the attention of judges, practitioners and academics who are familiar with the international selection processes. A key criticism concerns the potentially distorting effects that political influence can have on the goal of selecting meritorious and independent candidates. In 2007, for example, Senator Miriam Defensor Santiago, the candidate of the Philippines for the International Court of Justice, gave this assessment of the relative importance of merit and politics in the election process to the court:

> I will be representing not myself but a developing country. Generally, in this international voting, it is the candidates of developed countries who are certain of victory.

[4] E. Voeten, 'The Politics of International Judicial Appointments', *Chicago Journal of International Law* 9(2) (Winter 2009) 389.

[5] K. Alter, 'Who are the "Masters of the Treaty"?: European Governments and the European Court of Justice' *International Organization* 52(1) (1998) 121.

A candidate of a developing country must work twice as hard because the decision is not made on the individual's merits and qualifications but on the diplomatic clout of the country concerned.[6]

Similar claims have been made in relation to other courts. Regarding the European Court of Human Rights, for example, it has been noted that nominations are often a reward for political loyalty rather than on merit.[7] Similarly, a former UK Law Lord, Lord Hoffmann, has argued that the Court lacks 'constitutional legitimacy' as a result of its 'totally opaque' judicial appointments process.[8] More generally, *The Economist* newspaper questioned in 2008 whether the selection processes to the international courts led to the appointment of 'government hacks and lickspittles, with little or no judicial experience'.[9] To date, however, there has been a lack of reliable data against which to assess the validity of such claims.

Against this background, the primary aim of this work is to produce a systematic empirical picture of the workings of the judicial appointments processes in the international courts. The research focuses on nomination and election practices across different countries for two of the leading international courts: the International Court of Justice (ICJ) and the International Criminal Court (ICC). Using survey data, interviews and case studies,[10] we have sought to identify the key features of the selection processes of these two courts.[11] Given the range and varieties of international courts and selection processes, this study was faced with a choice between prioritizing breadth or depth of analysis, either by opting to produce a broad overview of the whole panoply of courts and selection processes or a detailed examination focusing on a limited number of examples. In an attempt to reconcile these conflicting aims, we have focused our attention on two courts while drawing on comparative data about other courts, so as to place the practice in these courts in a wider context.

The ICC and ICJ were selected as our primary data sources because of their global significance and both courts fall broadly within the same judicial selection model: candidates are nominated through a national process and put

[6] Senate of the Philippines, 14th Congress, 'Press Release: July 30, 2007: Transcript of interview with Senator Miriam Defensor Santiago', available at: <http://www.senate.gov.ph/press_release/2007/0730_santiago1.asp> (accessed 28 October 2008).

[7] J. Limbach et al, *Judicial Independence: Law and Practice of Appointments to the European Court of Human Rights*, op. cit., 9.

[8] Lord Hoffmann, 'The Universality of Human Rights', Judicial Studies Board Annual Lecture, 19 March 2009, available at: <http://www.jsboard.co.uk/downloads/Hoffmann_2009_JSB_Annual_Lecture_Universality_of_Human_Rights.doc> 22–3 (accessed 20 March 2009).

[9] 'Wanted: Better judgment, fewer crowd-pleasers and lickspittles' *The Economist* 22 November 2008, 78–9.

[10] In addition to a questionnaire-based survey, more than one hundred interviews were conducted for the study. Some of these were with individuals with an overview of the way in which the election process worked for one or more international courts, as well as some specialist knowledge of a particular state and/or region: diplomats, judges and candidates; other interviews focused much more closely on the nomination of candidates at the domestic level in nine states: here, interviews were conducted with a wide range of stakeholders and involved individuals within and outside government.

[11] See Appendix 1 for more details of the research methodology of the project.

forward to be elected by an intergovernmental body. Given their broad, potentially global, membership, it is not possible for each state party to have its own 'national' judge on either court. In many other respects, however, the two courts differ, and these differences shed light on some important tensions and conflicting goals. The ICJ, as the 'principal judicial organ of the United Nations', reflects the traditional selection process which is short on formal rules, leaving many of the practices to be determined by states acting in political fora. In contrast, the newer ICC has a more complex and prescriptive selection process which aims to influence the balance of the court in terms of factors such as gender, as well as ensuring a particular range of legal expertise. In this work, we seek to discover to what extent the selection processes for these courts differ in practice.

The second, more tentative aim of the research is to assess, in the light of the empirical findings, what changes, if any, might be appropriate for the judicial selection processes of international courts both in the short term and the long term. The analysis is exploratory and provisional at this stage but we hope that our findings will provide the groundwork for others to undertake more detailed work (both academic and policy-orientated). This could lead to the development of 'best practices' in international judicial selection, and facilitate assessments as to whether some models are more likely than others to weed out weaker candidates and ensure that only the most well-qualified, independent and talented judges are appointed.

Our hope that this work will contribute to a developing interest in the field is bolstered by evidence of a growing willingness of the international courts to scrutinize their own selection processes. The Parliamentary Assembly of the Council of Europe, for example, has recently completed an extensive review of the rules and practices for the selection of judges to the European Court of Human Rights and, as a result, has proposed a number of reforms.[12] In more recently created tribunals such as the Caribbean Court of Justice, the European Union Civil Service Tribunal, and the African Court of Human and Peoples' Rights, new appointments processes have been created or stronger guidance on nomination of candidates given after considerable debate about the different models and their likely effects. These recently created courts and their judicial appointments processes are being watched with interest by more established courts, as well as by academics, policy-makers and a variety of stakeholders. In a similar way, as proposals for new courts arise in the future, choices between different models and selection practices are most likely to be made in the light of the experience of existing international courts.

This is a dynamic and evolving area, and one of intellectual and practical significance which is likely to attract increasing attention in the near future. It is not obvious which appointment models will become more popular given that two

[12] Committee on Legal Affairs and Human Rights, *Nomination of candidates and election of judges to the European Court of Human Rights,* 3 September 2008 AS/Jur, 34 (2008).

apparently contradictory trends can be identified. On the one hand, there is evidence from some selection processes of greater political involvement, with more emphasis on backroom 'deal-making' between states.[13] On the other hand, there are moves towards greater professionalization, with the introduction of more rule-based, open and formalized practices.

In seeking to understand current judicial selection processes and to identify the underlying trends at international level, we do not presume that any particular model of judicial selection is inherently superior or preferable. Instead, the work is based on the assumption that there is scope for a diversity of models at the international level (as there is in the national courts), in the light of the history, role and function of each particular judicial body. Just as the US judicial appointments process has a much higher degree of political involvement, both at state and federal level, than the continental civil law systems, so neither model can be said to be inherently superior to the other as each is the product of its own legal, political, and historical context. It has long been recognized when comparing judicial selection at national level that there is no one-size-fits-all process.[14] Moreover, even when looking at the selection processes that operate within any one jurisdiction, the differences between types and tiers of courts make generalizations difficult. What is appropriate, for example, in selecting judges for the criminal courts, both in terms of appointments process and selection criteria, may be quite different for the commercial courts. Similarly, the right balance between the requirements of independence and accountability in the selection processes of constitutional court or supreme court judges is likely to be very different from that of trial judges or magistrates.

International courts and tribunals are diverse in their mandates and in their judicial selection processes. This presents a methodological problem for a study of this kind, which seeks to paint an empirical picture from which some general conclusions might be drawn. In terms of jurisdiction and functions, international courts cover as wide a spectrum as national courts: they may be global or regional, general or specific, first instance, appellate or hybrid. Their members may require highly specialized skills in a narrow area of the law, or a broad legal knowledge and general 'court-craft' experience. The circumstances of each particular court are also different: some are long established with a settled jurisprudence; others are new and relatively fragile, and have yet to develop a substantial caseload or gain public recognition.

Just as we do not presume that there is an ideal model for a judicial appointments process, we do not subscribe to any particular vision of what constitutes a 'good international judge', beyond the claim that those appointed should be

[13] M. Wood, 'The Selection of Candidates for International Judicial Office: Recent Practice' in T. M. Ndiaye and R. Wolfrum (eds), *Law of the Sea, Environmental Law and Settlement of Disputes*, op. cit., 357.

[14] K. Malleson and P. H. Russell (eds), *Appointing Judges in an Age of Judicial Power: Critical Perspectives from Around the World* (Toronto: University of Toronto Press, 2006).

independent and highly qualified within the terms laid down for each court. Reasonable people will differ as to whether they believe judges in the international courts should adopt a minimalist view of their role as dispute resolvers, or a maximalist view of their role in pushing forward the boundaries of law and policy. These differences mirror long and intense debates over the proper function of judges in the national courts, particularly in North America and Europe. These debates are more recent in relation to the international courts, though no less contested, as is illustrated by the sharp division between Eric Posner and John Yoo, on the one hand, and Laurence Helfer and Anne-Marie Slaughter, on the other, over the appropriate role of judicial independence in the international courts.[15] Some have characterized this as being a divergence of opinion between two ideal types of judges—those who act as 'trustees' and those who see themselves as 'agents'.[16] In relation to the international judicial selection process, these alternative positions are relevant to many key questions, including whether and to what extent states should have a free hand in nominating their candidates, the appropriate selection criteria for international judges, and whether the judicial election process should be insulated from the election processes for other political appointments in intergovernmental organizations. These and other issues are often informed by views as to the correct balance between state and supranational sovereignty. These views are, in turn, underpinned by familiar, if sometimes unarticulated, normative assumptions about the appropriate boundaries of the power of judges versus politicians.

Whether or not an expansionist role for the international courts is a good or a bad thing is not the subject of this work. We assume only that if the trend towards a greater role for the courts continues—as seems likely—it is vital that these international judicial decision-makers should be appropriately qualified and independent-minded individuals who are selected through rigorous, open, and legitimate processes. It is equally important that they should command widespread international respect and authority, including before national courts. The processes of nomination and election lie at the heart of such authority.

[15] E. A. Posner and J. C. Yoo, 'Judicial Independence in International Tribunals' *California Law Review* 93(1) (2005) 1–74; L. R. Helfer and A-M. Slaughter, 'Why States Create International Tribunals: A Response to Professors Posner and Yoo' *California Law Review* 93(3) (2005) 899–956; E. A. Posner and J. C. Yoo, 'Reply to Helfer and Slaughter' *California Law Review* 93(3) (2005) 957–74.

[16] See E. Voeten, 'The Politics of International Judicial Appointments', op. cit., and K. Alter, 'Agents or Trustees? International Courts in their Political Context' *European Journal of International Relations* 14(1) (2008) 33–63.

1

The International Court of Justice and the International Criminal Court in Historical Context

A. Introduction

The design and operation of international judicial selection processes over the last century have taken place in the context of the ad hoc emergence of international courts and tribunals. There are no principles or rules of general application governing the selection of judges at international level and there has been no clear elaboration of any one particular model of judicial selection. Different processes have developed for each court, arising from the particular circumstances in which it was established, and states have developed a heterogeneous set of models borrowed and adapted from one court to another. This chapter traces the key stages in the emergence of the various international judicial selection processes of the International Court of Justice (ICJ) and the International Criminal Court (ICC).

A critical step in the early twentieth century was the move from a system of ad hoc arbitral tribunals, where states directly appointed adjudicators for specific disputes, to the establishment of the first permanent international dispute settlement bodies. This development represented a fundamental change in the nature of international adjudication and led gradually to the acceptance of the appointment of non-national judges, selected by international intergovernmental bodies, based on criteria related to individual qualities and regional (or other) criteria of representation. A key distinction arose (which still affects judicial selection processes today) between 'full representation' courts, where each state has a judge of its nationality on the court permanently, and 'selective representation' courts, where there are fewer seats than the number of states that are parties to the court's statute.[1] In the latter type of court, a choice has to be made between candidates from different states, thus giving rise to a greater degree of competition in which political influences, amongst other factors, can and do hold sway.

[1] E. Voeten, 'The Politics of International Judicial Appointments', *Chicago Journal of International Law* 9(2) (Winter 2009) 401–402.

In 'full representation courts', such as the European Court of Justice (ECJ), states are guided by the statute of the court as to the criteria that a judge has to meet, but in general terms there is very little procedural guidance and still less external supervision of the choice of judge. However, this is not always the case: the selection process of the European Court of Human Rights (ECtHR), for example, now requires that states must select three candidates who are then 'vetted' by the Parliamentary Assembly of the Council of Europe, which has the power to reject lists of contenders on particular grounds and change the ranking of the candidates selected by the states. The Parliamentary Assembly then votes, normally (but not always) electing the first ranked candidate. Full representation may be more likely at the regional court level, both for political reasons (to encourage integration) and practical reasons (there will normally be fewer state parties than for international courts). Nonetheless, many regional courts still reflect the 'selective representation' approach.

In 'selective representation courts', such as the ICJ, the ICC and the International Tribunal for the Law of the Sea (ITLOS), procedures are established for the nomination of candidates and their election by the relevant intergovernmental body that established the court. In most cases, the governing statute imposes rules as to the overall composition of the court. Alternatively, or additionally, there will be accepted conventions to that effect, setting out how seats on the court are to be shared amongst the state parties, usually on the basis of regional representation.

The differing degree of state control in the selection processes over, respectively, full and selective representation courts is one example of a tension between the independence of the courts and state sovereignty. International courts are themselves a departure from the dominant global model of *national* judicial authority. It is therefore inevitable that states seek to retain some control over an institution that has the capacity to limit sovereignty over important state affairs. The two main ways in which states can do this are by controlling the court's budget and by appointing its judges. It is no surprise that the judicial selection process is therefore an important arena in which the balance of power between the state and the supranational judicial authority is played out. The further tension, of course, is that while states may endeavour to secure representation on a court through the appointment of their nationals, once appointed a judge is expected to be independent and, indeed, may be called upon to decide against the interests of the nominating state.

In very general terms, it is possible to identify a trend in which international judicial selection processes are, in theory at least, gradually being distinguished from processes for making other international political appointments. There is some evidence that emphasis is being placed less on the authority of states and more on the goal of selecting independent and highly qualified judges, according to pre-determined merit-based judicial selection criteria and through a more formalized judicial selection process. This trend is not peculiar to international courts, as is becoming apparent in many national judicial selection processes.[2] In some cases there is evidence of a cross-fertilization of approaches between international and national jurisdictions and the development of principles for judicial appointments that favour transparency and independence. At one end of the spectrum, this involves the introduction of practices such as public advertising of posts, more formal and developed selection criteria, and nascent 'best practice' principles being incorporated into the pre-existing traditional nomination and selection process. At the other, it involves the creation of new independent screening or selection bodies designed to remove the process from political influence altogether. The most recent and clear example of the latter is the selection process adopted for the Caribbean Court of Justice (CCJ), established in 2005. After long and often heated debate, it was decided that the process should prioritize the need for the judges to be seen to be entirely independent of the governments of the Caribbean signatory states. This resulted in the direct appointment of the judges of the court by a Regional Judicial and Legal Services Commission, rather than by the state parties to the court.[3] Less far-reaching examples of the introduction of greater transparency into the selection processes are found in the ICC and the ECtHR, where non-governmental organizations have become informally involved in the judicial selection procedures by making recommendations on nomination procedures, as well as by screening candidates, and lobbying and commenting on election procedures.

These developments, however, are neither universal nor linear. In some courts they are very much in evidence; in others they are embryonic, and in some they are non-existent. Moreover, there is no clear consensus as to the desirability of moving away from existing politically based judicial selection processes. Although there is general agreement that the role of the international judge differs substantively from those of other international decision-makers—and that this has implications for the judicial selection process—it is apparent that courts do not operate in a manner that is detached from the surrounding political arena.[4] Many of the issues decided by courts are politically sensitive. Just as the debate about the appropriate selection process for national constitutional and supreme court judges is an ongoing and contentious one, so the same issues arise at international level. The following historical overview of the

[2] K. Malleson and P. H. Russell (eds), *Appointing Judges in an Age of Judicial Power: Critical Perspectives from Around the World* (Toronto: University of Toronto Press, 2006).

[3] The Commission comprises the President of the CCJ as Chair; two lawyers; two lay people; two academics and two chairs of the public service commissions and judicial services commissions of the member states. Full details of the membership of the RJLSC can be found at: <http://www.caribbeancourtofjustice.org/about_rjlsc.html> (Accessed 28, April 2010).

[4] See the debate between Helfer and Slaughter, and Posner and Yoo about the role of the international courts and judicial independence: E. A. Posner and J. C. Yoo, 'Judicial Independence in International Tribunals' *California Law Review* 93(1) (2005) 1–74; L. R. Helfer and A-M. Slaughter, 'Why States Create International Tribunals: A Response to Professors Posner and Yoo' *California Law Review* 93(3) (2005) 899–956; E. A. Posner and J. C. Yoo, 'Reply to Helfer and Slaughter' *California Law Review* 93(3) (2005) 957–74.

establishment and early years of the ICJ and the ICC, and the debate about the best method of selecting the judges to those courts, illustrates the underlying tensions between the political and legal functions of the international courts. This issue is equally evident in the later chapters, which review the current judicial selection processes to the ICJ and the ICC.

B. From ad hoc arbitration to permanent courts of justice

The early years of the international court system demonstrate the origins of the tension between state control and judicial independence. Prior to the establishment of permanent dispute settlement institutions, international legal disputes were decided by ad hoc arbitrators chosen directly by the parties to determine the particular dispute between them. Treaties entered into between the United States and the United Kingdom, such as the Jay Treaty of 1794[5] and the Treaty of Washington of 1871,[6] were early attempts to provide for the establishment of mixed commissions and tribunals to resolve certain types of international disputes. Under Article 1 of the 1871 Treaty, one member each was appointed by the heads of state of the United States, the United Kingdom, Brazil, Italy, and Switzerland to the five-member tribunal. The last three states were not involved in the disputes under consideration by the tribunal. This tribunal determined the Alabama Claims[7] and established the modern precedent for the use of arbitration to settle certain international disputes. Following this decision, recourse to international arbitration and the use of compromissory clauses in agreements between states increased notably.[8]

Reaching agreement as to the procedure for the appointment of judges was a major obstacle to be surmounted before the first permanent international court could be established. The Hague Peace Conference of 1899 discussed the possibility of a permanent international court, but these proposals were not taken up, largely because of difficulties in agreeing a procedure for the choice of judges that

[5] The Jay Treaty. Treaty of Amity, Commerce, and Navigation, signed in London, 19 November 1794, available at: <http://avalon.law.yale.edu/18th_century/jay.asp> (accessed 18 March 2010).

[6] Treaty between Her Majesty and the United States of America, for the Amicable Settlement of all Causes of Difference between the two Countries, *British and Foreign State Papers*, vol. 61 (London: HMSO, 1877) 40.

[7] '*Decision* and *Award* made by the tribunal of arbitration constituted by virtue of the first article of the treaty concluded at Washington, 8 May 1871, between the United States of America and Her Majesty the Queen of the United Kingdom of Great Britain and Ireland' in John Bassett Moore (ed), *History and Digest of the International Arbitrations to Which the United States Has Been a Party*, vol. 1 (Washington: Government Printing Office, 1898) 653, 656–7.

[8] M. O. Hudson, *The Permanent Court of International Justice, 1920–1942: a treatise* (New York: The Macmillan Company, 1943) para 1.

'presaged the great difficulties that would resurface with all subsequent discussions of a permanent international court'.[9] Instead, the Conference established the Permanent Court of Arbitration (PCA), comprised of members organized into 'national groups'. These national groups consisted of up to four individuals whom state parties were entitled to nominate under the 1899 Convention for the Pacific Settlement of International Disputes (the 1899 Hague Convention) and the 1907 Convention for the Pacific Settlement of International Disputes (the 1907 Hague Convention) to be placed on a roster of arbitrators maintained by the PCA International Bureau.[10] The members of the PCA make up a pool of potential arbitrators who can be appointed by states on a case-by-case basis.[11] Thus, although at this stage a permanent court was not created, the Conference represented 'a point of inflection, a turn in the river'[12] towards the establishment of a permanent court.

When the 1899 Convention was reviewed at the Second Hague Peace Conference convened in 1907, a number of states made proposals to move beyond ad hoc arbitration and establish a permanent international court of general jurisdiction, with the proposed name of the Court of Arbitral Justice. A Draft Convention Relative to the Creation of a Court of Arbitral Justice of 1907 was eventually annexed to the Final Act of the Second Hague Peace Conference with the recommendation (that did not receive support from all forty-four states at the Conference) that states adopt the Draft Convention and bring it into force as soon as agreement was reached as to the selection of judges and the constitution of the court.[13] The Draft Convention did not deal with the issue of appointment,

[9] D. Caron, 'War and International Adjudication: Reflections of the 1899 Peace Conference' *American Journal of International Law* 94(1) (2000) 17. See also S. Rosenne (ed), *The Hague Peace Conferences of 1899 and 1907 and International Arbitration: Reports and Documents* (The Hague: T. M. C. Asser, 2001) 111–12 and generally, A. Eyffinger, *The 1899 Hague Peace Conference* (The Hague: Kluwer Law International, 2000).

[10] 1899 Convention for the Pacific Settlement of International Disputes, concluded at The Hague on 29 July 1899 ('1899 Hague Convention' in following text), and the 1907 Convention for the Pacific Settlement of International Disputes, concluded at The Hague on 18 October 1907 ('1907 Hague Convention' in following text).

[11] PCA arbitrators must be of known competency in international law and high moral reputation (Article 23, 1899 Hague Convention; Article 44, 1907 Hague Convention). More than one state may select the same individual to act as a PCA member. PCA members serve six-year renewable terms. There are currently approximately 265 arbitrators included on the list. The list is transmitted periodically by the PCA International Bureau to the parties to the 1899 and 1907 Hague Conventions (Article 23, 1899 Hague Convention; Article 44, 1907 Hague Convention). Hudson notes that the PCA member 'cannot be said to form a *body*' but that '[t]hey form instead a panel from which *ad hoc* tribunals may be constituted': M. O. Hudson, *The Permanent Court of International Justice, 1920–1942: a treatise*, op. cit., para 4.

[12] D. Caron, 'War and International Adjudication: Reflections of the 1899 Peace Conference', op. cit., 4.

[13] M. O. Hudson, *The Permanent Court of International Justice, 1920–1942: a treatise*, op. cit., para 76. For the text of the Draft Convention: S. Rosenne (ed), *The Hague Peace Conferences of 1899 and 1907 and International Arbitration: Reports and Documents*, op. cit., 216–21 and the Final Act, at 411.

save to say that the judges should be appointed 'as far as possible, from members of the Permanent Court of Arbitration'.[14]

In these early years the tension between the more powerful and less powerful states could already be seen in the debates over the appropriate models of judicial selection. Some states preferred selective representation, in which certain states would be accorded greater weight, and others supported a full representation model. Amongst the myriad of suggested arrangements put forward during the Conference were proposals from Bulgaria for the appointment of a competent person by each state who would sit together to elect the judges of the court from amongst themselves.[15] In contrast, the United States, United Kingdom and Germany proposed that certain states should be permanently represented, in relation to population and industry and commerce, and that the judges from the other countries should sit on the court according to a rotation system.[16] A number of states argued that there should be sovereign equality in the appointment of judges and that they should all have a seat on the court, while the 'Great Powers' assumed they would be represented in the court but that smaller states would have to share the other seats amongst them.[17] The United States delegation proposed a free election of fifteen members of the court, based on one candidate nominated by each state and a vote conducted through the International Bureau of the Permanent Court of Arbitration in accordance with representation rules based on population, language and jurisprudence.[18] But the states were unable to reach agreement on the matter and the proposal was defeated.[19] Later attempts were made by the United States to revive the proposals for a Court of Arbitral Justice based on the appointment of one judge per state, with judges serving on a rota system that was annexed to the International Prize Court Convention of 1907. These efforts failed because the Prize Court Convention never entered into force.[20]

However, developments at the regional level were more successful and in 1907 the first international court was established in Central America. The Central American Court of Justice came about as a result of the Central American Peace Conference that took place shortly after the adjournment of The Hague Peace Conference in 1907, largely influenced by discussions in The Hague. The creation of a full representation court was possible as it had only five state parties

[14] S. Rosenne (ed), *The Hague Peace Conferences of 1899 and 1907 and International Arbitration: Reports and Documents*, op. cit., 216.

[15] M. O. Hudson, *The Permanent Court of International Justice, 1920–1942: a treatise*, op. cit., para 78.

[16] ibid.

[17] D. Caron, 'War and International Adjudication: Reflections of the 1899 Peace Conference', op. cit., 22.

[18] ibid.

[19] M. O. Hudson, *The Permanent Court of International Justice, 1920–1942: a treatise*, op. cit., para 78. See also S. Rosenne (ed), *The Hague Peace Conferences of 1899 and 1907 and International Arbitration: Reports and Documents*, op. cit., 157–67.

[20] M. O. Hudson, *The Permanent Court of International Justice, 1920–1942: a treatise*, op. cit., para 79.

(Costa Rica, El Salvador, Guatemala, Honduras and Nicaragua).[21] Judges were required to have 'the qualifications which the laws of each country prescribed for the exercise of high judicial office', and to enjoy 'the "highest consideration, both because of their moral character and their professional ability"'.[22] One of each of the five was to be appointed by each party's legislature to serve for a period of five years. However, the court was not a great success. It was noted that '[u]nfortunately, the justices of the court seem to have been looked upon not as international officials of all five States, but as officials of their respective States... as there was no method for a cooperative election of the justices'.[23]

The next major step came in the aftermath of the First World War and the creation of the League of Nations, with the establishment of the Permanent Court of International Justice (PCIJ) in 1922. The PCIJ was the first selective representation international court, which meant that states had to build on the attempts made to establish the Court of Arbitral Justice at the Second Hague Peace Conference and to arrive at a formula for nominations and elections of judges, and the composition of the court. Thus under Article 14 of the Covenant of the League of Nations,[24] the Council of the League (consisting of permanent members Great Britain, France, Italy, and Japan and four non-permanent members)[25] was given responsibility for formulating plans for a Permanent Court of International Justice to hear 'disputes of an international character... [and] also give an advisory opinion upon any dispute or question referred to it by the Council [of the League of Nations] or the Assembly [of the League of Nations]'.[26] Before the Covenant came into force in 1920, the Committee of Jurists was established to formulate a plan for the Court. The Committee consisted of ten members, with Baron Descamps of Belgium as President. Most members had been involved in The Hague Peace Conferences, and some were subsequently elected to the court,[27] but the appointment of judges became a contentious issue.

In 1920 the Committee of Jurists submitted a report, via the Council, setting out draft proposals to the Assembly of the League of Nations.[28] The Committee

[21] A. Eyffinger, *The 1899 Hague Peace Conference*, op. cit., 460. The court ceased operations on 12 March 1918. A new Central American Court of Justice was established in 1962, under the Charter of the Organization of Central American States of 1951 (as amended) and only became active after the 1991 Protocol of Tegucigalpa and the Agreement on the Statute of the Central American Court of Justice of 10 December 1992: see <http://www.pict-pcti.org/courts/CACJ.html> (Accessed 28 April 2010).

[22] M. O. Hudson, *The Permanent Court of International Justice, 1920–1942: a treatise*, op. cit., para 44.

[23] ibid. Hudson notes that this was reinforced by the fact that the judges took the oath prescribed by law before their appointing authority and some of them received salaries directly from the states that appointed them.

[24] The Covenant of the League of Nations, concluded at Versailles on 28 June 1919, as Part I of the Treaty of Versailles.

[25] The Covenant of the League of Nations, Article 4.

[26] ibid, Article 14.

[27] M. O. Hudson *The Permanent Court of International Justice, 1920–1942: a treatise,* op.cit., para 109.

[28] ibid, paras 110–113.

and Sub-Committee of the Assembly revised the proposals and the Assembly adopted them in December 1920 in the form of a Statute of the Permanent Court of International Justice (the Statute), providing for its adoption by individual states by ratification of a Protocol of Signature.[29] The Statute entered into force on 1 September 1921.

Interestingly, in 1920 the Committee of Jurists also adopted a recommendation that states establish a High Court of International Justice to try crimes against public order or the universal law of nations. While this proposal was not taken up, the discussions it provoked and other current events led to two conventions of 1937 negotiated under the auspices of the League of Nations: the Convention on Terrorism and the Convention for the Creation of an International Criminal Court. The latter's purpose was to establish an International Criminal Court that would be responsible for the trial of persons for offences under the Convention on Terrorism. However, neither Convention entered into force. Under the second 1937 Convention, the five judges and five deputy judges of the International Criminal Court were to be elected by the PCIJ for a term of ten years from among jurists of acknowledged authority on criminal law who were currently or previously qualified to be judges of national criminal courts and who had been nominated by state parties.[30]

Meanwhile, in relation to the individual selection criteria for the judges of the PCIJ, Article 2 of the Statute provided that the Court:

> shall be composed of a body of independent judges, elected regardless of their nationality from amongst persons of high moral character, who possess the qualifications required in their respective countries for appointment to the highest judicial offices, or are jurisconsults of recognized competence in international law.

These two last alternatives were intended to reconcile the preference in civil law jurisdictions for the appointment of non-judges as international judges, and the preference of common law jurisdictions for national judges.[31] Article 3 provided that the court would be a selective representation court consisting of fifteen members.[32] Article 4(1) set out the double election process through which judges would be selected: 'by the Assembly and Council from a list of persons nominated by the national groups in the [Permanent] Court of Arbitration'.

The Assembly and Council would vote independently,[33] bearing in mind 'that not only should all the persons appointed as members of the Court possess

[29] The Statute of the Permanent Court of International Justice, annexed to the Protocol of Signature of 16 December 1920, as amended by the Revision Protocol of 14 September 1929 (Statute of the PCIJ in following notes).

[30] M. O. Hudson, *The Permanent Court of International Justice, 1920–1942: a treatise*, op. cit., para 85.

[31] ibid, para 138.

[32] Until the amendments of 1929 that took effect in 1936, the court consisted of eleven judges and four deputy judges.

[33] Statute of the PCIJ, Article 8.

the qualifications required, but the whole body also should represent the main forms of civilization and the principal legal systems of the world'.[34] Candidates obtaining an absolute majority of votes would be elected.[35] Articles 11 and 12 provided for multiple voting rounds and the establishment of a joint conference if a sufficient number of candidates were not elected. Article 13 provided for a term of nine years and allowed for the possibility of re-election.

As Manley Ottmer Hudson notes, linking the election with the League of Nations allowed states to reconcile demands for equality of states with the expectations of the 'Great Powers' for permanent representation on the court. This conflict had doomed plans for a court at the Second Hague Peace Conference in 1907.[36] However, the result reached was somewhat open-textured, which may have been considered an advantage by the negotiating states since it allowed for political flexibility.[37] As an important part of obtaining state consent to the new court and election arrangements, the Statute also included in Article 31 the possibility of appointing an ad hoc judge when the state in a dispute did not have a judge of its nationality on the court. This was a crucial provision, and has been retained to this day at the ICJ.[38]

As to the mechanics of nominations, the United States and the Netherlands had proposed the use of the PCA national groups to nominate candidates as a way of 'preventing political intrigues in the elections, because of the "moral weakness of all political bodies" '.[39] Because it had previously been proposed that the PCA itself would elect the judges, this was a means of establishing a link between the PCA and the PCIJ. Under Article 5 of the Statute, national groups were entitled to nominate four candidates; a maximum of two of their own nationality.[40] Article 6 recommended that each national group 'consult its highest court of justice, its legal faculties and schools of law, and its

[34] ibid, Article 9.

[35] ibid, Article 10(1). Note Rosenne who states that the PCIJ in fact only required a simple, rather than an absolute majority: S. Rosenne, *Rosenne's The World Court: What It Is and How It Works*, Legal Aspects of International Organization Series No. 41, edited by T. Gill, 6th edn (Leiden: Martinus Nijhoff, 2003) 51–2.

[36] M. O. Hudson, *The Permanent Court of International Justice, 1920–1942: a treatise*, op. cit., para 140. See also: O. Spiermann, *International Legal Argument in the Permanent Court of International Justice: The Rise of the International Judiciary*, Cambridge Studies in International and Comparative Law (Cambridge: Cambridge University Press, 2005) 7.

[37] E. Reut-Nicolussi, 'The Reform of the Permanent Court of International Justice', *Transactions of the Grotius Society, Problems of Peace and War, Papers Read before the Society in the Year 1939*, 25 (1939) 135–49.

[38] Statute of the ICJ, Article 31.

[39] M. O. Hudson, *The Permanent Court of International Justice, 1920–1942: a treatise*, op. cit., para 140. It is noted that the Netherlands objected to this on the basis that candidates of certain countries are permitted to be members of the PCA and that the PCA national groups had been organized for another object.

[40] It was suggested that this might allow the PCA national groups to express such similar views that the 'election would thereby be virtually decided' and that it would also allow them to nominate candidates not of their nationality but of universally recognized competence: M. O. Hudson, *The Permanent Court of International Justice, 1920–1942: a treatise*, op. cit., para 144.

national academies and national sections of international academies devoted to the study of law'.[41] No further detail was provided as to the procedure to be followed by national groups in making nominations, nor how they were to relate to their governments in undertaking this function. Nor was there any provision for establishing a supervisory mechanism for determining whether candidates met the relevant criteria for nomination.[42]

The first elections of the PCIJ were held on 14 September 1921.[43] Eighty-nine candidates were nominated by thirty-four national groups[44] and forty-two member states of the League of Nations voted for the candidates. The number of candidates was high compared to modern elections at the ICJ. The Council and Assembly proceeded to vote simultaneously and they elected the eleven judges in six ballots and the three of the four deputy judges in four ballots, the final deputy judge being elected after the constitution of a joint conference under Article 12 on the request of the Assembly.[45] Ten of the fifteen members elected were also members of the PCA.[46] Eleven further elections were held between 1921 and 1938.[47]

Hudson observes that although the role of national groups in the nomination process was intended to ensure independent selection of qualified candidates 'by men who are not necessarily under Government influence', in some cases the national groups 'clearly conceived it to be their function to express their

[41] It was made clear by the Committee of Jurists that this would not be a legal obligation, therefore failure to consult would not render a nomination void, nor would refusal to follow any recommendations made by bodies consulted. Britain and Italy tried to remove the provision but it was retained: M. O. Hudson, *The Permanent Court of International Justice, 1920–1942: a treatise,* op. cit., para 145. As to 'national sections of academies devoted to the study of Law', the Committee of Jurists listed: 'the Institute of International Law, the American Institute of International Law, the Union Juridique Internationale, the International Law Association and the Iberian Institute of Comparative Law': ibid, para 252.

[42] See the criticism of this, as enduring under the ICJ Statute by Lauterpacht: H. Lauterpacht, *International Law: being the collected papers of Hersch Lauterpacht,* Volume 5, *Disputes, war and neutrality,* Parts IX–XIV, systematically arranged and edited by Elihu Lauterpacht (Cambridge: Cambridge University Press, 2004) 103.

[43] J. B. Scott, 'The Election of Judges for the Permanent Court of International Justice', *American Journal of International Law* 15(4) (1921) 556–8.

[44] M. O. Hudson, *The Permanent Court of International Justice, 1920–1942: a treatise,* op. cit., para 235.

[45] ibid.

[46] M .O. Hudson, *The Permanent Court of International Justice, 1920–1942: a treatise,* op. cit., para 249. For a profile of the first judges elected, see O. Spiermann, *International Legal Argument in the Permanent Court of International Justice: The Rise of the International Judiciary,* op. cit., 134–40.

[47] According to Hudson, judges of the nationality of the 'Great Powers' were permanently represented (except when Germany was not a member of the League of Nations) and that even when the number of states in the Council were increased and theoretically states could refuse to elect candidates from the 'Great Powers' it would be 'practically inconceivable' that this would happen: M. O. Hudson, 'The Election of Members of the Permanent Court of International Justice' *American Journal of International Law* 24(4) (1930) 725–6. It was expected that an American, British, French, German, Italian and Japanese judge would be permanently represented: ibid, 727.

Government's will',[48] and nominations were usually conveyed via the Ministry of Foreign Affairs.[49] In Hudson's view, national groups did 'not always select the strongest nominees', sometimes using nominations 'for the purpose of paying compliments'.[50] With the outbreak of the Second World War, the court sat for the last time on 4 December 1939 and ceased to exist when the League of Nations was dissolved on 18 April 1946.

C. The International Court of Justice

During the Second World War, a number of states expressed support for the establishment of an international court once hostilities had ceased.[51] For a time it was unclear whether the PCIJ would be retained in its existing form in the post-war period. The proposals made at Dumbarton Oaks (or Washington Conference on International Peace and Security Organization) in 1944 did not address this issue although a preference was expressed for retaining at least the form of the PCIJ Statute.[52]

In 1944 China, the USSR, the United Kingdom and the United States convened a meeting of a Committee of Jurists in Washington, in which forty-four countries participated, to draft a statute for consideration at the 1945 San Francisco Conference. The proposed statute set out a new court, the International Court of Justice (ICJ), as a replacement for the PCIJ.[53] However, the Committee did not make decisions about the election of judges, the place of the proposed court in the UN organization or whether the jurisdiction of the court should be compulsory.[54] Once the fifty states at the San Francisco Conference had decided that the PCIJ's consensual basis for jurisdiction would be retained, and that the court would be part of the UN, the provisions relating to the election of judges were adopted, almost without amendment, from the PCIJ statute. For the purposes of election, the Assembly and Council of the League of Nations were replaced with the Assembly and Security Council of the UN.

[48] M. O. Hudson, *The Permanent Court of International Justice, 1920–1942: a treatise*, op. cit., para 252.

[49] ibid. The previous political links of candidates elected was noted by Reut-Nicolussi as potentially impugning the independence of the Court for potential state parties: E. Reut-Nicolussi, 'The Reform of the Permanent Court of International Justice', op. cit., 135–49.

[50] M. O. Hudson, *The Permanent Court of International Justice, 1920–1942: a treatise*, op. cit., para 252.

[51] G. Marston, 'The London Committee and the statute of the International Court of Justice' in V. Lowe and M. Fitzmaurice, *Fifty Years of the International Court of Justice: Essays in Honour of Sir Robert Jennings* (Cambridge: Cambridge University Press, 1996) 40–60.

[52] S. Rosenne, *Rosenne's The World Court: What It Is and How It Works*, op. cit., 17.

[53] Article 92, Charter of the United Nations, 26 June 1945, 59 Stat. 1031, T.S. 993, 3 Bevans 1153, *entered into force* 24 October 1945 ('UN Charter' in following notes).

[54] S. Rosenne, *Rosenne's The World Court: What It Is and How It Works*, op. cit., 18.

Various proposals to alter the PCIJ nomination and election procedures were put forward by states, including the replacement of nominations by PCA national groups with direct government nominations, the reduction in the number of judges on the court, and provision for a system of staggered triennial elections (rather than the old PCIJ system of full bench elections every nine years).[55] The last proposal was adopted, although there has subsequently been some criticism of this approach on the basis that it has tended to increase the politicization of elections and may undermine continuity in the work of the court.[56] The proposal to reduce the number of judges was rejected, and the vote by the Committee of Jurists on conferring the right to nominate candidates on governments was tied. The San Francisco Conference eventually voted for the retention of nominations by PCA national groups.[57] The system of double elections was also challenged, but retained in the end.[58] The majority required for election was also increased.[59] The first ICJ elections took place on 6 February 1946 and the court commenced operation on 18 April 1946.[60]

The Statute of the Court offers minimal guidance as to individual selection criteria for judges,[61] but provides that PCA national groups or their equivalents are the sole bodies entitled to nominate candidates for the court, and that they should operate independently of governments, consulting widely as to the nomination of candidates.[62]

Judges are elected in accordance with a convention of geographical representation (discussed further in Chapter 2) and the 'P5 Convention' (which ensures that the five Permanent Members of the UN Security Council are represented on the Court). The UN General Assembly and UN Security Council vote independently, with candidates requiring absolute majority of votes in each body.

Under Article 7 of the United Nations Charter, the ICJ is designated as the principal judicial organ of the UN. Thus the court becomes an integral part of the UN, in contrast to the relationship of the PCIJ to the League of Nations. Article 93 of the UN Charter provides that all members of the UN are *ipso facto* parties to the ICJ Statute and that non-UN members may become party to the

[55] G. Abi-Saab, 'Ensuring the Best Bench: Ways of Selecting Judges: Presentation by Professor Georges Abi-Saab' in C. Peck and L. Roy (eds), *Increasing the Effectiveness of the International Court of Justice: Proceedings of the ICJ/UNITAR Colloquium to Celebrate the 50th Anniversary of the Court* (The Hague: Martinus Nijhoff Publishers/UNITAR, 1997) 177.

[56] S. Rosenne, 'The Composition of the Court' in L. Gross (ed), *The Future of the International Court of Justice*, 2 vols (Dobbs Ferry, New York: Oceana, 1976) 377.

[57] G. Abi-Saab, 'Ensuring the Best Bench: Ways of Selecting Judges: Presentation by Professor Georges Abi-Saab', op. cit., 178.

[58] ibid, 182.

[59] B. Fassbender, 'Chapter I. Organization of the Court: Article 10' in A. Zimmerman et al, *The Statute of the International Court of Justice: a commentary* (Oxford: Oxford University Press, 2006) 288–9.

[60] Information about the current composition of the court is available at: <http://www.icj-cij.org/court/index.php?p1=1&p2=2&p3=1> and a list of all previous judges at: <http://www.icj-cij.org/court/index.php?p1=1&p2=2&p3=2> (Accessed 27 April 2010).

[61] See Chapter 2.

[62] Statute of the ICJ, Articles 4–6.

Statute on the fulfilment of particular conditions. This secures the prospect of greater participation in the court, but with it greater demands for representation on its bench.

D. The International Criminal Court

The Statute of the International Criminal Court (ICC) was adopted in 1998. The ICC is the first permanent court established to try individuals accused of committing crimes of genocide, crimes against humanity and serious violations of the laws of war. It may also in the future have jurisdiction over the crime of aggression. A number of earlier proposals were put forward for an international criminal court, but it was not until the end of the Cold War that the UN was able to move towards the establishment of a permanent court. The International Law Commission (ILC) first addressed the topic in 1948, at the request of the UN General Assembly, but was unable to proceed further due to political divisions caused by the Cold War. In 1989, the UN General Assembly requested that the ILC continue its work, but it was not until 1994 that the ILC presented a first draft statute to the General Assembly.

In 1995, against the background of the atrocities in the Balkans and Rwanda, and the creation of the ad hoc International Criminal Tribunal for the former Yugoslavia (ICTY) and the International Criminal Tribunal for Rwanda (ICTR) by the Security Council, a Preparatory Committee was convened by the UN General Assembly to draft a consolidated statute. It met from 1996 to 1998 and at the conclusion of this work, a United Nations Diplomatic Conference of Plenipotentiaries on the Establishment of an International Criminal Court (known as the 'Rome Conference') was convened from 15 June to 17 July 1998.[63] At the end of the Conference, the Rome Statute was adopted and opened for signature and the Statute entered into force on 1 July 2002.[64] The court commenced operation on 11 March 2003 and by 31 August 2009 110 states had become parties to its Statute.

In contrast to the ICJ, the Rome Statute provides detailed guidance as to the individual qualifications of judges and criteria and guidance for their nomination and election. It allows the nomination procedure to follow either the ICJ procedure or that used for the appointment of national superior court judges. States must also provide information on how the candidate they have nominated meets the criteria laid down by the Statute. Candidates are elected by the Assembly of State Parties (ASP), the management oversight and legislative body of the

[63] R. Lee, 'Introduction' in R. Lee (ed), *The International Criminal Court: The Making of the Rome Statute: Issues, Negotiations, Results* (The Hague: Kluwer Law International/UNITAR, 1999) 2–5.

[64] Rome Statute of the International Criminal Court, 2187 U.N.T.S. 90, entered into force 1 July 2002 (Rome Statute).

court,[65] voting in accordance with the minimum voting requirements set out in relevant ASP resolutions[66] and the Statute, based on a two-thirds majority of votes. The Rome Statute also provides for the possible establishment of a 'screening' body, an Advisory Committee on Nominations; however, this has not yet been established.

The proposed rules for the composition of the court and the nomination and election of judges prompted a wide-ranging and heated debate. One key issue was whether judges should be eligible for re-election, as ICJ judges are, but it was eventually decided that ICC judges should not be re-elected because of the particular nature of the ICC as a criminal court.[67] There was also discussion as to whether there should be an age limit for judges, but this too was rejected.[68] One particularly problematic issue concerned the professional qualifications of judges and the need to ensure an appropriate range of expertise in criminal law and international law (known as the 'List A' and 'List B' requirements). The formula now found in Articles 36(3)(b)(i) and 36(3)(b)(ii) of the Statute appeared in its current form in the draft debated at the Rome Conference and requires that candidates:

1) have established competence in criminal law and procedure, and the necessary relevant experience, whether as judge, prosecutor, advocate or in other similar capacity, in criminal proceedings (List A); or
2) have established competence in relevant areas of international law such as international humanitarian law and the law of human rights, and extensive experience in a professional legal capacity which is of relevance to the judicial work of the Court (List B).

The United Kingdom and a number of other states argued that these requirements should be specified in greater detail, in particular by providing that judges should have legal professional practice experience. These states also argued that overall the pre-trial and trial divisions of the court should predominantly consist of judges with criminal law experience and that the appeals division should be predominantly composed of judges with international law experience.[69] In the final Statute, no fixed quotas for the divisions were established; rather the organs were to be constituted depending on their functions and the particular experience of the judges elected,[70] with the trial and pre-trial divisions to be composed 'predominantly of judges with criminal and trial experience'.[71] To provide sufficient numbers of adequately qualified judges for this purpose, Article 36(5) was inserted, requiring that at least nine List A judges and five List

[65] Information about the ASP can be found at: <http://www.icc-cpi.int/Menus/ASP/> (Accessed 27 April 2010).

[66] See ASP Resolution ICC-ASP/3/Res. 6, Appendix 3.

[67] M. Rwelamira, 'Composition and Administration of the Court' in R. Lee (ed), *The International Criminal Court: The Making of the Rome Statute: Issues, Negotiations, Results* (The Hague: Kluwer Law International/UNITAR, 1999) 156–7.

[68] ibid, 157.

[69] ibid, 159–60. See also Rome Statute, Article 39(1).

[70] ibid, 157–61.

[71] Rome Statute, Article 39(1).

B judges be elected in the first elections, and that this proportion be maintained. The proposed requirement for experience of professional legal practice was not incorporated.

Discussions also took place as to how candidates should be nominated. The United States proposed a Nominating Committee made up of the ASP.[72] The role of the Committee would be to nominate a number of candidates, of any nationality, equal to the number of vacancies. However, the proposal was rejected as some other states considered that it overly restricted their right to nominate candidates and believed that it would be undesirable to open the court to non-nationals of state parties.[73] The other main option considered was nomination by a state party or, as proposed by the United Kingdom, by the PCA national group, as for the nomination procedure for the ICJ.[74] This proposal was eventually incorporated into the Statute, with the requirement that nominations be accompanied by a statement as to how the candidate meets the qualification requirements of the Statute.[75] Nominations made by state parties were constrained by the further addition of Article 36(4)(a)(i) which provided that nomination by a state party should be in accordance with the 'procedure for nominations to the highest judicial offices of that state'.

A related discussion was held as to whether there should be some type of screening body to provide more information on candidates to guide states in electing judges.[76] The United Kingdom proposed a screening committee to be composed of:

> The Chief Justices of each State Party which would examine nominations of all candidates and, where necessary, seek further information from them... [t]he proceedings of this committee would not be binding..., but it would make recommendations and proposals to States Parties collectively...[77]

A number of states were concerned about the role of such a committee and eventually, as a result of Egyptian and French proposals, the committee was reframed as an 'advisory' committee. However, it was left open to state parties when and how it might be established and, to date, no such committee has been established.[78]

[72] As the ICC is not an organ of the UN, but a treaty-based court, judicial elections for the ICC do not take place in the UN General Assembly and Security Council, but in the ASP, the intergovernmental body composed of state parties to the Rome Statute.

[73] M. Rwelamira, 'Composition and Administration of the Court', op. cit., 163.

[74] ibid, 162.

[75] Rome Statute, Article 36(4)(a).

[76] T. Ingadottir, 'Nomination and Election of Judges' in T. Ingadottir (ed), *The International Criminal Court: Recommendations on Policy and Practice: Financing, Victims, Judges, and Immunities* (Ardsley, New York: Transnational Publishers Inc, 2003) 173–6.

[77] M. Rwelamira, 'Composition and Administration of the Court', op. cit., 163–4. Ingadottir notes that the terms of Article 36(4)(c) do not limit the membership of the potential committee in any way: T. Ingadottir, 'Nomination and Election of Judges', op. cit., 176.

[78] Rome Statute, Article 36(4)(c). M. Rwelamira, 'Composition and Administration of the Court', op. cit., 164.

A debate also arose as to the formulation of the provisions on the overall composition of the court, particularly whether there should be 'equitable geographical distribution' (which implied strict quotas) or 'equitable geographical representation' (which implied minimum thresholds). The latter formulation was chosen as a compromise position and no formal geographical allocations were agreed.[79] The adoption of the recommendations as to fair representation of male and female judges and the inclusion of judges with legal expertise in violence against women and children were included after intensive lobbying from the Women's Caucus for Gender Justice. The Caucus argued for gender mainstreaming in relation both to the jurisdiction of the courts and its composition, and their success in both these respects was unprecedented in the international court system.[80]

The Rome Statute, as adopted, provided a new framework for the nomination and election of judges. It set down detailed individual criteria and minimum quotas for judges with criminal law, human rights law and humanitarian law expertise, and made recommendations to states as to the overall composition of the bench. However, it was not until the first session of the ASP that final details were decided, including the detailed minimum voting rules for elections.[81] It was agreed that guidance should be given to states as to the overall composition of the bench, to ensure that the most appropriate judges would be elected so that the court could carry out its functions effectively and earn the respect of the international community. The first elections of judges were held from 4 to 7 February 2003. The second regular elections were held in January 2006, and the third in January 2009. Elections for vacancies were held in November/December 2007 and November 2009.

E. Conclusion

A chronological account of the kind set out in this chapter has a tendency to leave the impression of a process which naturally and inevitably led towards the present arrangements. In reality, there was nothing preordained about the choice of systems for selecting the judges to either the ICJ or the ICC. The arrangements ultimately adopted were products of the particular time and context in which the two courts were created. They were the outcome of political lobbying by state parties and other groups jostling to ensure that their interests would be sufficiently represented in the courts, having regard to different legal approaches.

[79] ibid, 166.

[80] See P. Spees, 'Women's Advocacy in the Creation of the International Criminal Court: Changing the Landscapes of Justice and Power' *Signs* 28(4) (Summer 2003) 1233–54. Ingadottir notes that the requirements as the overall composition of the bench must be taken to apply to both the nomination and election stages: T. Ingadottir, 'Nomination and Election of Judges', op. cit., 157.

[81] ibid, 146.

Some lobbying was conducted openly, but much more was carried out behind the scenes. As a result, the processes which were decided upon were inevitably a compromise between different powerful groups in the context of various legal systems and traditions, all of whom adopted very different approaches.

One notable difference in the histories of the selection processes for the two courts is the relatively detailed attention which each attracted. In the process leading up to the creation of the ICJ, a surprisingly small amount of time and effort was devoted to determining the specifics of the arrangements for appointing the judges. In contrast, the question of judicial appointments formed a central part of the debate in the creation of the ICC. These differences are reflected in the complex and detailed provisions for the ICC, both in terms of composition and procedure, compared to the relatively sparse arrangements for the ICJ. This discrepancy is partly a general reflection of the differences in attitude towards judicial selection in the 1940 and the 1990s. By the time of the creation of the ICC, there was far greater awareness of the significance of the selection processes in influencing the ultimate conduct, effectiveness, and legitimacy of the courts. Were the ICJ being created from scratch today, there is little doubt that debates over the selection process would be far more complex and contentious, with greater awareness of the need to accommodate a far wider range of perspectives and interests.

Despite the differences in context in which the two courts were established and the divergence in the detail of the processes to which these differences gave rise, the selection model of the two courts is in very broad terms the same, both being processes of national nomination followed by election. But it is important to remember that this selection model is not replicated in all other areas of the international court system. The following chapters present current empirical evidence about the way the ICC and ICJ selection processes function in the light of alternative arrangements in other international courts—some old and some new. Moreover, just as newer courts have adopted different processes in the light of their own particular contexts, so the story of the development of the ICJ and ICC processes does not end here. Change, whether detailed or structural, is likely in both systems in the coming years, influenced no doubt by developments in other courts. The political and cultural context in which the international courts operate is a dynamic one. But whereas the history of the debate and developments of the selection processes for the two courts to date have been largely self-contained (determined by input from a relatively narrow group of insiders), it is likely that future developments will be subject to broader engagement. Academics, practitioners, and policy-makers from outside the world of international courts are increasingly interested and involved in proposed changes and are likely to play a greater role in the future development of judicial selection processes.

2

The Composition of the International Courts

A. Introduction

A number of different factors determine the composition of the international bench. The most important are the court's governing rules and conventions, including individual selection criteria for judges and rules about the composition of the bench as a whole; the available pool of candidates; and the practice and priorities of member states. This chapter reviews the interplay of these factors as they affect the ICJ and the ICC. It also considers current debates and trends in relation to the composition of international courts more generally, including questions about the composition of the bench as a whole, in terms of geographic representation and the place of the five permanent members of the UN Security Council; the representation of different legal systems; the need for certain types of legal expertise and a particular combination of legal experience on the bench; and the promotion of gender balance. In relation to individual judicial selection criteria, the debate reveals differing views about the appropriate professional background, experience and skills required for international judges.

At national court level, debates about the composition of courts in many countries are ongoing with certain issues being hotly contested, particularly in relation to supreme courts and constitutional courts.[1] At the international level, such debates are more recent, more sporadic in their development, and mainly arise at the point when international instruments establishing new international courts are being negotiated. Tensions at the national level are reflected at the international level, but with differences of emphasis. Most notably, the relationship between legitimacy and representation takes on another meaning at the international level in two different respects. First, there is increasing agreement in relation to most common law and civil law national courts that the judiciary needs to be broadly reflective of the make-up of society in order for it to command public confidence and maintain political legitimacy as an unelected institution of power. Issues such as the gender balance and the ethnic background of members of top national

[1] K. Malleson and P. H. Russell (eds), *Appointing Judges in an Age of Judicial Power: Critical Perspectives from Around the World* (Toronto: University of Toronto Press, 2006).

courts now attract considerable interest and media attention. At international level, these questions are only just starting to find their way on to the political agenda. Moreover, they are generally focused not on ethnicity and gender but on issues of geographic representation and the representation of different legal cultures. Nevertheless, it is clear that there is growing awareness at the international level of the strong link between the composition of a court and its legitimacy, hence the guidelines for the nomination of judges for the first African Court on Human and Peoples' Rights (ACHPR), which stated that 'the moral authority, credibility, and reputation of the African Court on Human and Peoples' Rights will, to a large extent, depend on the composition of its first bench'.[2]

The second area of difference between international and national courts concerns the approach to the principle of judicial independence. At the national level there is, at least at a rhetorical level, a universal commitment to the idea that judicial independence requires judges to act entirely independently of the government in power.[3] At international level the relationship between the judges and the states which nominate and elect them is more complex and nuanced. While most international judges and observers would subscribe to a version of judicial independence in which judges decide cases on the basis of the law rather than the interests of their state, there is also recognition that judges cannot entirely leave their nationality at the door of the court and that the continuing commitment of states to international justice derives, to a significant degree, from the belief that having a national on the bench furthers the interests of the state in some way. Indeed, some observers go further than this and reject the idea that international court judges should be seen as wholly independent, arguing that there will be more effective decision-making in international courts if the vested interests of the judges are acknowledged and accepted. The debate about the appropriate nature of judicial independence in the international courts is a lively one.[4]

[2] The Protocol to the African Charter on Human and Peoples' Rights on the establishment of an African Court on Human and Peoples' Rights, available at: <http://www.achpr.org/english/_info/court_en.html> (ACHPR Protocol) and Note Verbale, Commission of the African Union, 5 April 2004, Reference BC/OLC/66.5/8/Vol.V (ACHPR Guidelines) 1. Judges of the ACHPR were elected in 2006 but as at May 2009, the ACHPR was still not in operation. Note that in 2004 the African Union had decided to integrate the African Human Rights Court and the Court of Justice of the African Union, but in 2005 it decided that the establishment of the ACHPR should continue pending the drafting and ratification of an instrument to create the African Court of Justice and Human Rights (ACJHR), that will be the main judicial organ of the AU. The Protocol of the merged court is currently being ratified by AU member states: as at April 2009, fourteen states had ratified the Protocol—fifteen ratifications are needed to bring the Protocol and the Statute into force: see <http://www.africa-union.org/root/au/Documents/Treaties/list/Protocol%20on%20Statute%20of%20the%20African%20Court%20of%20Justice%20and%20HR.pdf>. See Protocol on the Statute of the African Court of Justice and Human Rights, available at: <http://www.africa-union.org/root/au/Documents/Treaties/text/Protocol%20on%20the%20Merged%20Court%20-%20EN.pdf> (ACJHR Protocol) (Accessed 28 April 2010).

[3] UN Basic Principles on the Independence of the Judiciary, GA. Resolution 40/32, 29 November 1985; 40/146, 13 December 1985.

[4] E. A. Posner and J. C. Yoo, 'Judicial Independence in International Tribunals', *California Law Review* 93(1) (2005) 1–74; L. R. Helfer and A-M. Slaughter, 'Why States Create International

Whatever the merits of the different approaches to state representation in the international courts, it is clear that the issue of geographical distribution impacts on the composition of the international judiciary in novel ways.[5]

Debates about composition, particularly concerning the individual selection criteria, are also strongly influenced by national legal cultures. Factors at play include legal training, national judicial appointment criteria and the status of judicial power in the domestic constitutional system. The interpretation and application of the principles of judicial independence and the rule of law, and their particular status in national jurisdictions, also play a role. These variables differ widely between states, and in many cases are in flux, creating dynamic and shifting cross-influences between the national and international levels.

These issues, and others, were discussed at length with many of the interviewees. The material gathered highlights the fact that those involved in the international courts see a correlation between the composition of the courts and issues of public confidence, judicial competence and independence. Perceptions as to the quality and background of the judges and the broader representativeness of the bench clearly impact upon perceptions of the legitimacy of the courts.

B. General selection criteria for the bench

Almost all international courts are governed by rules which address the composition of the bench as a whole. These requirements provide for representation across a range of different criteria. For many, the primary consideration is that of geographical representation.[6] The development of accepted means of allocating seats to different geographically defined groups of states has been a key to the establishment of selective representation courts. In the ICJ, the P5 convention additionally provides that the five permanent members of the UN Security Council are continuously represented on the court. This provides an additional level of state representation, based on the political position of those states; accordingly, ICJ distribution is based on both 'power and geography'.[7] For many states, securing a seat on one of the principal international courts is a means of bolstering the influence and reputation of that state in the international arena. As one international judge put it, 'Somehow you are an ambassador of your country.

Tribunals: A Response to Professors Posner and Yoo' *California Law Review* 93(3) (2005) 899–956; E. A. Posner and J. C. Yoo, 'Reply to Helfer and Slaughter' *California Law Review* 93(3) (2005) 957–74.

[5] Although some parallels may be drawn with constitutional or supreme courts in federal or quasi-federal systems (for example, Canada) where geographical representation is a live issue.

[6] See ICJ Statute, Article 9; ITCOS Statute, Article 2(2); WTO Dispute Settlement Understanding, Article 17(3) (on the membership of the WTO Appellate Body).

[7] B. Fassbender, 'Chapter I. Organization of the Court: Article 9' in A. Zimmerman et al (eds), *The Statute of the International Court of Justice: A Commentary* (Oxford: Oxford University Press, 2006) 270.

People will certainly think about what you're doing, and sometimes you receive a note of congratulations from the Minister of Foreign Affairs for an opinion you gave because your country is very proud of that.'[8]

Geographical representation on the ICJ

The requirements of the ICJ Statute with regard to the composition of the bench as a whole is characteristically sparse: Article 9 encourages states to have some regard to diversity of representation on the bench in casting their votes:

> [a]t every election, the electors shall bear in mind not only that the persons to be elected should individually possess the qualifications required, but also that in the body as a whole the representation of the main forms of civilization and of the principal legal systems of the world should be assured.

Article 3 also provides that each judge must be of a different nationality.[9] Some observers have noted that Article 9 is considered by most states to be satisfied by the convention of equitable geographical distribution.[10] Others consider that Article 9 requires a more nuanced approach, and that particular 'forms of civilization' or legal systems should be represented. The concept of equitable geographical distribution is referred to in Article 23 of the UN Charter that sets out the composition of the UN Security Council:

> The Security Council shall consist of fifteen Members of the United Nations. The Republic of China, France, the Union of Soviet Socialist Republics, the United Kingdom of Great Britain and Northern Ireland, and the United States of America shall be permanent members of the Security Council. The General Assembly shall elect ten other Members of the United Nations to be non-permanent members of the Security Council, due regard being specially paid, in the first instance to the contribution of Members of the United Nations to the maintenance of international peace and security and to the other purposes of the Organization, and also to equitable geographical distribution.

The convention as to equitable geographical distribution allocates the ten non-permanent seats of the Security Council between five UN General Assembly geographical groups known as the UN regional groups: Western European and Other Group (WEOG); Eastern Europe; Latin America and the Caribbean

[8] T65, 13.

[9] However, note that Article 2 states that judges must be 'elected regardless of their nationality', although this provision has not been interpreted to in any way override Article 9: C. F. Amerasinghe, 'Judges of the International Court of Justice—Election and Qualifications' *Leiden Journal of International Law* 14(2) (2001) 345–6.

[10] S. Rosenne, *The Law and Practice of the International Court, 1920–2005*, vol. I : *The Court and the United Nations* (4th edn, The Hague: Martinus Nijhoff, 2006) 360; R. Mackenzie and P. Sands, 'Judicial Selection for International Courts: Towards Common Principles and Practices' in Kate Malleson and Peter H. Russell (eds), *Appointing Judges in an Age of Judicial Power: Critical Perspectives from Around the World* (Toronto: University of Toronto Press, 2006) 222.

(GRULAC); Africa; and Asia.[11] As noted in Article 23, five seats on the Security Council are automatically reserved for the five permanent members.[12]

The adopted practice is that the ICJ bench follows this distribution and is composed of one judge from each of the five permanent members of the Security Council and ten additional judges from different geographical regions of the world.[13] Across the bench, WEOG has five seats, Africa and Asia each have three seats, GRULAC and Eastern Europe each have two seats.[14] Taking into account the P5 convention, the seats available to other WEOG and Asian states are reduced to two each and there is one seat for Eastern European states other than Russia.[15] Given that Germany and Japan have been almost continuously represented on the court, non-P5 WEOG and Asian states must in effect compete for one seat each.

The distribution of seats on the ICJ is based on a convention which was firmly established by the late 1960s[16] but that now arguably reflects an outdated distribution of world power. Nevertheless, some interviewees saw the convention as secure and relatively uncontroversial. One diplomat noted that 'On the ICJ there is actually no formal regional distribution; one of the really interesting things is that actually we have a very disciplined system of ensuring representation. There

[11] The current regional groups (except the addition of the Caribbean to the Latin American group in 1987, discussed in a note below) and the distribution of non-permanent member seats on the Security Council can be traced back to 1963: United Nations General Assembly, *Question of Equitable Representation on the Security Council and the Economic and Social Council*, GA. Res. 1991 (XVIII), para 3. In accordance with this resolution, the ten non-permanent seats on the Security Council are allocated as follows: five from African and Asian states, one from Eastern European states, two from Latin American states and two from Western European and other states. This is the allocation that still applies today: UN Security Council, *Annotated Preliminary List of Items to be Included in the Provisional Agenda of the Sixty-Third Regular Session of the General Assembly*, UN Doc. A/63/100, para 105.

[12] The P5 convention is discussed further in the next section.

[13] P. Sands, R. Mackenzie and Y. Shany (eds), *Manual on International Courts and Tribunals* (London: Butterworths, 1999) para 1.5. Rosenne notes that this understanding regarding the ICJ emerged in the mid-1960s after the dissatisfaction following the *South West Africa* case: S. Rosenne, *Rosenne's The World Court: What It Is and How It Works*, Legal Aspects of International Organization Series No. 41, edited by Terry D. Gill (6th revised edn, Leiden: Martinus Nijhoff, 2003) 45.

[14] B. Fassbender, 'Chapter I. Organization of the Court: Article 9', op. cit., 272.

[15] See generally: S. Rosenne, *Rosenne's The World Court: What It Is and How It Works*, op. cit., 44–9 and <http://www.icj-cij.org/court/index.php?p1=1&p2=2> (Accessed 28 April 2010).

[16] Note that there have been shifts in the representation of different regional groups on the court to accommodate the sharp increase in UN members from Africa and Asia (mainly due to decolonization). Fassbender notes that in the 1951 elections, the seat held by WEOG was lost to Asia. In the 1963 elections, Latin America, who had held four seats since the first elections, had its seats reduced to two by the election of judges from Senegal and Pakistan. Africa was then given another seat in 1966, taking that seat from WEOG. In 1969 Africa was then given a 'North African' seat which was taken from the Asian Group, bringing the court to its current composition: B. Fassbender, 'Chapter I. Organization of the Court: Article 9', op. cit., 271–3, and S. Rosenne, op. cit., 46–7. Rosenne points out that the elections of 1987 were also significant because they resulted in the election of a judge from the English-speaking Caribbean (Guyana) for the first time, expanding the Latin American group to become the Latin American and Caribbean group: see Rosenne, 47.

is this understanding that an outgoing judge from Africa will be replaced by a judge from Africa, for example.'[17] Others, however, felt that the conventions were less stable, as a Western European former legal adviser explained:

> Because they're conventions, and they're so loose, there is always room in them for argument, for contestation . . . they only exist in the minds of people, and sometimes the memory just fades away, or the expectations fade away, because governments know that they simply are going to have to be in there and join the battle and it's no good simply relying upon some sort of regional convention.[18]

Equitable geographical distribution and the P5 convention are maintained through simultaneous and independent elections by the General Assembly and the Security Council.[19] The involvement of both the General Assembly and the Security Council in electing the judges of the ICJ was a compromise reached to balance the demands for representation of the 'Great Powers' and more universal representation of state parties, enabling the establishment of the first global selective representation court.[20]

Geographical representation on the ICC

The Rome Statute requires that states, when selecting judges, should take into account the need for: '(T)he representation of the principal legal systems of the world, equitable geographical representation and a fair representation of female and male judges.'[21] Each judge must be of a different nationality.[22] Equitable geographical representation has been defined and enforced by resolutions of the court's establishing and administrative body, the Assembly of States Parties (ASP). The minimum voting requirements relating to the election process, namely those concerning the selection of judges with List A and List B expertise and the requirement for gender balance are discussed in the following sections.

The judges are elected by the states parties of the Rome Statute during a meeting of the ASP.[23] The resolutions of the ASP bind states parties to elect a bench containing at least three judges from each of WEOG, Africa, GRULAC and two from each of Eastern Europe and Asia.[24] This development was an innovation

[17] T3, 5. [18] T35, 16. [19] ICJ Statute, Articles 2 and 4(1). See further Chapter 4.

[20] See Chapter 1 for more details on the historical origins.

[21] Rome Statute, Article 36(8)(a)(i)–(iii). [22] ibid, Article 36(7).

[23] ibid, Article 36(6)(a). See also Rule 85 of the Rules of Procedure of the Assembly of States Parties, *First Session, New York, 3–10 September 2002, Official Records*, ICC-ASP/1/3, which refers to the procedure under Articles 36 and 37.

[24] The minimum voting requirement is calculated in accordance with paragraph 20(b) of Assembly of States Parties, *Procedure for the Nomination and Election of Judges of the International Criminal Court*, ICC-ASP/3/Res.6 as '2 minus the number of judges from that regional group remaining in office or elected in previous ballots. If the number of States Parties of any given regional group is higher than 16 at that moment, the minimum voting requirement for that group shall be adjusted by adding 1'. Note that the number of seats allocated to a regional group can increase in accordance with the number of states parties.

for international courts, representing an acceptance by states of more structured processes for the selection of international judges. During the negotiations on the resolutions, some states parties raised the possibility that states could renegotiate the UN regional groups for the ICC context. However, according to one interviewee, the consensus was that 'there was no way they wanted to reconsider renegotiating a separate regional group system for the ICC, because [the UN regional groups are] part of the furniture'.[25] The geographical representation requirements in the ASP resolutions act as minimum quotas leaving some 'free' or 'floating' seats to be allocated amongst the regional groups, hence the reference in Article 36(8)(a)(ii) to equitable geographical *representation* rather than *distribution*.[26] In this way, the ICC regional representation requirements, although they are set out in the voting requirements for the court, are in practice less rigid than those of the ICJ and provide greater flexibility in the allocation of seats across different regional groups.[27]

In practice, of eighteen judges elected, the first bench of the court consisted of the following numbers of judges from each of the regional groups: three from African states, three from the Asian states, one from Eastern European states, four from Latin America and Caribbean states and seven from Western Europe and other states.[28] In the second elections in 2006, one seat was lost by the Asian Group (Tuiloma Neroni Slade (Samoa)) and one gained by Eastern Europe (Ekaterina Trendafilova (Bulgaria)).[29] The casual elections in 2007 (to replace two WEOG and one GRULAC judge), to which no geographical minimum voting requirements applied, resulted in the election of one Asian judge (Fumiko Saiga (Japan), bringing Asian representation to three), one WEOG judge (Bruno Cotte (France), bringing WEOG representation down to six) and one African judge (Daniel David Nsereko (Uganda), bringing African representation up

[25] T4, 4.

[26] An interviewee who was involved in the negotiation of the election provisions of the Statute and the minimum voting rules said that states decided that it was not possible to have the legal experience requirements of List A and B *and* strict regional quotas as this would require significant cross-regional co-ordination (T3, 11). Another observer said that as it was not possible to negotiate with the regional groups and decide how many women, List A and List B, etc each would have, it was decided that the overall composition of the bench would be regulated through the election process: (T4, 3).

[27] Also note that they do not apply if there are insufficient candidates nominated (as provided by para 20(b)) for a regional group or if any of the conditions in para 21 apply: ASP Resolution 6. These provisions are discussed further in Chapter 3.

[28] Assembly of States Parties, *First Session (First and Second Resumptions), New York, 3–7 February and 21–23 April 2003, Official Records*, ICC-ASP/1/3/Add.1, paras 15–31. There was only one judge from Eastern Europe elected. There were no Eastern European candidates that reached the two-thirds threshold in the first four ballots and in accordance with para 7 of *Procedure for the Election of the Judges for the International Criminal Court*, ICC-ASP/1/Res.3, the minimum voting requirements ceased to apply (the predecessor of the current provision in para 21 of ASP Resolution 6). Judge Anita Ušacka (Latvia) was elected in the ninth ballot.

[29] However, the number of judges from Asia was left at two, as required under the Rome Statute. Assembly of States Parties, *Resumed Fourth Session, New York, 26–27 January 2006, Official Records*, ICC-ASP/4/37, paras 15–20.

to four).[30] In the third triennial elections in 2009, a total of six judges were elected from the following regions: two from each of Africa and WEOG, one from GRULAC and one from Asia, therefore increasing African seats to five and decreasing Asian seats to two.[31] In August 2009, the ICC comprised five judges from Africa, one from Asia,[32] two from Eastern Europe, three from GRULAC[33] and six from WEOG.[34] At present, Africa and WEOG share the 'floating' seats, with two and three seats respectively.

The adequacy of geographical representation

States wish to see their national candidates appointed to international courts for a number of reasons. In the interviews, the reasons given indicated that in most cases international judges are seen as indirectly representing their respective states. As noted previously, representation is closely linked to perceptions of the legitimacy of international courts. One legal adviser at a Permanent Mission to the UN summed up this perspective: 'No matter what national interest or prestige is at stake, they are aware of the perception, the legitimacy of the court and the way it is perceived will be better if there is better regional representation on the courts.'[35] Given the importance of ensuring that states feel that there is an acceptable level of representation on the courts, it is perhaps not surprising that there are diverse views as to the adequacy and fairness of the current allocation of seats in the international courts generally and in the ICJ and ICC specifically. Interviewees highlighted the adequacy of the allocation of seats to different regional groups, the distribution of seats within regional groups and other issues relating to the impact of size, power and level of development on a state's prospects of being represented on the courts.

The current distribution of seats on the ICJ is now generally accepted, although there is some criticism as to whether it is fair in the current global context.[36] A former ICJ judge explained that 'The present division of the court is virtually the same as it was in 1946. And times have changed much since then. It ensures

[30] Assembly of States Parties, *Sixth Session, New York, 30 November–14 December 2007, Official Records,* Volume I, ICC-ASP/6/20, paras 26–33.

[31] Assembly of States Parties, *Seventh Session (First and Second Resumptions), New York, 19–23 January and 9–13 February 2009, Official Records*, ICC-ASP/7/20/Add.1, paras 15–24.

[32] A judicial vacancy existed as a result of the death while in office of Judge Saiga (Japan). An election was held in November 2009.

[33] Judge Blattmann (Bolivia) was due to remain in office until Trial Chamber I delivered its decision in the *Lubanga* trial. Judge Shahabuddeen (Guyana), elected in January 2009, had notified the ASP that he was unable to assume his position on the court, and an election to fill the vacancy was scheduled for November 2009.

[34] For the current composition, see: <http://www.icc-cpi.int/Menus/ICC/Structure+of+the+Court/> (accessed 28 April 2010). At the elections held in November 2009, Kuniko Ozaki (Japan) and Silvia Fernández de Gurmendi (Argentina) were elected to the ICC.

[35] T6, 7.

[36] Amerasinghe suggests that the current distribution of seats on the court may be contrary to the 'spirit of Article 9': C. F. Amerasinghe, 'Judges of the International Court of Justice—Election and Qualifications', op. cit., 347.

that Western Europe is over-represented and I don't understand why some other regions are not correctly represented.'[37]

Other interviewees shared similar concerns. An Eastern European PCA national group member described the regional distribution as 'not representative'.[38] Another interviewee described Eastern Europe as being over-represented, following the ending of the Cold War,[39] because 'the earlier distinction between the grouping of east and west Europe is becoming blurred'.[40] An international judge said: 'The court is basically a European court because the UN has kept this fiction of a separate Eastern European region and they are all members of the European Union now.'[41]

It was suggested that Asian states are 'underrepresented':

> Asia is culturally the most heterogeneous continent... you have [South East and North Asia], the Indian subcontinent and then you have all these lands from central Asia to the Mediterranean, with the addition of all these little islands in Oceania and the central Asian republics that emerged from the Soviet Union, it really is the most difficult campaign as we are all competing for one seat.[42]

Similar concerns were expressed by Eastern European interviewees regarding the first elections to the ICC, although some attributed this not to a lack of available seats on the court but rather to the lack of a coordinated election strategy within the Eastern European Group that led to the group not winning its full allocation of seats in the first elections.

The allocation of the 'floating' seats on the ICC has also led to some criticism. A Caribbean diplomat in New York said that there is a general perception that 'WEOG is over represented. The Africans complain about that a lot, saying that in terms of the most states parties in the ICC, I think they have the largest number of states parties. And they complain. Within the group of Latin American and Caribbean states, I think we are reasonably well served.'[43] Other interviewees thought that the flexibility in the allocation of certain seats on the ICC was an advantage. One Eastern European diplomat said: 'I was happy to see the African candidates trying to get the former Western post [in the second elections]. I guess that would be something I personally would like to see, so the Court does not become as petrified as the ICJ.'[44]

In relation to the 2007 elections to the ICC, a WEOG diplomat acknowledged that 'WEOG is already over-represented among the judges, so while it's a WEOG judge coming off, I'm not entirely convinced it need be a WEOG judge going back on. Particularly given that Japan is on the verge of becoming a party.'[45] Interviewees also expressed broader concerns about the limited possibilities for certain states to be represented on the ICJ. This is particularly so in the light of the number of seats taken up as a result of the P5 convention and the fact

[37] T31, 8. [38] T33, 14–15. [39] T44, 20–21. [40] T59, 13.
[41] T81, 10–11. [42] T81, 10–11. [43] T2, 13. [44] T6, 1. [45] T11, 17.

that certain states—Japan and Germany—have maintained virtually permanent membership on the court.[46]

Interviewees from some states complained of limited access to the bench because 'some countries tend to think that they have a permanent seat and that limits the possibility for the smaller ones to get in'.[47] These issues are also compounded by the fact that judges may be re-elected. One commentator has noted that the re-election of candidates from countries such as Germany, Japan and Brazil, based on political elements such as size and economic importance, may undermine the individual selection criteria of Article 2 as it prioritizes political factors over merit.[48] A superior court judge in a WEOG state criticized the system as being 'too institutionalized in favour of countries and groups of countries having expectations in relation to seats'.[49]

As to the claim that Japan considered that it should be permanently represented on the court,[50] one interviewee put it rather colourfully: 'Japan is like Zsa Zsa Gabor—if Zsa Zsa wants something, Zsa Zsa gets it. So they, with their money and their efficiency, they go and they get it. They shouldn't have a permanent judge on the court.'[51]

Although there is no P5 convention as such in the ICC, the P5 members that are States Parties to the Rome Statute have nevertheless been continuously represented on the bench so far. The conventions regarding representation from Japan and Germany also appear to have been carried over to the new court. When Japan joined the ICC, a number of interviewees from ASP delegations argued informally that Japan should be represented, if for no other reason than to secure from Japan a significant ongoing financial contribution to the court, to ensure greater representation of Asian judges (even though at that time all minimum geographical representation quotas had been met) and as a symbolic gesture. Moreover, there has been a German judge on the ICC since the very first elections.

An important subsidiary issue relating to geographical representation is that of sub-regional representation, which is the informal allocation or rotation of the seats of a regional group amongst different recognized sub-regions within that group. From the interviews it appears that all five regional groups at least adhere to some broad concept of 'rotation' of seats amongst their members. Rotation is not formalized, but rather depends on which state believes it has a good candidate and which has the strongest argument for claiming that it is its 'turn'. It can also depend on agreements between individual states as to which of them will contest a particular election as well as broader claims within the regional group. A member of the Eastern European group also explained that it can be difficult

[46] Amerasinghe also indicates a number of countries that have spent long periods on the bench, such as Algeria, Brazil, Nigeria, Senegal and Italy: C. F. Amerasinghe, 'Judges of the International Court of Justice—Election and Qualifications', op. cit., 347.

[47] T13, 10.

[48] C. F. Amerasinghe, 'Judges of the International Court of Justice—Election and Qualifications', op. cit., 348.

[49] T17, 2.

[50] T44, 19.

[51] T81, 10–11.

for Eastern European states who are EU members to gain representation on international bodies because there is a perception that they are already represented by their WEOG EU counterparts.[52]

In some regional groups, there are conventions (of varying degrees of acceptance) as to how the group's seats are to be divided. These conventions influence which states nominate candidates and which candidates will be endorsed, and have a significant impact on the likelihood of success. Examples include the northern and southern Europe seats in WEOG, the allocation of the three African seats between Northern Africa (Arab countries), francophone Africa and anglophone Africa,[53] and a looser rotation of the two GRULAC seats between 'the south, the north of South America, continental Central America and the English speaking Caribbean'.[54] Asia and Eastern Europe do not appear to have any particular sub-regional conventions. One African interviewee attributed the lack of Asian sub-regional distribution to the fact that there is 'no across-the-board regional organization'.[55]

These conventions often amount to little more than arguments used by a particular state as to why its candidate should have regional endorsement, or as a basis for tacit agreements between groups of states. According to one interviewee, the conventions are 'not strict'.[56] Another noted that they 'can be broken', as they may be subject to the power plays of the election process and can be overturned by lobbying and vote-trading.[57] Thus they may be displaced in the face of more pressing political concerns.

In relation to representation of Western European countries, and more broadly, WEOG states some interviewees complained of a north–south divide: 'For the past few elections there were no people from southern Europe, you know, from Portugal or Spain. I mean, invariably the Germans and the Dutch are more efficient and they win.'[58] A southern European diplomat complained that: 'We feel that southern Europe in general, not only here but also in other bodies, is sidelined by northern Europe or central Europe and the Commonwealth WEOG states.'[59]

The representation of southern Europe was also a contentious issue in the 1996 ICJ elections that resulted in the appointment of a Dutch judge, Pieter Kooijmans, and in the 2005 ICJ elections that appointed a New Zealand judge, Sir Kenneth Keith. The southern European states had considered that in both cases 'the post was for a national of a southern European country',[60] but they had only sought the support of other southern European countries, not to compete with them.[61] They were not successful in securing support amongst states in other regional groups.

[52] T15. Many interviewees also spoke about what they perceived to be structural disadvantages for small or developing states in the nomination and election processes that are discussed in Chapters 3 and 4.

[53] T47, 2.

[54] T53, 14.

[55] T47, 6.

[56] T82, 10.

[57] T47, 5.

[58] T81, 10–11.

[59] T9, 6.

[60] T39, 2.

[61] T39, 12.

A number of interviewees also asserted that there is evidence of a 'right' to replace a judge who has resigned or died before his or her term was completed with another judge of the same nationality. This argument was often combined with others relating to the continuity of representation of a particular sub-regional group. As one interviewee put it in relation to the ICC: 'At present the geographical area of Latin America and the Caribbean is represented by three judges from the Latin American area, with no representation from the English-speaking Caribbean area.'[62] In the ICC, the outgoing judge from this sub-regional group was not replaced by a judge from the same sub-regional group. Amongst some there is also a perception that there is a Nordic seat on the ICC, but it is 'all very informal as there is no such thing as a Nordic place anyway. But we try to use the argument saying, especially in judicial bodies that there is a specific Nordic legal culture that should be represented. It's different from the continental legal tradition.'[63] Again, any convention as to the mid-term replacement of a judge with another judge of the same sub-region or region may be overturned by lobbying and other political factors.

Despite the divergence of views about the strengths and weaknesses of the current system of geographical representation in the ICJ, the ICC and the international courts more generally, a clear consensus emerged from the interview data that representation on the courts remains an important political concern for many states. Several interviewees noted that the equitable geographical distribution convention in the ICJ had resulted in regional groups '"producing the number of candidates to fit the number of seats available for that group". Such a practice was referred to as a "clean slate".'[64]

Although clean slates are discouraged by the ICC nomination and election rules, they are still possible if states consider themselves bound by regional representation conventions.[65] Clean slates may occur by consensus, under pressure from a powerful country in the regional group, or simply because one state submitted their nomination first. As one diplomat from a WEOG country observed: 'Once a nomination is out there in a regional group it can be very hard politically for other countries to come forward with more nominations.'[66] Some interviewees commented that where clean slates have been put forward, this reflects a view that seats 'belong' to a regional group and that they can determine who will represent their region, without having this choice vetted through a contested election. Although it is not impossible that states would refuse to elect a clean slate candidate, at least in the ICJ it would be extremely unlikely in the context of the equitable geographical distribution convention. Not all candidates proposed on a clean slate are necessarily poor quality. However the absence of competition raises the prospect that a candidate could be elected without meeting the individual selection criteria.

[62] T27, 2. [63] T16, 8. [64] T37, 1.
[65] See Chapter 3 for a more detailed discussion of clean slates. [66] T3, 8.

All states reap the benefits of the universal acceptance of a principle of geographical representation, but they know that it comes with potential costs. One interviewee put it bluntly: 'Regional quotas per se are rather bad for quality.'[67] Another interviewee saw advantages and disadvantages of the practice: 'My personal view would be that regional distribution is still good because you don't want to have only one group represented. But it's also bad, because there could be better candidates out there.'[68] Another interviewee put it rather more starkly: 'Equitable geographical representation can be problematic, for example, if you expect a dictatorship to come up with an independent candidate.'[69] Yet another was pragmatic: 'Equitable geographical distribution is the most important thing, it is okay if politics are a big factor in these elections and sometimes the best are not elected, as long as there is representation.'[70]

It was also pointed out that geographical representation is a crucial part of what many diplomats described as the 'buy-in' factor for the court: 'We all know that we don't live in an ideal world, we live in a political world, and if all the best candidates for a full election or the majority of the candidates we would deem to be the best would come from the same geographical region, that wouldn't be received very well by the larger membership.'[71] Another asked: 'Should [states] throw out the concept of geographical representation if there is someone who is outstanding but would not get on the court due to these rules?' However, she conceded that however meritorious an idea this might be, it would be unlikely to happen.[72] Some interviewees were clear, nonetheless, about the need to produce high-quality candidates and that representation is a rather empty concept without this minimum standard: 'As for geographical representation, the problem is not quantitative it's qualitative. It must be ensured that the candidates have the correct profile.'[73]

The suggestion was also made that national pride might serve to ensure that at least adequate candidates are nominated. Few states would wish to have the reputation of having put forward a wholly incompetent judge.

Overall, the interviews demonstrated that geographical representation is still a live and divisive issue and one that leads to political compromise at the heart of the international judicial selection process. This has been confirmed by recent developments in relation to geographical representation in the International Tribunal for the Law of the Sea (ITLOS).[74] It is vital that existing rules and

[67] T3, 8. [68] T15, 9. [69] F22, 2.

[70] T62, 15–16. On this point, see S. Rosenne, *Rosenne's The World Court: What It Is and How It Works*, op. cit., 48–9. [71] T16, 8.

[72] F39, 2. [73] F43, 2.

[74] In 2009, the states parties to the UN Convention on the Law of the Sea decided upon a new arrangement for the allocation of seats on the tribunal after negotiations on proposals made by the African and Asian groups. The new arrangements allocate the seats on the twenty-one-member tribunal as follows: five members each from the Group of African States and Group of Asian States, four members from the Group of Latin American and Caribbean States, and three members each from the Group of East European States and Group of Western European and other

conventions ensure sufficiently wide and flexible representation that states accept and support the courts. Yet it is also recognized that this 'buy-in' can come at a cost in terms of the real or perceived quality and independence of the judges appointed.

The P5 convention

Tensions regarding the adequacy of representation are most clearly expressed in discussions about the P5 convention.[75] As noted in the previous section, the operation of this convention significantly limits the opportunities for states from the same region as P5 members to put forward successfully candidates for election to the ICJ. A number of interviewees expressed considerable frustration with the convention, particularly those from WEOG states. One commented that 'We, non-permanent members are at a disadvantage because already three posts are for practical purposes taken by nationals of the United States, UK, and France, because the election takes place both in the Security Council and in the General Assembly.'[76]

A former WEOG ad hoc ICJ judge complained that EU expansion has increased the difficulties for WEOG states because

> One of the criteria has been to keep permanently a post for a national of the five permanent members of the Security Council, therefore already two of our posts are taken by France and the UK...And with so many European states, it's impossible especially as now Germany took a post and they want to be there all the time.[77]

Non-Western European members of WEOG also described this situation as frustrating: 'with those five countries, it's a pretty big bite of the court membership when you think there are 190 potential candidates for the seats. Anyway, Canada, Australia and New Zealand have to come in sometime.'[78]

Some had concerns about the impact of the P5 convention on the representation of less powerful countries: 'No one is saying that the P5 does not promote

States (WEOG), and the one remaining seat elected from among the African and Asian Groups and WEOG: Press Release, SEA/1920, UN Department of Public Information (29 June 2009). In contrast to the composition of the ICJ and ICC, it is notable that only three seats are 'reserved' for judges from WEOG states.

[75] As noted above, Article 23 of the UN Charter provides that 'The Republic of China, France, the Union of Soviet Socialist Republics, the United Kingdom of Great Britain and Northern Ireland, and the United States of America shall be permanent members of the Security Council'. The only absence from the bench of any P5 member was during the period 1967–85 when China was not represented on the court: B. Fassbender, 'Chapter I. Organization of the Court: Article 9', op. cit., 270. Due to a struggle regarding the recognition of the People's Republic of China in the UN, the Republic of China (Taiwan) withdrew its candidate in the 1966 triennial elections and it was only in 1984 that the People's Republic of China nominated a candidate to take up the 'Chinese' seat: S. Rosenne, *Rosenne's The World Court: What It Is and How It Works*, op. cit., 45 and C. Harland, 'Special Report: International Court of Justice Elections: A Report on the First Fifty Years' *Canadian Yearbook of International Law* 34 (1996) 323 and 331–3.

[76] T9, 7.

[77] T44, 9.

[78] T60, 17.

good candidates; most of the candidates, in fact all, are highly qualified. But there is some concern that smaller countries are not as represented on the ICJ as they should be.'[79] The apparent sense of entitlement was also a cause of annoyance, as 'the P5 clearly sort of believe that they should be represented, every single one of them'.[80] It was questioned whether the convention had any rational basis 'because what is the fundamental reason why they established the five permanent members? It is international peace and security, and the Security Council is the main organ of the system regarding international peace and security, but it has no role outside of that.'[81]

Others were more positive, or at least realistic about the practice and prospects for change. A former ICJ judge, from a non-P5 member state, said that he was in favour of the convention, particularly in the cases of the UK and France, because of the importance of those countries, the quality of their judges and the languages they spoke. For their part, interviewees from P5 countries felt that there were certain standards that they had to maintain: 'I think it would be looked at with astonishment if we did not put forward an absolutely first-rate nominee for the vacancy when it arises.'[82] One interviewee from a P5 state also challenged any suggestion that the P5 convention undermined the quality of the judges appointed: 'There is no issue regarding the competence of P5 judges as in those countries there is generally competition between people with a good level of competence.'[83] Another interviewee reiterated this point, suggesting that the P5 convention was 'like the House of Lords, it is completely unjustifiable, but it works'.[84]

Yet, according to a number of diplomats, the P5 convention ensured the engagement of five powerful countries in the ICJ and in international legal processes. 'From a political point of view, since we are talking about very influential countries, there are some gains from a political perspective in having them on board in the ICJ.'[85]

Others stressed the role of the convention in promoting the court's effectiveness: 'The P5 convention is natural and normal as it is not very useful to have a decision if these countries do not participate.'[86] One PCA national group member was similarly pragmatic but questioned whether the convention fully achieved the 'buy-in' of the leading states: 'There's no use having a fully democratic tribunal if the major countries in the world aren't prepared to at some stage contemplate they might make themselves subject to it. Unfortunately, however, P5 control doesn't really seem to be reflected in complete adherence to the system.'[87] It is notable in this regard, of course, that notwithstanding the P5 convention, of the five Permanent Members of the Security Council, only the

[79] T2, 7. [80] T16, 9. [81] T58, 12. [82] T35, 2. [83] F19, 1.
[84] F32, 3. [85] T13, 9. [86] F29, 2. [87] T17, 10.

UK maintains a declaration under Article 36 of the Court's Statute accepting the court's jurisdiction as compulsory.[88]

Some interviewees, while critical of the P5 convention, accepted that it was a political reality and that states had to 'live with it'.[89] Acceptance does not, however, necessarily mean that states are resigned to its existence in the long term: 'Democratization is desirable in international organs but states can understand and accept that there are permanent members because it is in the Charter. It is *realpolitik* but they are not entirely happy with it. It should be different and many countries will soon start agitating for this.'[90] Indeed, there have been recent signs that the P5 convention may be under pressure, at least at the margins. Some interviewees from P5 countries themselves acknowledged that 'the convention has been vulnerable for a number of years'.[91] Another P5 interviewee said that he '[doesn't] have a sense that there is a P5 convention. The reality is that there is the election of candidates by the Security Council and the General Assembly and the inclusion of the Security Council shifts the balance in favour of the P5. But there is no sense that the P5 can always rely on that.'[92] An interviewee from a non-P5 state said: 'I don't think that people any longer consider that the P5 should be entitled as of right to be on either the ILC or the ICJ.'[93]

Although there is no P5 convention in other international courts, there are also, to varying degrees, expectations that the P5 states will need to be represented. P5 candidates have often—but not always—secured seats on the International Tribunal for the Law of the Sea (ITLOS) and the International Law Commission (ILC), and have to date been represented on the ICC.[94] Elections to the ILC and, more recently, to ITLOS have been taken as an indication of the strength of the P5 convention, even though some interviewees said that the failure of P5 candidates to be elected was owing to the particular political circumstances at the time, and did not signify a rejection of the P5 convention itself. In 1986, Sir Ian Sinclair, the member from the United Kingdom, was not re-elected to the ILC. According to one interviewee, this happened 'because the African and Asian countries were angry at Margaret Thatcher',[95] another said it was perhaps because of a desire to bring in 'new blood'.[96] The United Kingdom, according to an interviewee, took it as 'a blip on the screen; or it has proved to have been a blip on the screen, as it was probably produced by extraneous political events having nothing to do with that election'.[97]

Another 'blip' occurred for the United Kingdom in the 2005 ITLOS elections, when Judge David Anderson was not re-elected.[98] The following year

[88] A list of declarations recognizing the jurisdiction of the ICJ as compulsory is available on the ICJ website at <http://www.icj-cij.org> (accessed 28 April 2010).

[89] T18, 7.

[90] F17, 1.

[91] F32, 3.

[92] F48, 3–4.

[93] T19, 15.

[94] UK and France, the two P5 states that are states parties to the Rome Statute.

[95] F29, 2.

[96] T36, 3.

[97] T35, 15.

[98] Doc SPLOS/135. Although there is no formal convention that P5 members would be represented on the tribunal, the re-election of a sitting judge might normally have been expected.

a further challenge to the P5 convention arose, when Michael Matheson of the United States was not re-elected to the ILC.[99] One diplomat commented that 'The P5 convention is a strong convention, people take that into account, but apparently not strong enough. It was a big surprise to everybody that the American, Professor Matheson, wasn't elected to the ILC. It was a big, big surprise.'[100] Some attributed the result to a protest against the policy of the United States in Iraq, while one interviewee pointed to the election strategy of the United States and the fact that they 'didn't put Matheson in the Indonesian lounge' (the lounge at UN headquarters in New York where much of the lobbying for votes takes place).[101] Increasingly, there is a sense that 'there's nothing automatic' about P5 representation, even though 'it's still easier to get someone elected to the ICJ, because of the electoral system, than it is other courts'.[102] In contrast, elections to the ILC were described as 'just a straightforward vote and the Western group are always oversubscribed with candidates'.[103]

The failures of P5 candidates in ITLOS and the ILC elections have been cause for reflection. There was no suggestion in the interviews that these results were in any way a consequence of a lack of merit in the candidates concerned, but rather they were attributed to politics and lobbying. One US interviewee talked through the implications of the weakening of the P5 convention in terms of a changing approach to the selection process:

> I think the first time we lost an election was Michael Matheson for the International Law Commission... and I think the implications of that are still sinking in. It means that we need a different style. It was not that he was not qualified, but we'd never campaigned, we'd never done that sort of thing. For us, the whole selection process is a nomination process and that's pretty much the end of it...[104]

There are also indications that some P5 members feel that they must now make greater efforts in lobbying for their ICJ candidates in order to cover for 'the contingency, however small, that they will not be able to get their candidate elected'.[105] The P5 convention therefore appears to be increasingly open to challenge, although there is no immediate sign that it will disappear.[106]

[99] Michael Matheson obtained 114 votes of 186 states present and voting. The required simple majority was 94 votes, but eight candidates (the required quota for WEOG in accordance with: United Nations General Assembly, *Enlargement of the International Law Commission: Amendments to Articles 2 and 9 of the Statute of the Commission*, GA. Res. 36/39 (1981), para 3) received a higher number of votes: United Nations General Assembly, *Election of the Members of the International Law Commission*, UN Doc. A/61/PV.54 (2006) 6.

[100] T16, 9.

[101] F48, 3.

[102] T36, 1.

[103] T36, 3.

[104] T72, 9.

[105] T72, 9. It mainly appears to be France, the United States and the United Kingdom who are increasing their lobbying efforts. According to interviewees, China and Russia generally do not lobby or campaign for their candidates.

[106] Chapter 5 considers the prospects for its reform in more detail.

Legal systems

Article 9 of the ICJ Statute recommends that states ensure that the bench as a whole represents 'the main forms of civilization and . . . the principal legal systems of the world' while Article 36(8)(a)(i) of the Rome Statute requires that when electing judges of the ICC, states 'take into account the need . . . for the representation of the principal legal systems of the world'. These requirements have generally been regarded as being met through the convention of equitable geographical distribution for the ICJ, and the minimum voting requirements for the ICC. However, some states have suggested that the representation of different legal systems on the international bench requires the selection process to look beyond the allocation of seats in accordance with the UN regional groups to consider the overall diversity of the legal traditions of the judges on the bench.

Such an exercise poses a challenge in that it requires a classification of legal systems and cultures, and may explain why, until now, the representation of different legal systems has not been included in the more formal bench requirement rules or minimum voting requirements of any international court. As one interviewee explained: 'There was no requirement as to representation of different legal systems in the ICC Statute because there was no commonly accepted list of different countries and their legal systems and there were already three representation criteria.'[107]

A diversity of legal systems represented in the courts is seen by some to have potential benefits. The inclusion of judges who have developed their skills in a broad range of legal cultures may extend the reach or acceptability of the court's findings, as they will be developed and explained in a manner that takes into account the full range of legal systems. It also ensures that disputes which have a basis in national law are fully understood by the court.[108] In the case of the ICC, the presence of judges from different legal cultures can contribute to ensuring that the court is properly informed about the nature of preceding national criminal investigations or prosecutions before making decisions on jurisdiction.

Against these benefits, one disadvantage of seeking to select judges from diverse legal cultures is that international courts which draw heavily on one system of law can prove to be difficult environments for judges from other legal traditions. One interviewee with civil law training from one of the ad hoc international criminal tribunals said: 'I had to study this new kind of law, because

[107] T4, 4–5.

[108] This is a function that is also intended to be performed by judges ad hoc: see E. Lauterpacht, 'The Role of *Ad Hoc* Judges: Presentation by Professor Elihu Lauterpacht' in Connie Peck and Roy S. Lee (eds), *Increasing the Effectiveness of the International Court of Justice: Proceedings of the ICJ/UNITAR Colloquium to Celebrate the 50th Anniversary of the International Court of Justice* (The Hague: Kluwer Law International, 1997) 371–8 and S. Schwebel, 'National Judges and Judges Ad Hoc of the International Court of Justice' *International and Comparative Law Quarterly* 48(4) (1999) 889–900.

in terms of substantive and procedure it is quite frankly new to me, because it is Anglo-Saxon. It is not easy for me to deal with.'[109]

Nevertheless, these problems are generally accepted as inevitable given the reality of the increased complexity and extended reach of international jurisdictions. It was clear from the interviews that the representation of different legal systems is recognized as necessary and valuable: 'I think it's essential the International Court be composed by people from different legal systems and different civilizations.'[110] This view was particularly strongly held by interviewees from states with legal systems that stand outside main legal traditions (for example, those of Nordic countries), or that are the minority in a particular regional group (for example, the Commonwealth Caribbean countries in GRULAC). A diplomat from a Nordic country emphasized: 'It is really important to have all the major legal systems in all the corners of the world represented, even though it is not mandatory in any way.'[111] The point was reiterated by another Nordic diplomat: 'The different legal cultures have to be represented; you cannot have a majority of judges from one legal system and the other systems severely under-represented because it wouldn't produce a balanced judicial examination of cases.'[112]

A Ministry of Foreign Affairs legal adviser from a legal system based on Islamic law noted:

> In terms of regional factors, the geographical regional grouping is not so important in terms of who should be on the court. What is more important is that judges should represent different legal systems; this is more important than geography. There should ideally always be an Arab/Islamic legal system judge on the bench. The ICJ system is a fairly good one, as there is fair geographical distribution, but there is also a need to ensure all legal systems are represented. It is not a political body so there is not only pure geographical distribution, but also a need to ensure the diversity of legal systems is taken into account.[113]

Some of the divisions of sub-regional representation in UN regional groups are based on legal systems, suggesting that states seek to address some of these concerns at sub-regional level. One interviewee explained that in Africa the seats are notionally divided between judges from 'continental, common law and Arab legal systems'.[114] In GRULAC, the common law Caribbean countries have also sought to be represented. In relation to the ILC,[115] in the WEOG group it was proposed that: '... within the group there should be at least one, arguably two out of the eight WEOG seats reserved for the common law countries, so it is an argument that one uses.'[116]

One interviewee from a civil law state also expressed concern at 'the increased number of common law lawyers on the ICJ over the last decades'.[117] A judge from

109 T34, 13. 110 T44, 19. 111 T13, 10. 112 T16, 11. 113 F26.
114 T47, 5.
115 Article 8 of the ILC Statute is in the same terms as Article 9 of the ICJ Statute.
116 T19, 4. 117 T44, 16.

a common law jurisdiction questioned whether this was the case: 'In so far as the common law world is concerned, there is an American and a Sierra Leonean, and a British judge and a New Zealander so that is only four out of fifteen, which is hardly over-representation.'[118]

Linguistic competence

Views on linguistic diversity reflect many of the concerns relating to the representation of legal systems. Language is often tied to the specificities of a particular legal system, enabling the expression of concepts that may not be readily translated into other languages.[119] Nonetheless, international courts must have official languages to be able to function efficiently. The requirement of competence in those languages is essential even though it does narrow the selection pool and act as a potential barrier to appointment for some high-quality candidates: 'Few potential candidates in [state x] had adequate language skills in French or English which would have impacted on their ability to participate in the work of the court, so candidates were not nominated.'[120] In another state, an interviewee noted that 'For the ICC nomination, the selection pool consisted of one person who was a diplomat, because national judges did not have sufficient language skills.'[121]

The failure to assess properly the official language skills of potential candidates during the selection process, or the absence of candidates with appropriate skills, has in some instances undermined the ability of some judges to participate adequately in the work of the court in question. This problem has attracted particular attention in relation to the European Court of Human Rights (ECtHR) as a result of its rapidly expanding membership and its full representation structure.[122]

Even when judges have competence in an official language, concerns were also expressed that the international courts are becoming increasingly anglophone as a result of the increasingly widespread use of English in international communications:[123]

I think many judges want to speak more in English because now it is more common and entrenched as the language for negotiations. Another fundamental reason is that

[118] T60, 25.

[119] See, for example, Report of the Brandeis Institute for International Judges 2009, *International Justice: Past, Present, and Future* (Brandeis University, 2009) 19–25; available at: <http://www.brandeis.edu/ethics/pdfs/internationaljustice/biij/BIIJ2009.pdf> (Accessed 28 April 2010).

[120] General, T33, 21–2.

[121] T39, 9.

[122] Committee on Legal Affairs and Human Rights, Parliamentary Assembly, *Nomination of candidates and election of judges to the European Court of Human Rights,* Doc. 11767, (1 December 2008), available at: <http://assembly.coe.int/Documents/WorkingDocs/Doc08/EDOC11767.pdf> (Accessed 28 April 2010).

[123] Note, however, that the working language of the European Court of Justice is French, while the official languages are those of the EU member states.

those who speak French can speak English. Many of those who speak English don't speak French at all, and therefore the only common language to understand each other is English.[124]

This is a matter of concern for francophone judges:

Those who are Francophone or closer to the French culture are a little upset because at present English is almost the working language of every judge. The problem is that the number of judges who have French as a working language is now only three or four. In the past, it was more or less 50/50, but in the new composition of the Court this has changed, because for instance, the German judge can understand French but he opted for English.[125]

According to a hispanophone judge, even though interpretation is available, the dominance of English gives judges from English-speaking jurisdictions an advantage: 'To speak English is to be able to have more influence over the decisions of the Court. To speak with other colleagues in the caféteria, in corridors, it is necessary to speak a little bit of English.'[126]

Some states have sought to promote linguistic diversity through sub-regional representation. The sub-regional divisions in Africa and the GRULAC, in particular, seek to ensure the representation of particular language groups in those regions, and hence greater linguistic diversity on the bench as a whole.

The English-speaking Caribbean countries have sought 'to ensure that there is at least one English speaker within the region in elections where geographical representation is a factor'.[127] The division of seats within the African region is based on legal system and linguistic lines, so that common law countries are anglophone, the civil law countries are francophone and the Arab legal system countries speak Arabic. Some interviewees suggested that there are different ways in which the fulfilment of geographical, linguistic and legal system expectations can be achieved across all African seats; for example, if one judge from the region speaks a number of languages, it might be argued that there does not need to be a judge from each language group, thereby opening seats to candidates from other parts of Africa or legal systems.[128] Countries from outside regional groups often support campaigns of candidates who speak their language, particularly when those candidates come from their ex-colonies; for example, in relation to an anglophone African candidate who won an ICJ seat: 'It was put to states, by many, including the British, that this is an anglophone.'[129] International organizations such as l'Organization de la Francophonie also often endorse candidates.

One interviewee suggested that judges should 'ideally have competence in both French and English',[130] and that 'mastery of these languages is more important than which geographical region a judge comes from'.[131] This suggests

[124] T44, 30. [125] ibid, 29. [126] T39, 14. [127] T25, 12.
[128] See T82, 9–10. [129] T47, 5. [130] T48, 12. [131] ibid.

the linguistic competence of international judges is an important factor in their ability to play an active and influential role in an international court and perhaps that language ability will become an increasingly important requirement in the eyes of states.

Judges with specific expertise

The statutes of the ad hoc international criminal courts and the ICC include provisions requiring that, in the election of judges, states take into account the need for judges with particular legal expertise on the bench. In relation to the ICC, Article 36(5) of the Rome Statute sets out two lists from which the judges must be drawn. At least nine judges must be appointed with experience in the areas set out in List A:[132] 'Criminal law and procedure and the necessary relevant experience in criminal proceedings as a judge, prosecutor, advocate or similar;'[133] and at least five judges with experience from List B: 'Relevant areas of international law (such as international humanitarian law and human rights law) and extensive experience in a professional legal capacity that is relevant to the work of the ICC'.[134]

In addition, Article 36(8)(b) requires state parties to 'take into account the need to include judges with legal expertise on specific issues, including, but not limited to, violence against women or children'. The List A and List B quotas are mandatory and enforced by the minimum voting requirements set down by the ASP whereas Article 36(8)(b) leaves a degree of discretion.

Interviewees expressed a range of views as to whether the List A and List B requirements of the ICC were an effective way to ensure an efficient and well-qualified bench, and whether the overall balance it seeks to strike in terms of the composition of the bench is the right one. Amongst those who could see the merits of a mixed bench in terms of experience, views varied on whether the formula was appropriate: 'now whether this list A and B requirement really is conducive to having better candidates, I'm not so sure. To some extent, I would question the wisdom of having such a high number of international lawyers required.'[135]

International NGOs also expressed the view recently that more List A judges should be elected to the ICC as it moved into its trial phase.[136] The List A and B criteria were agreed to satisfy the demands of certain states that wanted the pre-trial and trial divisions of the court to comprise judges with criminal law

[132] See also ASP Resolution 6, para 20(a).
[133] Rome Statute, Article 36(3)(b)(i).
[134] Rome Statute, Article 36(3)(b)(ii).
[135] T3, 11.
[136] Coalition for the International Criminal Court, 'CICC Recommended Criteria for States Parties to Nominate and Elect Judges to the ICC', available at: <http://www.iccnow.org/documents/CICC_Judicial_Nomination_Election_Criteria_FINAL.pdf> (accessed 3 October 2008) and Human Rights Watch, 'Nomination of Candidates for the 2009 ICC Judicial Election: Letter to Foreign Affairs Ministers of ICC States Parties', available at: <http://www.hrw.org/en/news/2008/08/19/nomination-candidates-2009-icc-judicial-election> (accessed 3 September 2008).

experience and the appeals division to comprise judges with international law experience,[137] but in the end no such fixed quotas were established.[138] Nevertheless, the final compromise model was intended to ensure that judges with different but appropriate types of experience were responsible for different stages of the judicial process:

> Because there was a great divergence of view between people who wanted to have professorial judges, and people who wanted to have real judges. We wanted real judges. And that's what led both to the rather curious structure for the election of the two categories of people. And that was very carefully calculated to ensure that at the levels in which it mattered, the pre-trial chamber and the trial chamber, you would inevitably have a preponderance of people with professional experience, whereas, as you moved up the judicial hierarchy, you could have more people with purely abstract experience.[139]

This resulted in a bench which, according to one interviewee, was problematic because 'more than 50% had no prior experience or knowledge of a judicial process'.[140] Whilst another said: 'The gender requirements and List A and B are a complete mess. In the first round only women from Africa and criminal lawyers were elected. Does the court have greater legitimacy? This is hard to measure.'[141] Concerns about the outcome produced by the List system were shared by many other interviewees. Some felt, however, that 'the balance in the Statute between List A and B is fine'.[142]

The interview data reveals that views differ as to the ideal composition in terms of expertise for particular courts. Similarly, interviewees had differing views as to whether this type of representation is best secured through formal rules or looser guidelines and recommendations. In the majority of courts, notably the ICJ, there are no composition requirements at all based on specific categories of expertise. Although the issues around such provisions are still contentious, the experience of the ICC demonstrates that it is possible to shape the overall composition of expertise on the bench and to specify criteria relating to expertise that it may not be realistic or desirable for *all* members of the bench to have, but which are extremely valuable if they can be included for a particular court. As new, increasingly specialized international courts are created, this may become a more common feature of the overall bench requirements for those courts. Ensuring that the slate of candidates presented for election adequately reflects the desired range of expertise is problematic where—as remains the case in most international courts and tribunals—there is no pre-election screening of the qualifications and experience of candidates, either individually or by reference to the slate as a whole.

137 M. Rwelamira, 'Composition and Administration of the Court' in Roy S. Lee (ed), *The International Criminal Court: The Making of the Rome Statute: Issues, Negotiations, Results* (The Hague: Kluwer Law International/UNITAR, 1999) 159–60. See also Rome Statute, Article 39(1).

138 Rome Statute, Article 36(5).

139 T35, 11–12.

140 T24, 10.

141 F19, 3.

142 T7, 13.

Gender balance

In comparison to the increasing focus on gender balance in national courts, the low numbers of women appointed to the international courts has attracted relatively little attention.[143] The claim by the most senior woman judge in the UK that 'a diverse judiciary is an indispensable requirement of any democracy' is widely accepted in debates on gender balance at national level.[144] Although few would explicitly reject the suggestion that the argument has equal applicability in the international courts, this rhetorical approval has yet to translate into widespread support for proactive measures designed to improve gender balance in the international courts. Nevertheless, the interviews indicated a range of views about the need for gender balance, including some diversity as to the best way to encourage it.

There are no requirements as to gender representation in the ICJ Statute. There has been only one female judge on the court, apart from judges ad hoc,[145] Dame Rosalyn Higgins (United Kingdom), who served as a judge from 1995 to 2009 and as President from 2006 until 2009.[146] According to Senator Miriam Defensor Santiago, a female ICJ candidate in 2008, geographical representation and political considerations are generally considered by states to be more important in the ICJ context than gender representation.[147] By contrast, the ICC Statute requires states, in selecting judges, to 'take into account' the need for a fair representation of female and male judges.[148] The minimum voting requirements require that the bench have at least six judges of each gender.[149] As at December 2009, there were eleven female judges[150] and seven male judges on the court.[151]

[143] R. Mackenzie and P. Sands, 'Judicial Selection for International Courts: Towards Common Principles and Practices', op. cit., 224–5.

[144] Baroness Hale of Richmond, 'The Appointment and Removal of Judges: Independence and Diversity', International Association of Women Judges, 8th Biennial Conference, 3–7 May 2006, Sydney, Australia, available at: <http://www.iawj.org/what/Session3Hale.doc> (accessed 20 November 2008). See also B. McLachlin, 'Why We Need Women Judges', International Association of Women Judges, 8th Biennial Conference, 3–7 May 2006, Sydney, Australia, available at: <http://www.iawj.org/what/Session4BMcLachlin.doc> (accessed 20 November 2008).

[145] The first female ad hoc judge, Judge Suzanne Bastid was designated by Tunisia in Application for Revision and Interpretation of the Judgment of 24 February 1982 in the Case concerning the *Continental Shelf (Tunisia/Libyan Arab Jamahiriya)* (*Tunisia v Libyan Arab Jamahiriya*) Judgment, ICJ Reports 1985, 192. She is the only judge ad hoc to have ever voted against his or her appointing state on the merits. She was followed by Judge Christine Van Den Wyngaert designated by Belgium in *Arrest Warrant of 11 April 2000* (*Democratic Republic of the Congo v Belgium*) Judgment, ICJ Reports 2002, 3. She sat between 2000 and 2002 and is currently a judge of the ICC.

[146] Judge Higgins (UK, 1995) and Senator Miriam Defensor Santiago (Philippines, 2008) are the only women to have been nominated for election to the ICJ.

[147] M. Lim Ubac, 'Santiago Blames "Power Game"' *Philippine Daily Inquirer* 8 November 2008, available at: <http://globalnation.inquirer.net/news/breakingnews/view/20081108-171051/Sant> (accessed 12 November 2008).

[148] Rome Statute, Article 36(8)(a)(iii).

[149] ASP Resolution 6, para 20(c).

[150] The full list of judges is available at: <http://www.icc-cpi.int/Menus/ICC/Structure+of+the+Court/Chambers/The+Judges/> (Accessed 28 April 2010).

[151] Note the NGO activity on this issue, most notably by the Women's Initiatives for Gender Justice (<http://www.iccwomen.org>) in relation to the ICC, where they have produced

Amongst interviewees, there were mixed views about the desirability of mandatory gender representation requirements. A number were in favour of promoting greater representation of women on the courts and were concerned about the limited numbers to date, considering that 'it would be great if we had more female expertise on the court'. One diplomat said that 'it's a very important issue for us. For instance, if all other things are equal and we had a choice between a female and a male candidate, we would likely vote for the female candidate if women were underrepresented on that particular body'.[152] Another interviewee said in relation to the nomination and appointment of judges that the lack of a fair representation of female judges on international courts and tribunals was 'of some concern'.[153]

Of those who were in favour of a greater representation of women, however, there were few who could attest to taking concrete steps towards identifying and nominating women candidates. One PCA national group member said that 'in our group of the Permanent Court of Arbitration I thought that we must nominate a woman. I was taught by women who are very good professors of international law. That is the feeling we have in the group.'[154] Another interviewee took a more generalized view: 'As to gender, there is clearly a need to rebalance the court but it is important not to force things. There needs to be an institutionalization of sensitivity to gender and the need to put women forward.'[155]

However, one international judge doubted whether the concern about gender was as deep-seated as it seemed:

> I remember from the various UN bodies to which I belong that a lot of things are said and many crocodile tears are shed. But when it comes to a country really fighting [for women] to be elected then I have personally had the occasion of watching people shedding a lot of tears about the lack of women candidates who I know had pushed female candidates aside in their own country.[156]

Some interviewees clearly rejected the need for any provisions to encourage gender equality, seeing it as a problem that was no longer relevant, as one international judge explained: 'I don't see the necessity for emphasis on gender, because women in any event are holding their own there; they are more than 60 per cent of university entrants in the Western world now.'[157] Others had concerns about the potential impact of 'affirmative action' on the merit of candidates, maintaining

publications setting out the 'Profile of Judicial Candidates' for ICC elections, for example, Women's Initiatives for Gender Justice, *Profile of Judicial Candidates: Election—JANUARY 2009*, 10 November 2008, available at: <http://www.iccwomen.org/news/docs/Profile_of_Judicial_Candidates-Web_Final.pdf> (accessed 5 December 2008). See also C. Steains, 'Gender Issues' in Roy S. Lee (ed), *The International Criminal Court: The Making of the Rome Statute: Issues, Negotiations, Results* (The Hague: Kluwer Law International, 1999) 357–90 and L. Chappell, 'The International Criminal Court: A New Arena for Transforming Gender Justice' in Shirin M. Rai and Georgina Waylen (eds), *Global Governance: Feminist Perspectives* (Basingstoke: Palgrave Macmillan, 2008) 160–84.

152 T16, 11.

153 T27, 5.

154 T39, 7.

155 F43, 2.

156 T77–80, 8–9.

157 T24, 11.

that the appointment of female candidates is simply a political knee-jerk response: 'when you have this quota system, you compromise standards'.[158] There were also suggestions that some male candidates were resentful that seven of the seats on the ICC had gone to female candidates in the first election: 'I think there is a danger that the men, as the group which is more or less on the retreat in that regard, consider that a quota rule leads to people who wouldn't deserve to be elected to that body.'[159]

One diplomat saw gender as one factor amongst many which can be taken into account in determining the right candidate and producing a balanced court: 'The second best will work too. If [a second candidate] represents another legal system completely different from the first, and is a woman, that is going to achieve a greater good than having the absolutely top best.'[160]

Underlying some comments was a sense that women are in some way unfairly advantaged by the minimum voting rules in the ICC, so that they 'are more likely to win elections for the ICC',[161] even though male candidates also have at least six seats reserved for them. Some suggested that the gender requirements were a 'box ticking' exercise in the first round of the first ICC elections in 2003: 'What happened is that states apparently dealt with the gender issue. They selected the required number of women who should be on the bench and one other judge, one male judge, from Korea, was elected.'[162] It was also suggested that some states are pressing for a reduction in the number women on the court: 'I have heard that some state parties are not very inclined to keep that gender balance, but probably the NGOs will push for that. We need to have the gender balance. We have to fulfil the requirement established in the statute.'[163]

Such comments are an important reminder that measures to promote equitable gender representation on the international courts are still new and relatively controversial. Whereas the requirements for geographical, legal and linguistic diversity are widely accepted, in principle, as necessary to ensure a competent, politically legitimate court, attitudes towards gender balance are generally much more ambivalent.

C. Individual selection criteria for the ICJ and ICC

According to Article 2 of the ICJ Statute, the judges selected must be 'of high moral character' and should either 'possess the qualifications required in their respective countries for appointment to the highest judicial offices'

[158] T29, 15.

[159] T77-80, 9. See also C. Stephen, 'Women Judges Dominate World's New War Crimes Court' *Guardian* 9 February 2003, available at: <http://www.guardian.co.uk/world/2003/ feb/09/ warcrimes> (accessed 12 November 2008).

[160] T10, 24.

[161] T39, 10.

[162] T2, 11.

[163] T76, 6.

or 'be jurisconsults of recognized competence in international law'.[164] These alternatives, originally drafted for the Permanent Court of International Justice (PCIJ) and later adopted for the Statute of the ICJ, were intended to accommodate a common law preference for international judges with national judicial experience and a civil law preference for non-judges.[165] However, the first of the two qualification options does not require that an ICJ judge should have held the highest judicial office, merely that she or he is qualified to do so. In practice, states vary widely in their criteria for membership of their highest courts, and some do not require any legal background.[166] The ICJ Statute does not define the term 'jurisconsult', but it appears to mean an expert in law, particularly international law,[167] although not necessarily a person qualified as a lawyer in any national jurisdiction. It would seem that the original PCIJ individual selection criteria were intended to give credence to national law and standards for judicial selection and leave states a degree of discretion in deciding whom to nominate and elect.

In contrast to the rather general criteria for selection to the ICJ, the ICC Statute requires that each of the eighteen judges of that court:

- be of high moral character, impartiality and integrity;[168] *and*
- possess the qualifications required in their respective states for appointment to the highest judicial offices;[169] *and*
- have expertise in:
  - criminal law and procedure and the necessary relevant experience in criminal proceedings as a judge, prosecutor, advocate or similar (List A);[170] *or*
  - relevant areas of international law (such as international humanitarian law and human rights law) and extensive experience in a professional legal capacity that is relevant to the work of the ICC (List B);[171] *and*
- have an excellent knowledge of and be fluent in at least one of the working languages of the court.[172]

The ICC Statute uses the formulation of the ICJ regarding the qualifications required for highest judicial office. However, the ICC requirements are cumulative, as each judge must also meet the criteria in either List A or B. In this way, individual criteria are very closely tied to the overall composition of the bench. Some states also sought a requirement that ICC judges should have practical

164 ICJ Statute, Article 2.

165 M. O. Hudson, *The Permanent Court of International Justice, 1920–1942: a treatise* (New York: The Macmillan Company, 1943), para 138.

166 Amerasinghe notes that this first alternative in Article 2 is almost never used, and according to him has only been used once since 1966 as the sole basis on which a candidate was nominated: C. F. Amerasinghe, 'Judges of the International Court of Justice—Election and Qualifications', op. cit., 339.

167 ibid, 338.

168 Rome Statute, Article 36(3)(a).

169 ibid, Article 36(3)(a).

170 ibid, Article 36(3)(b)(i).

171 ibid, Article 36(3)(b)(ii).

172 ibid, Article 36(3)(c).

legal professional experience. List A reflects this, but List B allows for 'extensive experience in a professional legal capacity'. This has been interpreted by some states as not necessarily involving working as a practising lawyer.

The criteria for the ICC are clearly more detailed than those for the ICJ, and reflect the eras in which the courts were created as well as the subject-matter they address. At the international level, the judicial selection practice of the PCIJ and the ICJ, and other courts such as the European Court of Justice and the ECtHR, as well as the ad hoc criminal tribunals, provided additional experience on which states could draw in designing the ICC procedures.

The fact that the ICC is a criminal court underlined the need for a bench capable of adjudicating cases involving the potential deprivation of individual liberty. It also needed to cope with a range of procedural issues arising in criminal proceedings, including ensuring rights of the accused and the taking of evidence. ICC judges need to be skilled in specific areas of law and procedure to be able to deal effectively with these matters, and also to assure potential state parties that the court could deliver fair trials. This resulted in a consensus that judicial selection criteria should be more clearly defined and the latitude of states should be restricted.

The career profiles of judges in the ICJ and ICC

How have the ICJ and ICC judicial selection criteria translated into the actual composition of the bench? In practice, the profiles of ICJ judges have varied widely over the life of the court. Judges have generally been drawn from academia, national courts, the diplomatic corps or national civil service.[173]

In relation to the ICC, the candidates in the first elections were generally either diplomats who had been members of state delegations in the negotiations of the Rome Statute, academics with involvement in the drafting or ratification of the Statute, or national criminal judges. As with the ICJ, most candidates brought a range of different professional experiences including in legal practice, academia, the diplomatic corps and the civil service. The interviews revealed criticisms of the election of some judges appointed to the ICC to date, with particular concerns raised about individuals who did not appear to have academic legal training, and those with no knowledge of international criminal law or litigation experience. Some interviewees felt that the appointment of such judges could compromise the legitimacy of the court and even potentially raise grounds for appeal.

The careers of most international judges defy easy categorization, although some generalities do emerge. This has been the case since the inception of the

[173] D. Terris, C. P. R. Romano and L. Swigart, *The International Judge: An Introduction to the Men and Women Who Decide the World's Cases*, International Courts and Tribunals Series (Oxford: Oxford University Press, 2007) 20.

ICJ[174] and continues to be so, particularly amongst the younger judges who are increasingly joining the ranks of the international judiciary. The following sections will consider views on the propriety of experience in academia, the national judiciary and diplomatic or government service as preparation for work as an international judge. It is clear that there is no common understanding as to what constitutes an 'ideal international judge'. Perspectives about the relative merits of one group of potential candidates over another depend on the position, organization and status of that group at the national level, the legal and political culture of the particular country, as well as broader values held about the nature of the legal process and the role an international court, and its judges, should play. Views on the most appropriate experience and qualifications for judicial office also differ according to the court under discussion and its key functions and jurisdiction.[175] Further, the pool of available potential candidates depends on a range of factors. These include training and opportunities for development at the national level, access to decision-makers and the views of those decision-makers as to who would be an appropriate international judge, relative salary levels, post-bench career opportunities and the perception of the particular court amongst potential candidate groups.

Academia

Academia is traditionally acknowledged as a legitimate 'source' of international judges, particularly for the ICJ. A former judicial candidate expressed a widely held view on the background of a typical ICJ judge: 'it tends to be a little academic in a way, slightly diplomatic, but very slightly. Mainly, I think, you have to be a professor of international law'.[176] A PCA national group member said that academics have the ability to push the boundaries of international law and 'use their knowledge to develop a new theory and to go further into the new facts in front of them.'[177] Another expressed the belief that academics will often demonstrate greater independence: 'Professors are very good candidates because officials of government are necessarily very much influenced by the positions of their countries, whilst the professors have, I would say, more liberty.'[178]

[174] For example, Abdel Hamid Badawi of Egypt and Jules Basdevant of France: see A. Eyffinger, *The International Court of Justice: 1946–1996* (The Hague: Kluwer Law International, 1996) 266–7.

[175] Note that the debate regarding what the appropriate skills and experience are for judicial decision-makers is also alive at the national superior court level. Discussing whether lawyers should select High Court judges, Justice Michael Kirby of the Australian Court recently said: 'There is no reason to believe that lawyers with special skills in insolvency or trusts law have the essential skills for adjudicating the great constitutional conflicts in our nation. Politicians know this. Some lawyers never learn its truth': M. Kirby, 'Neville Wran—A Lawyer Politician—Reflections of Law Reform and the High Court of Australia', Inaugural Neville Wran Lecture, Parliament of New South Wales, Thursday 13 November 2008, available at: <http://www.nswbar.asn.au/circulars/november08/wran.pdf> (accessed 14 November 2008).

[176] T55, 10–11. [177] T50, 12. [178] T41, 3.

However, more critical views on this issue were expressed by those from countries where lecturers and professors have more limited academic freedom. Even in environments where there is a generally high level of academic independence, concerns about their reputation may constrain professors' freedom of decision-making. According to one former international judge: 'There is a tendency to ask, well, if I decide this way, what would my students think, or what would my university think?'[179]

On the other hand, some saw academic independence as a potential barrier to nomination as academics might not be seen as close enough to government to win a nomination, or might be perceived as unpredictable. In addition, some noted that academics might lack skills required for managing litigation: 'Everybody has had experience of lots of people with brilliant academic careers who'd be appalling judges.'[180] Others noted that academics may sometimes adopt the wrong approach to judicial decision-making, because 'they are not asking: who has the better argument?'[181] Instead, 'they may think that's a very interesting question that's not been addressed in the literature. This is an opportunity to clarify this interesting question',[182] rather than focusing on resolving the dispute.

One observer asserted that a court comprised mainly of academics and diplomats will be more inclined to seek the 'middle ground and avoid more robust, legally reasoned judgments'.[183] An international judge considered that this might be seen by some to be a 'cowardly approach' to international judicial decision-making that could lead to criticism of the international courts.[184] However, an interviewee with an academic background expressed the view that academics can make an important contribution to a complementary and balanced bench, by assisting judges with backgrounds as practitioners or diplomats to understand the underlying theory of the arguments being made.[185]

National judges

An equally wide range of opinions was expressed as to the merits of selecting national judges to sit on the international bench. A recurring concern in the interviews was that national judges lack substantive knowledge of international law. Referring to his own national jurisdiction, one PCA national group member said:

> I don't know whether the same could be said in other countries, but in my experience, and also during my many years at the legal bureau of the Ministry of Foreign Affairs, the degree of knowledge of international law in general by domestic judges is very, very low.[186]

[179] T37, 6. [180] T19, 3. [181] T37, 6. [182] ibid. [183] T26, 4.
[184] T26, 4. [185] F39, 1.
[186] T41, 13. In a number of countries, national judges are dually excluded by a lack of knowledge of international law and of competency in one of the official languages of the particular court, an issue that will discussed in the section on language.

Another PCA national group member said that in the selection of candidates for the ICJ, knowledge of international law was the most important consideration. It is not normally found amongst 'people who have experience in national courts'.[187] As one Western European PCA national group member said: 'I prefer a known lawyer to an unknown judge, because an unknown judge knows very, very little about international law.'[188] These types of concerns were expressed principally with regard to the ICJ.

As regards the ICC, particularly strong views were expressed as to the appropriate background for ICC judges and whether practical professional legal or judicial experience is necessary. One interviewee depicted the struggle between the common law and civil law countries at the Rome Conference over the criteria for the ICC as an attempt to prevent states from:

> ...putting forward hack diplomats in order to make sure that it would be [a] proper criminal court and to make sure all members had training as judges. Some civil lawyers thought this was a common law plot. Some also said there was a need for international humanitarian lawyers, and that this experience was unlikely to be found in national criminal judges.[189]

This tension between common law and civil law perspectives was evident across the board. Several interviewees held the strong view that in addition to substantive legal knowledge, international courts need judges who have practical judicial experience, particularly in the ICC. The view was expressed the view that a deficit of practical judicial experience on the bench would have an adverse impact on the image and legitimacy of the ICC. One former legal adviser put it as follows: 'The quality of the courts is going to be determined entirely by the quality of the judges, and the quality of the judge you needed for a criminal tribunal isn't the same...the experience, the background, is not the same as would fit a person for the other tribunals.'[190] A senior government official underscored that concern: 'A lot has been written with respect to the politicization, but worse than this, in these tribunals we have people who have not necessarily previously been judges.'[191] In some regions, people were 'shocked' to discover that there were only one or two former judges on the benches of some international courts.[192] One interviewee considered it 'ridiculous' to appoint judges to the ICC who did not have courtroom experience. [193]

As the ICC has begun to function, greater pressure has arisen for the selection of judges with practical judicial experience.[194] According to one international judge:

> The difference for the criminal courts is that you are dealing with different sorts of forensic problems. On the one hand there's the handling of witness evidence in chief. Then there is maintaining control over a court and obstructive individual defendants.

[187] T44, 5–6. [188] T41, 13. [189] F32, 2. [190] T35, 11. [191] T28, 5.
[192] T26, 4. [193] T24, 12. [194] See n 136.

There is also the assessment of the veracity of witnesses and reliability of written evidence.[195]

An interviewee described ICC judges who did not have a judicial background as: '. . . completely at sixes and sevens. They didn't know what a warrant was or what the originating procedure should be, or how you handle a trial . . . '[196]

According to another international judge:

There ought to be at least one judge on the bench, and possibly he or she should be the presiding judge, who has got real hands-on criminal experience and, if possible, criminal experience as a judge, handling cases day by day. Handling what happens in court is a skill that you can only learn by your day-to-day practice of it. It is very difficult to walk into court having watched a couple of episodes of a TV court drama and then do it.[197]

Another interviewee said that although he had no criticism of the criteria for the ICC, he hoped 'the court is never short of at least some judges and at the minimum one per trial and pre-trial chamber who have got first-hand experience of doing the business'.[198]

These concerns were echoed in comments on the ad hoc criminal tribunals. One senior Ministry of Foreign Affairs official from a common law country said that 'We would like to have some candidates at least who have experience of being judges in their own country.'[199] Another interviewee suggested that, in relation to the ICC, this could be dealt with by states 'nominating someone whom they would in any event have considered for a senior position of this kind domestically'.[200] A diplomat from a civil law country suggested that he would like to insert a criterion that 'Candidates for the ICC must have some judicial experience, be it in an international context or in a national context. Not necessarily only criminal law but they must have worked as judges for even just five years. I don't think they should go from a mission straight into a courtroom.'[201]

But how realistic is it to assume that states would have suitably qualified national judges to nominate? One former international judge felt that a requirement of litigation experience could easily be met as there is now 'a sufficient area of practice in international criminal law, and criminal law generally, to be able to get people who have experience in that area'.[202] This was not, however, felt to be the case for all countries. An interviewee from a developing country pointed out that 'most of the judges here do not have any knowledge of international criminal law, so the government gets some academic person or a person like the head of the administrative court'.[203] At the very least, it was felt that there would be no excuse for nominating a candidate who did not have any prior legal training, as: 'every country in the world has some type of legal training. I don't see why you would put someone up for election who doesn't have it'.[204] Another interviewee

195 T35, 14. 196 T24, 11. 197 T45, 9. 198 ibid. 199 T59, 15.
200 T45, 7. 201 T3, 13. 202 T24, 11. 203 T46, 17–18. 204 T27, 10.

felt strongly that 'you should have legal qualifications or you really ought not to be in a position of judging others, certainly not in serious criminal matters'.[205]

The view amongst interviewees that prior judicial experience was a valuable attribute for candidates was not entirely limited to the ICC.[206] An ICJ judge acknowledged that his previous judicial experience was a key factor leading to his election.[207] A former ICJ ad hoc judge from a civil law country said that national judges were 'well prepared to play this role'.[208] Another former international judge from a civil law country said that 'More attention should be paid to those candidates who have some experience in litigation. Because that's the most visible thing, the litigation business of a court and if you're familiar with the subject matter, it helps to some extent.'[209]

In terms of more general attributes, according to a PCA national group member, 'in principle judges are usually, we have to select our words, accustomed to being neutral'.[210] However, another interviewee pointed out that 'there are scandals in the national courts',[211] recognizing that judicial independence is not respected in all national jurisdictions.

Some also perceived possible shortcomings in the mindset of a national judge when operating in the international context. One interviewee pointed out that international courts are different from national courts and that national judges operating in an international environment are limited by their conception of their role and what a national court does; this may 'inhibit their vision' and their ability to think laterally about international law.[212] This was seen as a problem for a court which was intended to be 'ground-breaking'. In the context of the ad hoc criminal tribunals, a former judge thought that this was reflected in what he saw as the 'conflict between the very strict attitude of judges and the vision of professors':

> Judges who come from [national judiciaries] come with the mentality of a [lower domestic criminal judge]. For him, he doesn't understand yet and he hasn't got an international perspective so that he knows that he is dealing with something different. He is very strictly observant of the law. On the other hand, the others who are professors were not so bound by the words of the statute.[213]

[205] T25, 13.

[206] See, for example, the individual selection criteria for the soon to be established United Nations Dispute Tribunal and the United Nations Appeals Tribunal. Article 4 of the Statute of the UN Dispute Tribunal requires that judges: 'Possess at least ten years of judicial experience in the field of administrative law, or the equivalent within one or more national jurisdictions' and Article 3 of the Statute of the UN Appeals Tribunal requires that judges 'Possess at least fifteen years of judicial experience in the field of administrative law, or the equivalent within one or more national jurisdictions': United Nations General Assembly, *Appointment of the full-time and half-time judges of the United Nations Dispute Tribunal, Memorandum by the Secretary-General*, UN Doc. A/63/700, 3 February 2009.

[207] T60, 18–19.

[208] T48, 6.

[209] T37, 15.

[210] T50, 11.

[211] T50, 14.

[212] T29, 5.

[213] T49, 18.

One way to reconcile these concerns could be to proceed on the basis that judicial experience need not necessarily be gained at the national level. Some interviewees suggested that candidates with previous international judicial experience might be selected for another international court. As international courts increase in number, a number of individuals would already have experience as judges in more than one international forum.[214] Thus current and former international judges may form a distinct 'selection pool', particularly as individuals are joining the ranks of the international judiciary at earlier stages of their careers. According to one former international judge, those with international judicial experience may be inclined to be less partisan to a particular state than former national judges.[215] Nonetheless, this approach also has its limitations in that it is difficult to see, for example, how far judicial experience in the ICJ or ITLOS might equip a judge to preside over criminal trial proceedings in the ICC.

Civil servants and diplomats

The diplomatic corps and Ministries of Foreign Affairs are increasingly important recruitment pools for international judges, particularly the ICJ. This group includes diplomats (for example the Permanent Representative to the United Nations or ambassadors and their professional staff) and civil servants, including legal advisers to the Ministry of Foreign Affairs. As one observer noted: 'If you look at the current judges, you will find the majority of them were legal advisers. I think there are six or seven who have been on the International Law Commission, but I think 11 or 12 have been legal advisers.'[216]

Some states show a clear preference for nominating former legal advisers or diplomats for election to the ICJ. Yet, in common with the views expressed on academics and national judges, opinions also differ as to whether diplomats and legal advisers should become international judges. A PCA national group member explained why states often like to nominate diplomats for the international courts: 'Because they can manage them and they look all right. They know their stuff, they speak the language, they have good morals and so on, they're very civilized...'[217] It was felt that diplomats can be effective 'ambassadors' of a court in its fledging days because they are 'extremely good at going around the world and getting people to join the court, and extremely good at positioning the court'.[218] One African former judge said that he thought being 'a legal adviser prepares people extremely well for the ICJ'.[219]

It is also not uncommon for individual diplomats who have been heavily involved in the negotiation of the statute of a new court to be elected to its first bench. This was the case, for example, with ITLOS and the ICC, and may reflect

[214] For example, Judge Buergenthal and Judge Cançado Trindade of the ICJ previously served as judges (and presidents) of the IACHR; Professor Georges Abi-Saab has served as a judge of the ICTY and as a member of the WTO Appellate Body; Judge Odio Benito and Judge van den Wyngaert of the ICC have previously served as judges on the ICTY.
[215] T48, 6.
[216] T59, 10.
[217] T56, 4.
[218] T24, 11.
[219] T48, 8.

a tendency in the establishment phase of a tribunal to elect those seen to have a thorough familiarity and understanding of the court's governing instrument and its origins, and who are familiar to the electorate, that is the state parties to the statute of the tribunal in question.[220]

Nevertheless, the training and mindset of diplomats can also be seen as drawbacks. One legal adviser in a UN Permanent Mission said that ex-diplomats are often chosen because it is seen as a natural part of their career progression, 'without necessarily having much of a mind to the skills that you pick up along the way, and how they might equip you to be a judge as opposed to a political legal adviser'.[221] Diplomats, and in some cases, even legal advisers, do not necessarily have legal training. One interviewee felt strongly that only those who had had this training were well placed to be elected to the international judiciary.[222]

Diplomats may also, some suspected, be driven by the desire to find a compromise:

> By profession, they are successful because they make concessions, this way or the other. The mentality of a diplomat, I think, is not at all what I would consider to be compatible with the mentality of a judge. There are certain exceptions, but it remains very odd for me that a diplomat would change his mental behaviour when he sits as a judge. He will always be a diplomat trying to make concessions this way or the other, always in the middle of the road.[223]

One interviewee observed that diplomats often see 'the law as negotiable, not as a parameter you have to take as it is, although of course you have to interpret it'.[224] Another recounted an example of an ad hoc tribunal judge attempting to negotiate with the parties and persuade them to cooperate on a document production issue.[225] An international judge commented that he was 'incredulous' when his ex-diplomat colleagues demonstrated reluctance to rule that a particular witness lacked credibility, because they were concerned about the impact on states' willingness to bring cases to the court and the potential consequences for the witness himself.[226]

There were also concerns expressed that 'the ex-diplomat has been a government representative, so he is not neutral'.[227] According to a PCA national group member, the academic will be more neutral: 'You can find a judge who is not neutral, and you can find at the same time an ambassador who is very neutral. But this is the exception, because the training of a political man is different from the training of the judge. The academic man comes in between.'[228]

Suspicions remain, however: 'you wouldn't want somebody who obviously would take instructions from the government, you want an independent judge'.[229] These concerns have at times led to recusal challenges under Article 17(2) of the

[220] See further Chapter 4. [221] T11, 9. [222] F39, 1. [223] T48, 8.
[224] T61, 10. [225] F13, 3. [226] T26, 11–12. [227] T50, 12. [228] ibid.
[229] T16, 14.

ICJ Statute against former legal advisers in relation to their previous work,[230] although they have been unsuccessful.[231] Questions have also been raised as to the close involvement of diplomats and legal advisers in the nomination and election process and whether this may raise the possibility that diplomats who are less qualified are nominated.[232] One former legal adviser said that in making a nomination they were keen not to follow the practice of using former politicians or civil servants as all-purpose judges:

> One idea that we didn't want to give any fuel to was the thought that you just produced a retreaded government minister or a former leader or adviser of a senior government official or whatever, and this is an all-purpose person, you whack him into any court that you choose. We were looking for the qualities that matched particular courts.[233]

In addition to the question of which professional group was likely to be the best fit for the role of an international judge, interviewees also discussed the general skills or attributes which international judges should have, regardless of their professional background. A former ICJ ad hoc judge said:

> I do not believe that any person, even an intelligent, intellectual person, can become a judge. Because he should be a person who has a very calm sort of character, who knows how to listen to people, and how to talk very little. He must be willing to think a great deal about the reasoning of a decision with his colleagues and not to have preconceived concepts that he would like to direct in one way or another. These characteristics of neutrality, objectivity and impartiality are very important.[234]

The interviewee also stressed the importance of the 'ability to empathize'.[235] An ICC judge, meanwhile, highlighted the need for a general awareness of different legal cultures and the ability to work in cross-cultural legal environments as useful skills in the ICC context.[236] With regard to the ICJ, it was suggested that

[230] Article 17(2): 'No member may participate in the decision of any case in which he has previously taken part as agent, counsel, or advocate for one of the parties, or as a member of a national or international court, or of a commission of enquiry, or in any other capacity.' Evidently, this provision could equally give rise to a challenge against a former national judge who has previously 'taken part' in the case in proceedings before a national court, an international judge in relation to previous proceedings before an international court, or a previous lawyer or agent who has acted in the matter: C. Brown, 'The Evolution and Application of Rules Concerning Independence of the "International Judiciary"' *Law and Practice of International Courts and Tribunals* 2(1) (2003) 63–96.

[231] *Legal Consequences of the Construction of a Wall in the Occupied Palestinian Territory, Order of 30 January 2004,* ICJ Reports 2004, 3. See also: *Legal Consequences for States of the Continued Presence of South Africa in Namibia (South West Africa) notwithstanding Security Council Resolution 276 (1970), Order No. 1 of 26 January 1971,* ICJ Reports 1971, 3; *Legal Consequences for States of the Continued Presence of South Africa in Namibia (South West Africa) notwithstanding Security Council Resolution 276 (1970), Order No. 2 of 26 January 1971,* ICJ Reports 1971, 6; *Legal Consequences for States of the Continued Presence of South Africa in Namibia (South West Africa) notwithstanding Security Council Resolution 276 (1970), Order No. 3 of 26 January 1971,* ICJ Reports 1971, 9.

[232] This issue is explored in more detail in Chapter 3. [233] T35, 11. [234] T48, 7.

[235] T19, 13. [236] T45, 9.

a judge should be 'knowledgeable about international law and international relations, in a multi-disciplinary way'.[237]

Lastly, a few interviewees suggested that the individual qualities of judges may be less significant because the international courts operate in a collegial manner as a bench, in much the same way as many national supreme courts or constitutional courts.[238] A former ICJ ad hoc judge said that according to his experience: 'By and large the Court is better as a whole than each of its components... it is large enough so the weak parts don't influence its operation too negatively—the good people are the locomotive of the Court and they can bring out the best in what is available.'[239] This perception was echoed by others, a number of whom noted that there tended to be a core of more active judges that drove the work of the court. One interviewee noted that some judges remain relatively silent and follow the opinions of the active judges.[240] Another commented that accepting this division between active and passive members of the court can lead to problems: 'if the judges are not good enough, then that it will happen that the whole decisions are in the hands of a relatively small group of judges'.[241]

D. Conclusion

The composition of international courts, as with other courts, is a product of the interplay between rules governing eligibility and composition and the interests, values and political desires of those who apply them. A key factor which distinguishes the international courts from the domestic courts is the overriding role of geographical representation. Although the suggestion that judges are representatives of their governments is widely contested, in practice the principle of state representation strongly influences the composition of the international courts. The most pressing current debate on the make-up of the courts concerns the distribution of seats between regions, sub-regions and states. The extent to which states continue to support the international court system, as well as their willingness to comply with adverse findings against it, may be related to the patterns of geographical representation on the courts. These issues generally override all other considerations concerning the collective composition of the courts and the individual qualities of candidates.[242] For many countries, issues of merit are secondary to issues of representation and the primary interest is in selecting 'ambassadors' for the state. Thus the relationship between the judges and their state, even if characterized by meaningful independence in the adjudication process,

237 T48, 7.

238 S. Rosenne, *Rosenne's The World Court: What It Is and How It Works*, op. cit., 48.

239 F35. 240 T37, 17. 241 T33, 12.

242 C. F. Amerasinghe, 'Judges of the International Court of Justice—Election and Qualifications', op. cit., 348.

has a very real impact on who is selected and which attributes are considered to be preferable by a particular state for a specific court.

Despite the overwhelming importance of this political influence in determining the composition of the courts, the findings from this study show that a number of secondary factors also play a vital role. Moreover, their significance would appear to be growing as a result of a trend towards more developed composition and eligibility rules in the newer courts. More prescriptive and detailed formal requirements, such as those found in the ICC, are increasingly replacing the limited, open-textured and politically flexible rules found in older courts such as the ICJ. These differences account for a significant degree of divergence in composition between the courts, but equally important are the views of those engaged in the process of prioritizing certain qualities and characteristics. The interviews reveal a very wide range of attitudes towards criteria for the best judges. Different stakeholders disagree about the weight to be given to legal knowledge, political and negotiating experience and academic expertise. The consequence is that the make-up of the international bench is the product of compromises which lead to the selection of individuals from a range of professional backgrounds.

It is clear that competence is widely valued. It is broadly accepted that if the judges do not have sufficient skills to carry out their key functions the system of justice and the reputation of the courts will suffer. Likewise the reputation of individual states will be affected if their judicial 'ambassadors' are regarded as incompetent. Beyond this ability baseline, debate continues as to which types of candidate have the right skills for the different courts and how competencies should be defined and evidenced. Other aspects of judicial make-up, including the participation of judges from different legal systems, the need for linguistic diversity, the representation of judges with specialized legal expertise and equitable gender representation have gained varying degrees of acceptance in the newer international courts. Some of these aspects are covered by structured voting requirements or guidance, while others are simply raised at the level of debate and discussion. Many interviewees readily acknowledged the apparent contradictions and tensions between political considerations in the composition of the courts (and in the appointments processes, to be discussed in Chapters 3 and 4) and the principle of judicial independence enshrined in the statutes of the international courts.

One implicit concern running through the interviews was that the international courts suffer from the problem of 'high demand and low supply'. This suggests that there is perceived to be a relatively limited pool of well-qualified candidates. Similar claims have been made in many states at national level in the context of debates on the speed and extent of efforts to increase diversity on the bench. The validity of such concerns depends largely on how the recruitment pool is constructed, what selection criteria are considered essential and how the different qualities and qualifications are prioritized. The range of attitudes amongst those responsible for the nomination process illustrates that there is no universal agreement as to which qualities make for the ideal judge. This means that the scope and boundaries of the recruitment pool are not predetermined. If candidates are drawn from a small group of insiders with very limited and specific backgrounds, then the pool will indeed be narrow and will result in low supply as the court system grows. But a significantly wider pool can be created if diversity in terms of experience and background is valued and proactive efforts are made by states and other stakeholders to seek out high-quality but less highly visible or familiar candidates at the nomination stage.

The interviews demonstrate that, at some level, opinions on the composition of the international courts remain fluid, and polarized positions have not yet become entrenched, at least not to the extent that they are at national level (although discussions about the ICJ tend to be characterized by the institutional inertia that afflicts other parts of the UN). This is largely a reflection of the relatively new and dynamic nature of many components of the international court system, both in terms of changing rules and guidelines and in terms of attitudes and values. The views presented in this chapter provide a snapshot of perspectives on the make-up of the courts, and may be quite different in five, ten or twenty years' time. More recently established selection procedures, for example for the Regional Judicial and Legal Services Commission of the Caribbean Court of Justice, and screening mechanisms such as those used for the ECtHR, may result in different aspects of composition being prioritized. These systems have given greater emphasis to the representation of different legal systems and balanced gender representation. There is also evidence that particular courts want to define more precisely the types of professional background and expertise required. In addition, the interviews suggest an increasing preference, at least as regards the criminal tribunals, for the appointment of international judges with previous judicial experience. As international judicial practice becomes increasingly complex and demanding, it is possible that diplomats and civil servants may be considered to lack the requisite skills and mindset needed to develop and advance international jurisprudence.

The challenge for states is to accommodate these diverse and changing views on judicial composition in a way which produces top-quality courts within a highly politicized international environment. This task calls for a reconciliation of different national interests and perspectives in the light of shifting relationships between national and international courts and conflicting perspectives on the role and function of the international judiciary. The success with which these tensions and different perspectives are negotiated will ultimately determine the quality of the judges appointed, which in turn determines whether a court is effective, meritorious and legitimate: 'An entity is only as good as the individuals that are nominated and elected. We can have the best procedure and criteria, but that doesn't guarantee you a great court.'[243]

[243] T4, 19.

3

The Nomination Process

A. Introduction

The nomination process is critical in determining the quality of judges selected to the ICJ and ICC: 'if good candidates are not put forward, or do not come forward, the election procedure cannot lead to good results'.[1] Both the ICJ and ICC Statutes cover the nomination processes but the rules are open-ended and lack specificity as to the exact procedures to be followed. ICJ candidates are nominated by independent committees, known as the Permanent Court of Arbitration (PCA) national groups, or equivalent groups, that are recommended to consult with a range of outside bodies. ICC candidates can be nominated through this process or through the procedure used to select judges for the highest courts of the state. In the absence of more detailed guidance, states have been left to establish their own practices, in accordance with emerging conventions. Overall the subject has received remarkably little attention and until now discussion of how individuals emerge as candidates has generally been confined to conversations in the halls of the United Nations, the offices of the Ministries of Foreign Affairs and chambers of international lawyers.[2]

[1] M. Wood, 'The Selection of Candidates for International Judicial Office: Recent Practice' in Tafsir Malick Ndiaye and Rüdiger Wolfrum (eds), *Law of the Sea, Environmental Law and Settlement of Disputes: Liber Amicorum Judge Thomas A. Mensah* (The Hague: Martinus Nijhoff Publishers, 2007) 357–8.

[2] There have been precious few glimpses into this world in the literature; see, for example: C. Eagleton, 'Choice of Judges for the International Court of Justice' *American Journal of International Law* 47(3) (1953) 462–4; R. R. Baxter, 'The Procedures Employed in Connection with the United States Nominations for the International Court in 1960' *American Journal of International Law* 55(2) (1961) 445–6; J. D. Starke, 'Rules and Procedure Governing Election of Judges of International Court of Justice' *Australian Law Journal* 52(4) (1978) 230–2; J. D. Starke, 'Nomination by the Australian National Group of Candidates for Election to the International Court of Justice' *Australian Law Journal* 52(7) (1978) 396–7; J. D. Starke, 'Nominations by the Australian National Group of Candidates for Election to the International Court of Justice' *Australian Law Journal* 53(3) (1979) 115–16; L. F. Damrosch, 'Ensuring the Best Bench: Ways of Selecting Judges: Commentary by Professor Lori Fisler Damrosch' in Connie Peck and Roy S. Lee (eds), *Increasing the Effectiveness of the International Court of Justice: Proceedings of the ICJ/UNITAR Colloquium to Celebrate the 50th Anniversary of the Court* (The Hague: Kluwer Law International, 1997) 188–201; L. F. Damrosch, 'The Election of Thomas Buergenthal to the International Court of Justice' *American Journal of International Law* 94(3) (2000) 579–82; D. R. Robinson, 'The Role of Politics in the Election and the Work of Judges of the International

This chapter seeks to shed light on the nomination process, in the words of insiders who have been directly involved as candidates or potential candidates, decision-makers or observers. The information gathered has been drawn from a sample of the state parties of the two courts, with the aim of representing the range of approaches taken by states. It became clear in the interviews that some insiders lack detailed understanding of the nomination processes even in their own states; as a result, accounts are fragmented and contradictory, and only a few well-informed insiders appear to be familiar with the details. These factors have made it difficult to piece together a complete picture of the national processes in operation. For many states, including several of those surveyed for this study, nominations are made infrequently, and even within one state, significant variations in practice from one judicial nomination to another frequently occur.

Nonetheless, in piecing together an overview, two related issues emerge. First, processes differ considerably from state to state, ranging from the highly personal, informal and ad hoc, to the more structured, transparent and regulated systems,[3] though the majority of states sampled use informal nomination processes. No patterns can be discerned in the processes used within regions between ICJ and ICC nominations: processes depend on particular circumstances. There is no uniformity in the steps leading to nomination and it is often difficult to discern the decisive factor (or factors) that led to a particular decision. Second, the degree of formality in any particular process appears to be closely related to the level of politicization and political influence at play within the particular system. The more politicized the process, the more informal it is, and vice versa.

Informal nominations involve very little 'process'. Strikingly, in many states the selection criteria for the courts are not articulated at all, or if they are, lip service is paid to them. Nominations may emerge from informal personal discussions, followed by a decision by one or two key players within a small group of insiders. Usually, there is no identified 'selection pool', only a single candidate

Court of Justice' *American Society of International Law Proceedings* 97 (2003) 277–82; P. Sands, 'Global Governance and the International Judiciary: Choosing Our Judges' *Current Legal Problems* 56 (2003) 481–504; K. Keith, 'Member of the Permanent Court of Arbitration' in Tim L. H. McCormack and Cheryl Saunders (eds), *Sir Ninian Stephen: A Tribute* (Melbourne: Melbourne University Publishing, 2007) 155–75 and M. Wood, 'The Selection of Candidates for International Judicial Office: Recent Practice', op. cit. In the European Court of Human Rights context, see also the survey and review conducted by the Council of Europe Parliamentary Assembly: Committee on Legal Affairs and Human Rights, Parliamentary Assembly, *Nomination of candidates and election of judges to the European Court of Human Rights,* Doc. 11767, 1 December 2008, available at: <http://assembly.coe.int/Documents/WorkingDocs/Doc08/EDOC11767.pdf> (accessed 18 March 2010).

[3] The study of ECtHR nomination processes also indicates that a broad range of processes are used by states in that context: Appendix, 'Overview of National Selection Procedures'. See also Committee on Legal Affairs and Human Rights, Parliamentary Assembly, *Nomination of candidates and election of judges to the European Court of Human Rights,* Part B of the Appendix to Assembly Doc 11767: Overview of member states' replies to a questionnaire, AS/Jur (2008) 5 (1 December 2008), available at: <http://www.assembly.coe.int/CommitteeDocs/2008/20081201_ajdoc52.pdf> (accessed 2 December 2008).

who is known to the decision-makers, and who may initiate and lobby for nomination. The PCA national group or equivalent is often a bit-part player, usually comprised of government representatives or those with strong links to government. It frequently does not make the final nomination decision and may not even be involved at all. There is generally no outside consultation or, if there is, it is very limited. The lack of transparency limits accountability and confines knowledge about the process to a very small group of insiders.

At the other end of the spectrum, a small number of states have developed procedures that place greater emphasis on merit and transparency. These procedures draw on national judicial appointments procedures or have been specially developed for particular international courts. They include strengthening the independence of the PCA national groups, the use of independent expert selection committees, and selection procedures such as public advertisements, peer review, consultation and interviews. Some states have even legislated to regulate the process of nominations.[4] But these sorts of formalized processes are very much in the minority.

The ICJ and ICC nomination rules are meant to insulate nominations from political influence. In practice, a recurring theme across the interviews was the strong vested interest of governments in strictly controlling the nomination process in order to influence the composition of international courts. At a practical level, the state will most likely be actively involved in campaigning for a candidate to succeed, and therefore want to ensure that a candidate is politically acceptable and 'electable'. Equitable geographical representation also raises political issues as to who should be nominated and/or elected from the region in a particular election. Other domestic and international political considerations weigh heavily on whether a nomination is made, and if so, who is selected and how. Personal relationships and alliances frequently come into play.

This political context is not wholly inappropriate. As noted earlier, the complete de-politicization of the selection processes to the ICJ and ICC is neither possible nor desirable. Ensuring that states have some degree of control over nominations helps to promote continuing governmental engagement with international courts. Moreover, it is not axiomatic that the politicization of judicial selection reduces the quality of candidates selected. It is generally in the interests

[4] For example, the Slovenian *Law on Nomination of Judges from the Republic of Slovenia to International Tribunals/Courts* (17 July 2001), available at: <http://www.iccnow.org/documents/SloveniaLaw.pdf> (accessed 30 September 2006), that harmonizes the nomination process for all international courts and tribunals, providing for a parliamentary election procedure for international judicial candidates (section 7). Note also that Finland has carried out a review of its nomination processes for the European and international courts and proposals were made to amend the national law on the appointment of judges to provide for an expert committee and a detailed procedure for making international nominations. It is unclear whether any amendments have yet been made: Government Communications Unit, 'Greater transparency in the nomination of judges to serve in international and EU courts: Press Release 451/2006 7 December 2006', available at: <http://www.formin.finland.fi/public/default.aspx?contentId=84448&nodeId=15145> (accessed 22 June 2008).

of states to nominate competent candidates who will enhance their national reputation in the international community. But where there are embryonic nomination rules and informal nomination procedures operating within highly charged political environments, there can be a real risk that extraneous considerations enter into the process, which can detract from the selection of meritorious candidates. The extent to which the ICJ and ICC nomination processes are overtly politicized and may impinge on the selection of qualified candidates is the central question to be explored in this chapter. Chapter 5 will then address potential reforms, with reference to developments in other courts and contexts.

This chapter sets the scene by considering the rules for the ICJ and ICC and the composition of the national nomination committees. It then reviews the main elements of the process: the decision to nominate a candidate, the identification of potential candidates, and the practical mechanics of the nomination process. It considers the impact of political considerations along the way and highlights the key differences between the processes of the two courts.

B. ICJ and ICC nomination rules

The provisions on the nomination of candidates found in the ICJ and ICC governing statutes leave states a wide degree of discretion in respect of the nomination process. ICJ candidates are to be nominated by 'the national groups in the Permanent Court of Arbitration'.[5] If a state does not have a PCA national group, nominations are to be made by national groups specifically set up for the purpose.[6] More than three months before the election and no more than one month after a vacancy has arisen,[7] the Secretary-General of the UN sends a written request to PCA national groups (or their equivalents), requesting them to nominate potential candidates by a specified date.[8]

For ordinary (triennial) elections, national groups may nominate up to four candidates,[9] including a maximum of two nominees of the same nationality as the national group.[10] If there is only one seat available, for example when a judge has resigned or died, national groups may only nominate a maximum of two candidates.[11] Before nominations are returned, 'each national group is recommended to consult with its highest court of justice, its legal faculties and schools of law and its national academies and national sections of international academies devoted to the study of law'.[12] The nominations are then submitted to the Secretary-General of the UN who produces an alphabetical list of candidates

[5] ICJ Statute, Article 4(1).

[6] ibid, Article 4(2). Members of those groups must have the same qualifications as members of the PCA national groups.

[7] ibid, Articles 5 and 14.

[8] ibid, Article 5(1).

[9] ibid, Article 5(2).

[10] ibid.

[11] ibid.

[12] ibid, Article 6.

and the national groups that have nominated them.[13] The Secretary-General then submits the list of candidates to the General Assembly and the Security Council,[14] and the curricula vitae of candidates are also circulated prior to the elections.[15] There is no screening or other formal review or verification of the nominations submitted.

As noted in Chapter 1, the ICJ nomination process was agreed after much debate, negotiation and compromise. It is in principle a procedure that is intended to be apolitical, independent and focused on producing candidates of the highest quality. The process seeks to 'insulate the process of nomination from political considerations'[16] by requiring nominations to be made by non-state (albeit state-appointed) bodies, with the goal of promoting the independence of the court. It also seeks to embed the selection process within the broader international law community by recommending that potential candidates are reviewed by their peers at the national level.

In common with the ICJ Statute, the procedures set out in the Rome Statute for nominations to the ICC are sparse and open-ended. One important difference is that in the case of the ICC, states have two possible options for their nomination processes: nominations can be made either by the process for nominations to the highest national judicial offices of the state or by the procedure set out above for ICC nominations.[17] The Rome Statute does not require states to declare which procedure they will use, or to inform other states which procedure has been used for a particular nomination. As with the ICJ, there is no formal role for independent scrutiny.

The first step in the ICC process begins with a resolution of the Assembly of States Parties (ASP) which requires the Secretariat of the ASP to circulate invitations to state parties to submit nominations. These must include the text of individual criteria for the court, the resolution itself, and information on the application of the minimum voting requirements in the particular election.[18] The nomination period opens twenty-six weeks before the elections for a period

[13] ICJ Statute, Article 7(1). See, for example, United Nations General Assembly and United Nations Security Council, *List of Candidates Nominated by National Groups: Note by the Secretary-General*, UN Doc. A/63/187-S/2008/503.

[14] ICJ Statute Article 7(2). Note that Article 7(1) provides that apart from candidates exceptionally introduced through the procedure in Article 12, only candidates on this list are eligible for election to the court, see also Article 4(1).

[15] See, for example, United Nations General Assembly and United Nations Security Council, *Curricula Vitae of Candidates Nominated by National Groups: Note by the Secretary-General*, UN Doc. A/63/188-S/2008/504.

[16] International Court of Justice, 'Press Release 2005/23: United Nations General Assembly and Security Council proceed to the election of five Members of the Court', 8 November 2005, available at: <http://www.icj-cij.org/presscom/index.php?p1=6&p2=1&pr=638&search=%22armes%22> (accessed 20 November 2006).

[17] Rome Statute, Article 36(4)(a)(i) and (ii).

[18] Assembly of States Parties, *Procedure for the Nomination and Election of Judges of the International Criminal Court*, ICC-ASP/3/Res.6, paras 1 and 2.

of twelve weeks.[19] Each state party may nominate one candidate, who need not be a national of the nominating state, but must be a national of one of the state parties to the Rome Statute.[20] State parties then communicate their nominations to the Secretariat of the ASP.[21] The nomination period can be extended in certain circumstances.[22] Nominations must be accompanied by a statement that sets out how the candidate fulfils the criteria in Article 36(3).[23] The statement and the curriculum vitae of each candidate are posted on the website of the court[24] as soon as possible after their receipt by the Secretariat of the ASP.[25] A list of candidates, in alphabetical order, with the accompanying documents, is then prepared by the Secretariat of the ASP and circulated through diplomatic channels to all the state parties.[26]

The ICC nomination procedure seeks to draw on the advantages (at least notionally) at the heart of the ICJ process: that is, the independence and expertise of the PCA national groups. Permitting the use of national appointment procedures[27] imports a range of additional potential nomination procedures including direct appointment by government, the Executive or the President, depending on the national legal system. These procedures may be more or less open to politicization than the ICJ nomination procedure.[28]

[19] Paragraph 3, ASP Resolution 6.

[20] Rome Statute, Article 36(4)(b).

[21] Paragraph 5, ASP Resolution 6.

[22] Paragraphs 10–12, ASP Resolution 6. The nomination period can be extended for a period of two weeks up to three times if more than double the number of candidates are needed to fulfil the minimum voting requirements in relation to gender and regional criteria. It can be extended for an unlimited number of two-week periods if there are not as least as many candidates as are required to meet the List A and B requirements or at least the number of seats there are to be filled. See the discussion on the ICC criteria in Chapter 2.

[23] Rome Statute, Article 36(4)(a). Paragraph 6 of ASP Resolution 6 further elaborates on the required content of this statement.

[24] <http://www.icc-cpi.int> (Accessed 28 April 2010).

[25] Paragraph 8, ASP Resolution 6. See also T. Ingadottir, 'Nomination and Election of Judges' in Thordis Ingadottir (ed), *The International Criminal Court: Recommendations on Policy and Practice: Financing, Victims, Judges, and Immunities* (Ardsley, NY: Transnational Publishers Inc, 2003) 173.

[26] Paragraph 9, ASP Resolution 6. See, for example, Assembly of States Parties, *Third Election of Judges to the International Criminal Court,* ICC-ASP/7/33 and Assembly of States Parties, *Third Election of Judges to the International Criminal Court—Addendum,* ICC-ASP/7/33/Add. 1.

[27] As discussed in Chapter 1 the possibility of using national nomination procedures was introduced as a compromise between states that wanted unfettered control over nominations, and those who wanted greater institutional constraints, and also to encourage the nomination of candidates with criminal law backgrounds. It also accords with the requirement that each judge 'possess the qualifications required in their respective States for appointment to the highest judicial offices' (Article 36(3)(a)).

[28] Also note the language used in Article 36(4)(a), that nominations 'may be made by any State Party to this Statute, and shall be made either [the two procedures]' which places greater emphasis on the role of the state in making nominations. For an indication of the variety of national judicial selection procedures and their potential impact on ICC nominations, see D. Ten Brinke and H-M. Deml (eds), *Judges in the Service of the State? Procedures, Criteria and Political Influence on National Selection of Judges for the Highest Judicial Offices and their Possible Influence on the International Criminal Court* (Aachen: Shaker Verlag, 2002).

C. Nomination bodies

Composition of the PCA national groups

Permanent Court of Arbitration (PCA) national groups play a central role in the ICJ and ICC nomination processes and their composition is a significant factor in affecting how they participate in the process. The PCA was established under the 1899 Convention for the Pacific Settlement of International Disputes[29] as an intergovernmental international dispute resolution institution. The parties to the two founding conventions of the PCA can appoint up to four individuals as members of the PCA, who are known as the PCA national groups.[30] Members of the PCA serve as potential arbitrators to be appointed by parties to a dispute brought to the PCA. Two quite different features of the make-up of the PCA groups emerged from the interviews as being relevant to their role in the judicial selection system. On the one hand, many group members are government representatives, increasing government influence over the nomination process.[31] On the other hand, some groups also include members from a broad range of other institutions or professional backgrounds which may facilitate the independence of the group.

Members of the PCA must be 'of known competency in questions of international law, of the highest moral reputation, and disposed to accept the duties of Arbitrator'.[32] There is no vetting or election procedure for members and they are appointed for a six-year renewable term. One hundred and nine states have acceded to one or both of the Hague Conventions, and there are currently ninety-two national groups.[33] Of the states that are not parties to the Hague Conventions, or that have not yet established a national group for the PCA, it is unclear how many have established 'national groups' for the purposes of ICJ nominations. It would

[29] 1899 Convention for the Pacific Settlement of International Disputes, concluded at The Hague on 29 July 1899, later revised and followed by the 1907 Convention for the Pacific Settlement of International Disputes, concluded at The Hague on 18 October 1907. States may accede to either convention. Regarding the establishment of the PCA, see Chapter 1.

[30] Article 44 of the 1907 Hague Convention. See also Article 23 of the 1899 Hague Convention.

[31] 'Some [states] certainly respect the idea [that the PCA national group should operate independently to the government], others place their members under direct governmental pressure or indeed, their members may be legal advisers of their foreign office and so on': L. Dingle, 'Conversations with Professor Sir Elihu Lauterpacht, Fifth Interview: The Nineties and new Millennium', 28 March 2008, available at: <http://www.dspace.cam.ac.uk/bitstream/1810/197070/2/Eli%20Lauterpacht%20interview%205%20transcript%20-%2028%20March%202008.doc> (accessed 20 November 2008), 17.

[32] ibid. The members do not need to be nationals of the state that appoints them and members may be appointed by more than one member state.

[33] As at May 2009: <http://www.pca-cpa.org/showpage.asp?pag_id=1038>. The current list of members of the PCA, organized by national group, is accessible at <http://www.pca-cpa.org/showpage.asp?pag_id=1041> (Accessed 28 April 2010).

seem that, in most of these cases, ad hoc nomination groups will be established when it is decided by the state that a nomination should be made.[34]

PCA national group members are normally appointed by the Minister of Foreign Affairs or the legal adviser, but in some cases, the President or Prime Minister will make appointments. The process and criteria for appointment 'isn't really all that well understood',[35] even amongst PCA members. A number of those interviewed said they did not know why or how they were appointed, and there were even instances of individuals who were unaware that they had been appointed.

PCA national groups presently include current and former government representatives, academics, current and former international judges, international civil servants, national judges (particularly Chief Justices) and practising lawyers.[36] The members of the national groups are, on the whole, eminent international law practitioners. Of the 345 PCA members that formed the ninety-two PCA national groups in May 2009, only thirty-eight were women (11 per cent). One former WEOG Ministry of Foreign Affairs legal adviser said that in his state: 'I think nowadays one would make much more of an effort to see to it that there was at least one woman member, if not a balance.'[37] This approach is not, however, the norm.

There has been a recent shift away from more symbolic appointments (for example, retired national judges) to more active appointments, focusing on the international role of the national group,[38] while the composition of some national groups has been modified in an attempt to include representatives of bodies that the ICJ Statute recommends that PCA national groups should consult before making nominations.[39]

Whilst membership may be diverse, most PCA national groups include at least some serving government officials,[40] even though it is implicit in the

[34] One example was given by a diplomat from an African state that is not a member of the PCA, in which ICJ nominations have been made by a cross-departmental group consisting of 'the Attorney-General, the Minister of Justice and the Ministry of Foreign Affairs' (T5, 3).

[35] T60, 1–2.

[36] See also E. McWhinney, 'Law, Politics and "Regionalism" in the Nomination and Election of World Court Judges' *Syracuse Journal of International Law and Commerce* 31(1) (1986) 4–5.

[37] T35, 4.

[38] Some interviewees noted that members with experience in international court administration and the United Nations are often appointed to provide links to international legal networks and ensure that the group can obtain information from these networks to assess potential candidates.

[39] In a WEOG state, 'Most of the major judicial arms of government that the PCA national group might consult are on the national group' (T11, 3). One PCA national group also includes 'an official who "is involved in identifying people for appointment to a higher [domestic] court", providing a link to the national nomination process' (T22, 7).

[40] From the descriptions of professional backgrounds given in the list of PCA national group members of 8 May 2009, it appears that sixty-six PCA national groups have at least one member who currently holds a position as an elected official, in the diplomatic corps, the civil service or otherwise acting as an government or departmental adviser (note that three of ninety-two PCA national groups did not provide any details about their professional backgrounds). Only the Belgian PCA national group appears to have members without any current or former government

arrangements that members should be independent of government because they are appointed as potential arbitrators.[41] In the United States, for example, there is a convention that the current legal adviser to the Department of State and the legal adviser of the former administration are members, ensuring bipartisan participation.[42] In a number of states, an elected senior legal official, for example, the Attorney General or Minister of Justice, or non-elected legal officials such as the Solicitor General, are also included in national groups in an *ex officio* capacity. A number of national groups also include diplomats and other high-ranking civil servants. Most groups also include former government representatives or at least individuals with previous involvement with the government (for example, those who have formerly acted as legal counsel for government, consultants, or members of state delegations to international conferences).[43] According to one interviewee, PCA national group members are more likely to have government links in 'small countries, where the political class is small'.[44]

In some national groups, government representatives take a non-member 'secretarial' type role. However, the result of this, according to an academic from a GRULAC state, may be that 'the national group is a part of the Ministry, making it very difficult to draw the line between the national group and Ministry'.[45] Some considered that government representatives 'secure the link between the government and the national group'[46] while others felt that this link could be used to control the decisions of the group. However, the presence of a government representative or a member with links to government does not necessarily mean that the group lacks independence. A diplomat said that: 'Although the group is chaired by the legal adviser of the Ministry of Foreign Affairs, there are other people and it's not a ministry decision in any way.'[47] The presence of government officials does not automatically mean that a group will not challenge the views of government or propose unconventional candidates.[48] 'Those diplomats that are members of the PCA have a high degree of dignity, moral ethics and knowledge

affiliation. One hundred and eighty-eight members of the total of 345 members hold or have held such positions (ninety-three current and ninety-five former): <http://www.pca-cpa.org/showpage.asp?pag_id=1041>.

[41] As one interviewee said, 'no one would choose [a government representative] as an arbitrator, because he or she would be bound by the government' (T56, 3). The drafters of the Statutes of the Permanent Court of International Justice and ICJ expected that PCA national groups would be independent of their states, as this was the reason why PCA national groups were accorded the sole right to nominate candidates to those courts: see Chapter 1.

[42] L. F. Damrosch, 'Ensuring the Best Bench: Ways of Selecting Judges: Commentary by Professor Lori Fisler Damrosch', op. cit., no. 2, 193.

[43] Sixty–three of the ninety-two national groups based on the study described in the note above.

[44] T12, 4. [45] T53, 3.

[46] F1, 2. [47] T13, 6.

[48] F34.

of international law so I don't think they accepted all the candidates proposed by the government.'[49]

Moreover, one of the states surveyed for this study has 'a convention, which is probably unique to our country: we do not have serving officials as members of the National Group'; and not all PCA national group members have links to government. An African PCA national group member said that he is not involved in politics 'on the ground'.[50] Yet, an informed observer described this particular member as 'completely out of it'[51] and 'deadwood'[52] in terms of his influence over the nomination process, suggesting that the key players in that state were those with links to the Ministry.

Composition of other national nomination groups

As a result of the optional procedures for ICC nominations, a broader range of individuals may be formally involved in nominations to that court. One point to note regarding PCA national groups (where this procedure is adopted for the ICC) is that it is possible that none of the group's members will have any experience whatsoever of international or domestic criminal law.

If a state is not a PCA member, but wishes to utilize the equivalent procedure, a national group must be established in accordance with the same criteria as for the PCA national groups. In one GRULAC state, an ad hoc selection panel was established by the Cabinet, at the instigation of the Attorney General, to make ICC nominations, and comprised 'two senior practitioners, a member of academia and a former diplomat and a representative of the Ministry of Foreign Affairs, as a non-voting secretary'.[53] A senior Ministry of Foreign Affairs official explained that:

> The composition of the committee reflected the type of person we hoped to identify in the process, i.e. have the requisite knowledge, experience, academic qualifications, skills, but who would also have the other attributes: languages, understanding of other cultures and exposure to international issues.[54]

None of the states in our study had elected to use, without adaptation, the procedure for nominations to the highest national judicial offices. Instead, some states which had chosen this option established bespoke selection committees or used parliamentary vetting procedures that drew on some aspects of the procedure and criteria used for national appointments. In the United Kingdom, for example, an ICC selection committee was established as a 'national procedure'. The panel included the Foreign and Commonwealth Office Legal Adviser, the Permanent Secretary of the Lord Chancellor's Department, the Lord

[49] T53, 3. [50] T50, 1. [51] T61, 5. [52] ibid. [53] T28, 1.
[54] T25, 6.

President of the Court of Session and the Chair of the Equal Opportunities Commission.[55]

D. ICJ and ICC nominations in action

As already noted, ICJ and ICC nomination processes are diverse and do not follow any standard procedure or approach. Broadly, three steps can be identified in the procedure: (1) there is an initial decision to make a nomination; (2) potential candidates are identified; and (3) a candidate is selected.

In most states, political considerations emerge as a factor during all three stages, and where these play a determinative role in the selection process, there is a risk that meritorious candidates are blocked from being nominated and less qualified individuals emerge as candidates. In this regard, the ICJ and ICC processes are strikingly similar, even though the functions of the courts and the criteria for their judges are significantly different. ICC processes in most of the states studied indicate signs of overt politicization, perhaps to an even greater extent than the ICJ nomination process. This is a surprising finding considering the emphasis on the integrity of the selection process in discussions on the establishment of the ICC, considered in Chapter 1.

The following sections discuss the three stages of the nomination process in turn and then consider the particular issue of non-national nominations in relation to the ICJ. The discussion of the three steps relates to both the ICJ and the ICC, unless otherwise indicated.

Deciding to make a nomination

A state's decision to make a nomination is the crucial first step in the nomination process. It involves an assessment of the political issues surrounding a nomination, and in some cases, the decision to nominate is conflated with the selection of candidates: ie the government already has a specific candidate in mind. This may result in the government usurping the role of the PCA national group or other selection body. In most states we looked at, it is the Ministry of Foreign Affairs that makes the initial decision to nominate a candidate.[56] Interviews indicated that there tend to be four factors that are taken into account:

- the interest of the state in having a judge of its nationality on the court;
- the acceptability of putting forward a candidate at the domestic political level and the availability of sufficient resources to run an election campaign;

[55] Foreign and Commonwealth Office, 'Press Release—UK Candidate for International Criminal Court Judge Confirmed (02/10/2003)', 2 October 2003, available at: <http://www.fco.gov.uk/resources/en/press-release/2003/10/fco_npr_310702_iccjudgeukcand> (accessed 11 December 2008). The Equal Opportunities Commission has now been merged into the Commission on Equality and Human Rights.

[56] In a small number of states studied, the President or the Prime Minister makes the decision.

- the likelihood of success ('winability') based on regional political considerations and the political leverage of the state at the international level;
- the other international campaigns the state plans to undertake for election to other political and judicial offices.

The demands of lobbying, vote trading and obtaining regional support mean that campaigns must start early.[57] There is evidence that some states begin the process two or more years before the election and will often seek to identify a candidate at this pre-assessment stage. This might be done informally, by one or two Ministry of Foreign Affairs civil servants or, in some circumstances, the potential candidate may lobby the government directly to seek nomination, or there may be a 'star' or stand-out candidate that motivates the entire nomination process. States may then seek preliminary soundings at the regional and international levels to gauge support for the candidate; this could involve seeking vote trade agreements with other states and manoeuvring for regional endorsement of the candidate.

If the state has already decided to nominate a *particular* candidate, the PCA national group or other selection body may be cut out of the picture and merely act as a rubber stamp for the formal nomination. However, PCA national groups may also be brought into the pre-assessment stage to give their views on potential candidates. Alternatively, the state may decide to make a nomination, tell other states that it intends to do so, and then wait for the nomination period before an official nomination is made by the PCA and/or the government and the candidate is named.

In any event, the four issues mentioned above frequently came into play. A state must have an interest in being represented on the court.[58] The ICJ is seen as a 'highly respected organ'[59] and therefore it is 'an honour'[60] and 'prestigious'[61] for a state to have a judge of its nationality on the bench. A state may also want to demonstrate that it 'believes in the Court and believes in law',[62] to mark a significant change of government at the domestic level 'to demonstrate to the world just how stable it has become'[63] or to build its profile with a view to joining an international organization such as the European Union. There is also a sense that a state is 'entitled to be on the Court'[64] because it has never had a judge on the bench before, or not for a long period of time. In one state, it was said that a nomination was considered because a particular dispute appeared likely to come before the court and 'it was thought to be a very good thing to have a permanent judge [rather than only an ad hoc judge]'.[65] Conversely, another state decided not

[57] These issues are discussed in greater depth in Chapter 4.
[58] These questions do not affect the P5 which presumably will always make nominations to the ICJ because of the P5 convention. [59] T58, 2.
[60] T48, 13. [61] T21, 1. [62] T58, 7. [63] T36, 4. [64] T44, 11.
[65] T1, 9.

to make a nomination because 'the Court is so far away and we will never have a case there'.[66]

Some reasons for nominating ICC candidates were specific to the ICC context. States that identified themselves as 'active proponents and supporters of the Rome Statute'[67] felt that this contribution should be recognized with a seat on the court. Others, including a state that was formerly part of the Socialist Federal Republic of Yugoslavia, wanted 'to offer some of its direct experience of the ad hoc tribunals'.[68] An African diplomat suggested that a seat on the court could be a way for Africans 'to become more involved in the dispensation of international justice'.[69]

Nominations can also be used as political tools: a state may wish to reward an individual or to banish an individual. In one instance it was said that an ICC candidate was nominated 'as a way to get him out of the country'[70] because his presence had proved to be politically problematic. Conversely, for those close to, or in the government, they are seen as 'well-paid and secure posts'.[71]

The decision whether to nominate may turn on the personal ambitions of a particular foreign affairs legal adviser: 'his policy was to prevent anyone else from becoming a candidate to keep his own possibilities open for the future'.[72] Domestic political factors are also taken into account, so, for example, there must be sufficient resources available to run an effective election campaign. In two of the states studied, there were cross-partisan discussions as to whether an ICJ nomination should be made, and whether a proposed candidate should be nominated. In other states, opposition parties and parliaments were not engaged in the question of ICJ or ICC nominations at all.

In addition to these internal issues, an important consideration is often whether a seat on the court can be won. 'Winability' is crucial for states, because of the resources needed to run a campaign and the political consequence of defeat.[73] This may take into account the position of the state within its regional group and its broader political leverage. Winability will also depend on assessments of the international profile and cachet of potential candidates.[74]

Some regional groups coordinate at a regional level before they make nominations.[75] Priority can also be determined by bilateral 'gentlemen's agreements'.[76] Agreements may be at a sub-regional level, for example, where a geographical

[66] T56, 5. [67] T24, 1. [68] T6, 2. [69] T5, 2. [70] T56, 1–2.
[71] T56, 4. [72] T40, 5.
[73] One Eastern European diplomat said: 'We're a small country and a small Ministry, so we have had to prioritize candidates. It is a resource-intensive thing, lobbying, so why would you put so much effort and money to travel around the world if you don't stand a real chance of getting elected?' (T6, 15).
[74] Although it is possible that a particularly strong candidate may succeed in reversing the priority of these factors.
[75] According to interviewees, this is the approach in Africa, Asia and GRULAC.
[76] T8, 5.

or political sub-group bands together to support a single candidate.[77] In some regional groups, states may seek endorsement of their candidates by the regional group quite early, providing a distinct competitive advantage.[78] These arrangements may result in a clean slate, ie the same number of candidates as there are seats, ensuring that the candidates are elected.[79] Some consider this to be beneficial as it avoids splitting votes: 'it gives everyone an opportunity to be on the Court and avoids wasting money and time on lobbying'.[80] Others considered that there is a risk 'that groups for their own reasons might not nominate the best candidates'.[81] It is possible to challenge such regional arrangements, in order to bring forward a competing candidate, but it is 'not considered very friendly'.[82]

If there are no such arrangements, states will assess their chances against other states that intend to contest the election (and candidates, if they are already announced),[83] sometimes taking informal soundings to gauge support. There may be negotiations to seek the 'withdrawal' of particular candidates before nominations are made. Winability may also depend on factors such as perceptions of current government policy.[84] In the ICC, winability may be linked to the state's standing in the ASP (the body that elects judges to the court) and to general matters of international justice and human rights.[85]

A number of interviewees pointed out that smaller, less powerful states face unique challenges, particularly in ICJ elections. When competing against can-

[77] There is also a convention, that is not always adhered to, that if a judge dies or resigns before the end of his or her term, his or her state is entitled to nominate (and have elected) another national for the remainder of the term.

[78] A number of interviewees said that endorsement decisions are based on political considerations, rather than an assessment of the merit of the candidates. This issue will be discussed further in Chapter 4.

[79] In the ICC, clean slates are still technically possible, although there are disincentives against them—for example, there can be a number of extensions (maximum of three) if the regional minimum voting requirements are not matched by a least double the number of candidates that meet that requirement and if this threshold is not met in spite of extensions, any regional voting requirements will be reduced in accordance with a formula or in the case where there is only a single candidate from the region, they will be taken to no longer apply, ie the seat could go to a candidate from any regional group: see paras 11 and 20(b), ASP Resolution 6. However, in the absence of minimum voting requirements, there is nothing to say that states will not just follow the geographical representation rules on the court, hence allowing a candidate to be elected directly from a clean slate, in the same way this can happen in the ICJ context. Overall, however, the regional group is incentivized by these rules and the provision of open or 'floating seats' (discussed further in Chapter 4) to submit competing candidacies, if political considerations do not override these interests.

[80] T15, 9.

[81] T47, 8.

[82] T3, 5.

[83] 'If there is a very good candidate from the region, that would probably make the situation less conducive for us to nominate our own candidate... especially if there was immediate will to support that candidate.' (T10, 6).

[84] For example, Michael Matheson of the United States was not successful in seeking re-election to the ILC in 2006. Some interviewees attributed this, at least in part, to the foreign policy of the United States with regard to Iraq. See results at International Law Commission, '2006 Election of the International Law Commission', 25 April 2007, available at: <http://www.un.org/law/ilc/> (accessed 10 November 2008) and United Nations General Assembly, *Election of the members of the International Law Commission,* UN Doc. A/61/PV.54 (2006) 6.

[85] One interviewee referred to this as having 'momentum' behind a candidate: T6, 15.

didates from larger states they must have 'all the relevant ducks in a row'[86] in order to obtain enough support to win. Larger states in regional groups often have a sense of entitlement to a seat on the court and have a 'view of their turn'[87] so smaller states must fight to be given a chance. In less powerful states, assessing winability normally also involves a discussion of potential candidates and whether they would have the right profile to obtain sufficient votes. A diplomat from a small WEOG country said that 'your candidate's got to be demonstrably better, 50 per cent better, than the others even to get on the page'.[88]

Another related issue is whether the state intends to contest other international elections.[89] Success depends to a large extent on vote trading and campaigning and few states have the political capital and material resources to run several large campaigns simultaneously. As a result, they must make a strategic decision about which candidatures they will pursue. As one GRULAC diplomat said: 'If you have a candidate for the International Court of Justice, you've got to sacrifice some aspirations to other organs.'[90] An Asian Ministry of Foreign Affairs official explained the problem: 'The merit of the candidate of course is a factor but we feel that the reciprocities [vote-trading] are more important. If you have too many elections at the same time, then even having the best candidate is not enough.'[91]

Some states go so far as to undertake comprehensive studies of the potential candidatures and make detailed assessments of their likelihood of success in each election.[92] Even though the ICC operates under the auspices of the ASP, which is outside the UN system, it is still seen as part of the matrix of elections in the international system and makes equivalent demands on state resources as the major elections in the UN system. Therefore, states must conserve their political leverage if they wish to obtain an ICC seat. It was not suggested that ICJ or ICC elections are normally considered to be any different from other political and judicial elections for the purposes of assessing priorities, although some attached a higher priority to certain positions, such as the ICJ or non-permanent seats on the UN Security Council.

Nominations are therefore tightly bound up with the interests and position of the state. If the state considers that the political situation is not right, even the most meritorious candidate will not be nominated.[93] The risk of pre-judging the political viability of a campaign is that considerations of politics and merit will

[86] T19, 2. [87] T18, 7. [88] T19, 2.

[89] These elections may be for state political positions (for example, the non-permanent seats on the UN Security Council) or individual positions (for example, judicial positions or expert positions on the UN human rights treaty bodies). [90] T58, 4.

[91] T59, 2.

[92] One Ministry of Foreign Affairs official said that they 'look from anywhere between ten, fifteen or twenty-year horizons, to assess the major elections coming up' (T22, 4).

[93] For example, strong candidates have previously been blocked because their states thought they would be unable to obtain the endorsement of the regional group or because it was considered too early to seek a seat because another judge from the same state recently served on the bench. In another case, the potential re-election of a judge was prevented by the fact that his state had entered into an arrangement to support a judge from another country in the sub-region.

be blurred so that 'an outstanding, well recognized international law specialist from country A will not be proposed and someone from country B who is less qualified, but is from a large country, or an important country, will run and be elected'. The converse of this is that if the state decides the moment is right, it is likely to become highly invested in the process, insisting on the nomination of its 'preferred' candidate. At the same time, the high costs of running a campaign of this nature suggest that a state will want to field the best possible candidate, or at least one who is more likely to succeed.

Overall, the political considerations involved in the decision to nominate candidates may result in a state blocking a particular candidacy or seeking to control the nomination process.

The candidate pool

Political considerations play an equally significant role in shaping who is considered to be a potential candidate for the court and hence in the 'selection pool'. Two central themes were identified by interviewees: first, in most states it was perceived that a potential candidate must have political connections; and, second, that he or she should have an international 'profile'. These factors are often more important than the selection criteria themselves and can, in many cases, exclude qualified potential candidates. The extent to which these issues affect the outcome depends on the particular nomination process used.

In the majority of states in which informal selection processes are used the selection pool is confined to individuals with close proximity to the government or Ministry. Diplomats and other Ministry of Foreign Affairs civil servants (for example, legal advisers) and elected representatives (for example, ministers) 'use these international positions in judicial bodies to promote their own careers, and have the access to obtain them'.[94] A former African diplomat noted that the past three candidates for the ICJ from his country 'came either from the ranks of the foreign ministry or they were professionally associated with the foreign ministry'.[95] Another interviewee said that those who hold government positions

[94] The interviewee went on to note that 'professionals are progressively being excluded from the game' (T40, 4). Legal advisers are also in a strong position to obtain support for their own campaigns, according to another interviewee: 'All the legal advisers of the Foreign Ministries are a very important lobby and they help each other to become members of the International Law Commission and the International Court of Justice etc.' (T40, 4). However, one risk for the well-regarded potential candidate is that an admiring Minister or President may not be willing to let him or her go, as one interviewee noted with regard to a potential candidate: 'I don't think the President would nominate him, because the President likes him and would like to keep him here' (T51, 8).

[95] T51, 5.

or are otherwise 'close to power'[96] or are 'the best friend of the Minister of Justice'[97] are more likely to obtain ICC nominations.[98]

Groups with special access to the diplomatic corps, for example academics involved in training diplomats, are able to form special relationships that can lead to nominations. As noted earlier, PCA national group members themselves are often government representatives or closely linked to the government. It is unsurprising then that as experts in international law, well known within their own states, the PCA national group members might themselves be considered eligible for nomination to the courts.[99] Their intimate involvement in the process and unique access to government decision-makers places them in a privileged position[100] to obtain 'either an ICJ nomination or at least be chosen as an arbitrator'.[101] A former legal adviser said that 'the conflict of interest obviously involved in such a process is not often considered a serious matter'.[102] Individuals who are outside the government may obtain the right connections through 'good political contacts in the administration'[103] or personal relationships with the decision-makers.[104]

For government outsiders, involvement in party politics can be essential.[105] A former international judge pointedly noted that if a candidate 'is not a member of the party in government, or he is not well regarded in governmental circles, he will have no chance of being nominated'.[106] Another commented that it is a question of adherence 'to the governmental policy'[107] and that 'here in the

96 F39, 1–2.

97 F13, 3.

98 However, not all candidates have political connections. In some cases, deliberate attempts were made to exclude those with links to politics, in one state that made an ICC nomination: 'They really were looking for someone from outside the usual suspects and the apparatchik. They gave preference to people from the academia' (T32, 21).

99 E. McWhinney, 'Law, Politics and "Regionalism" in the Nomination and Election of World Court Judges', op. cit., 6–7.

100 One interviewee explained the connections of a former ICJ candidate who was a PCA national group member: 'He started the consultations within the national group. And, having been in the government, he also could approach the government. He had also worked for the President, and had links with other international law organizations. Having worked in all these various positions, he had the advantage of being able to approach all the people and get them together to make a nomination' (T59, 2).

101 F33, 3. See also E. McWhinney, 'Law, Politics and "Regionalism" in the Nomination and Election of World Court Judges', op. cit., 7. In one state, 'when it did happen quite frequently that the leading candidate was a member of the National Group, they would simply withdraw from further consideration of that nomination' (T35, 3).

102 F33, 1.

103 T33, 4.

104 It was noted that one should be 'a friend of the Under Secretary of the Foreign Ministry, and not an enemy of the legal adviser. Hence, one needs to be somehow engaged in politics' (T40, 4).

105 One interviewee noted that the strength of this factor depends on the degree of antagonism between opposing political parties at the national level. According to one African international judge, 'Political factors could have a very negative impact now, because you have political and social turmoil. For instance, a good international law professor, for instance, who is a leftist, or who used to be a counsel of opposition party, will certainly never make it' (T65, 17). National political rivalries are projected on to the international stage because 'no one wants someone from the other party being nominated internationally' (T56, 8).

106 T48, 9.

107 T48, 10.

Third World it's very important to be involved politically with the system'.[108] Establishing these relationships normally necessitates living in one's home state, and those who have left their home state in order to gain international experience are unlikely to form the necessary types of connections and could well be considered 'off the radar'.[109]

It may well be that individuals in or closely connected to government are highly qualified for appointment to the ICJ, yet any process that defines eligibility in terms of political affiliation risks excluding individuals or certain groups (those with certain politics, professional backgrounds, ethnicity or gender). One African interviewee noted that 'non-government people or people who are not intimate insiders cannot access these posts'.[110] An ICC judge expressed disapproval of the prevalence of political nominations: 'I think that a lot of other countries selected a candidate who they say would have been appropriate for a judge in their country, but who was simply selected, for instance, by the Minister of Justice or someone else without there having been any kind of competition leading up to that.'[111]

Such a focus on political connections as a key requirement may result in candidates of overriding merit being overlooked, because the 'political profile of the candidate is more important than the legal profile'.[112] One interviewee said:

> Generally persons with personal status and political clout land the nomination. The professional merits of the person appear to take a back seat even if they are not completely ignored... Winability is a criterion and a good background in international law is deemed desirable but the essential factor that is weighed in the selection process is political support the person has for his or her nomination.[113]

The second factor identified by a number of interviewees as necessary to obtain an ICJ or ICC nomination was whether or not the candidate had a profile at the international level. In order for an election to be winnable, one 'must be known to those who are going to vote',[114] as one interviewee explained: 'If you get someone who is not known internationally, even if he is the best lawyer in the world he will not get the votes. But being known is not that difficult for someone who lectures abroad and participates in seminars and conferences.'[115] Examples given of relevant international experience for the ICJ included participation in UN conferences,[116] membership of the Institut du Droit International and the International Law Association, and participation in international academic

108 T50, 2. 109 T51, 6. 110 T40, 5. 111 T45, 7–8. 112 T52, 25.

113 F33, 2.

114 T51, 4. In some cases, candidates who do not have international exposure are fielded in the UN General Assembly over a number of sessions before the elections to build their profiles. One interviewee referred to a candidate 'whose nomination had been announced two or three years before the elections and during that time he came to the General Assembly regularly' (T59, 4).

115 T47, 7.

116 An example given was the Vienna Conference on the Law of Treaties that resulted in the Vienna Convention on the Law of Treaties.

conferences.[117] Membership of the International Law Commission (ILC) also has a special role as a 'conduit'[118] for judges of the ICJ. A GRULAC diplomat noted that: 'If you have a promising jurist then you take him or her through the American Law Commission and the International Law Commission and in the final stage, you go for the Court.'[119]

A former ICJ judge said it is now 'a practice'[120] that ICJ judges come from the ILC. However, the selection process for the ILC itself is often based on the same political connections as ICJ nominations: 'diplomats that are working in that area simply tell the Ministry: "I want that".'[121] Nonetheless, a measure of transparency is introduced into the process, because 'everyone can see what the contribution of that person was to the ILC during his first term'.[122] In some states, prior involvement in advising the government on international disputes, whether in the ICJ or an arbitral tribunal is seen as an essential requirement for nomination to the ICJ.

In the ICC equally, candidates, particularly those with international human rights or humanitarian law experience (List B) are generally expected to have an international profile in order to be in the 'selection pool'. An ICC judge noted in relation to List B candidates that 'without an international background, especially in human rights, through academia, being a member of international organs in the United Nations, or in the diplomatic field, it's very difficult to get a nomination'.[123] One group that encompasses both political connections and an international profile is the members of government delegations to the Rome Conference.[124] An Eastern European ICC candidate was described as 'deeply involved in the drafting negotiations for the Rome Statute' as well as being 'very active in the debates on international criminal justice domestically, both at the governmental and non-governmental level'.[125] Another candidate's experience included involvement in the whole of the negotiations of the Rome Statute and having been present and active in the Security Council in the creation of the two ad hoc international criminal tribunals for the former Yugoslavia and Rwanda.[126] As a former WEOG legal adviser noted, 'many of the negotiators ended up as candidates for the Court themselves'.[127] Potential candidates in this category 'have a good mixture of the law and understand international politics',[128] though not all candidates had this type of international exposure, and at least one ICC candidate had 'no previous experience of UN bodies' prior to his nomination.[129]

Another category of potential candidates for nominations is that of Permanent Representatives to the United Nations in New York, who are seen

[117] T36, 5.

[118] T51, 3. See also E. McWhinney, 'Law, Politics and "Regionalism" in the Nomination and Election of World Court Judges', op. cit., 7.

[119] T12, 2.

[120] T31, 9.

[121] T56, 2.

[122] T48, 4.

[123] T76, 7.

[124] This group consists primarily of diplomats but also includes academics or other consultants who formed part of state delegations.

[125] T6, 2.

[126] T9, 2.

[127] T35, 13.

[128] T2, 10.

[129] T45, 3.

to have a triple advantage: national profile, international profile, and a direct line to the foreign ministry. According to a GRULAC PCA national group member, 'It is very easy if you are the Ambassador to the Mission in New York to convince your Minister that you should be a candidate.'[130]

In many cases, then, candidates with international experience will be members of the 'rarefied world'[131] of elite lawyers and diplomats involved in international appointments. It is a self-selecting and self-sustaining closed community that judges its members on its own criteria: 'Candidates who could integrate in the International Court of Justice are high level people who are very well known, and all these people are part of the community and in this community everybody knows them.'[132] Those on the outside will have little chance of breaking into this inner circle, however meritorious they may be, as one international judge commented: 'Maybe there is a brilliant academic somewhere in my country, but nobody knows of him. It will not help him, his brilliance.'[133]

In addition, this process of self-selection may limit the number of potential candidates because some do not want to give up their lucrative and varied careers: 'To be an ICJ judge means you're going to lock yourself away in The Hague for nine years, and turn your back on all the arbitrations, all the students. I don't think a lot of people are willing to do this.'[134]

There are other factors at play in shaping the candidate pool. In some states, the requirement that candidates are fluent in either French or English has an impact: an Eastern European diplomat noted that where there is a candidate who is fluent in one of these languages 'he or she usually stands out, because the pool of jurists that you can choose from is not so big'.[135] Age is also relevant, with some interviewees suggesting that candidates were appropriate for the ICJ at the age of seventy,[136] 'which is the moment to get a position or not because you finish

[130] T56, 12. [131] T9, 5. [132] T58, 2.

[133] T81, 4. An interviewee from an Asian country also noted that some professional groups, such as academics, are still judged by Western standards of 'eminence', such as publication in certain peer-reviewed journals that may not be as accessible to or prioritized by potential candidates from developing countries. [134] T72, 15.

[135] T6, 3.

[136] In some states, age is a consideration in this sense, although it is not considered a formal selection criterion. There is no formal age limit for ICJ judges, and this, combined with their possible re-election, has meant that a significant number of judges have died during their terms. This obviously differs from the majority of national jurisdictions that impose retirement ages and some international courts, such as the Caribbean Court of Justice, that imposes a compulsory retirement age of seventy-two years (Article IX, The Agreement Establishing the Caribbean Court of Justice of 2001, available at: <http://www.caricom.org/jsp/secretariat/legal_instruments/agreement_ccj.pdf> (Accessed 28 April 2010)) and the European Court of Human Rights (seventy years) Article 23(6), Convention for the Protection of Human Rights and Fundamental Freedoms, (ETS 5), 213 U.N.T.S. 222, entered into force 3 September 1953, as amended by Protocols Nos 3, 5, 8, and 11 which entered into force on 21 September 1970, 20 December 1971, 1 January 1990, and 1 November 1998 respectively. It is also particularly relevant in the ICC context, tying candidates' eligibility to 'the qualifications required in their respective States for appointment to the highest judicial offices'. Therefore, candidates who are too old to sit on the their highest courts could not be considered eligible, nor could they be considered eligible for the ICJ if they are seeking to be nominated only under

working as a diplomat at seventy years old'.[137] However, it appears that in most states there is a 'trend now towards nominating younger judges'.[138] In some circumstances, race and religion can be barriers to nomination to the ICJ, particularly where a particular race and/or religion is linked to political power.

However, the issue of gender appears to play a very small role in the decision-making process for nominations. The absence of any formal requirement in the ICJ Statute to promote an equitable gender balance on the court has meant that this issue has not been forced onto the political agenda. From the interviews, it appeared that very few states had considered female candidates for the court, and although some have debated whether efforts should be made to ensure that female candidates are included in the selection pool, they have yet to take concrete action. In contrast, in the ICC, it is generally considered 'an advantage'[139] to be a female candidate in an election because of the equitable gender representation rules in the Rome Statute. As a result, these rules appear to have had a knock-on effect in the nomination stage and have increased the likelihood that women will be considered as potential candidates. One Eastern European state recognized that it is 'absolutely excellent to have a female candidate',[140] while a potential male candidate from a WEOG state did not feel confident of his prospects and told the Minister of Foreign Affairs: 'If you want to have a candidate with good prospects of election you should choose a woman, preferably a woman with criminal law background.'[141]

Candidates with experience in issues relating to violence against women and children may also be favoured for the ICC as a result of the recommendation in Article 36(8)(b). It was also suggested by a number of interviewees that it is seen as an advantage to be running for election under the List A 'criminal law' head of the individual selection criteria as there are a more limited number of candidates worldwide who have appropriate experience for the court than under the List B 'human rights and humanitarian law' head.

Some interviewees noted that in some nomination processes there is no 'pool' as such, but rather one stand-out candidate and 'no obvious alternative'.[142] This arose more frequently in small or developing states that had fewer international law experts.[143] In these states, the presence of a world-renowned international law expert can motivate the entire campaign. But there might also be no 'pool' in circumstances where a particular candidate has been selected for very specific

the 'first leg' of Article 2 as a candidate that possesses 'the qualifications required in their respective countries for appointment to the highest judicial offices': see the discussion relating to the ICJ, but relevant to the ICC in C. F. Amerasinghe, 'Judges of the International Court of Justice—Election and Qualifications' *Leiden Journal of International Law* 14(2) (2001) 336–8.

[137] F12, 1. [138] T44, 32. [139] T1, 3. [140] T1, 5. [141] T9, 11.

[142] T22, 6.

[143] A Latin American academic suggested that political influence may be less in states where there are few credible candidates, suggesting that in some Latin American states 'it doesn't matter very much which political party is in government because you have only two or three candidates who are credible' (T53, 10).

political or personal reasons. Or, conversely, the pool could be expanded in places where individuals or entities completely outside government can propose potential candidates; for example, when the PCA national group consults with outside bodies, or advertises vacancies publicly, inviting applications. Finally, the pool could also be widened by an active PCA national group that is open to the introduction of less 'conventional' candidates into the nomination process.

Among the various factors that define who is considered appropriate to be an ICJ or ICC candidate, the most important appear to be the existence of political connections and the possession of an international profile. With such narrow parameters, it seems that merit may be sacrificed to political expediency, though the extent to which this occurs depends on the actual nomination process used.

The mechanics of the nomination process

The ICJ Statute simply provides that PCA national groups (or their equivalents) are to nominate ICJ candidates. It is silent on the relationship between the PCA national group and its government. In this vacuum, a wide variety of nomination practices have developed, ranging from informal models that rely heavily on personal contacts and about which 'little is really known' to highly structured and regulated selection procedures.[144] The process used in a particular state can vary over time depending on the prevailing political circumstances.

The ICC nomination process is even more indeterminate than that of the ICJ because of the extremely broad raft of procedures that are permitted under the Rome Statute. In the absence of any obligation to declare which procedure is being used, and the option of using national judicial nomination procedures, many different procedures have been used, some of which may barely be said to amount to a 'procedure' at all. In most states in the study, the nomination decision was made by just one or two government officials with no broader consultation. This is surprising given the high hopes placed on the ICC, and its political significance. When the court was established, and particularly during the first elections, non-governmental organizations that had been closely involved in the Rome Conference put pressure on states to use independent, transparent and merit-based selection procedures for nominating ICC judges.[145] The need for such processes was reiterated strongly in 2008 in

[144] S. Rosenne, *The Law and Practice of the International Court, 1920–2005*, vol. I: *The Court and the United Nations* (4th edn, The Hague: Martinus Nijhoff, 2006) 365, n 26.

[145] See, for example, Amnesty International, 'International Criminal Court: Checklist to Ensure the Nomination of the Highest Qualified Candidates for Judges', AI Index: IOR 40/023/2002 available at: <http://www.amnesty.org/en/library/info/IOR40/023/2002/en> (accessed 3 August 2006). Also see the website on the first elections of the Coalition for the International Criminal Court: <http://www.iccnow.org/?mod=electionjudges2003> (Accessed 20 April 2010).

recommendations produced by the Coalition for the International Criminal Court for the elections in 2009:

> We encourage all States Parties to nominate or support the nomination of candidates through a transparent and vigorous process, and involve broad consultation with Parliaments, the legal profession and civil society to ensure that all qualified candidates have been considered and that the process takes into account an array of perspectives.[146]

While some states established procedures that fulfil these objectives, others elected to retain tighter control over the nomination process and its outcome.

ICC nominations must be accompanied by a statement setting out how the candidate fulfils the statutory selection criteria.[147] In some cases, supporting statements are not provided, or, if they are, they set out only very limited information about the candidate's relevant experience. In some instances, it will be apparent from a candidate's accompanying statement that she or he does not meet the individual criteria. There is, however, no forum in which these statements—or conclusions relating to them—can be questioned or tested.[148] Nor does it appear that the requirement to provide such a statement has any significant impact on the nature or quality of the nomination process. While they might, in theory, have some effect on the individual voting decisions of states, in practice this is likely to be outweighed by the influence of mutual support arrangements and other political factors (to be discussed in Chapter 4).

The following three sections set out the typology of nomination processes identified across the states studied. The categories are broad and not all the processes used fit neatly into one or the other category. Further, the processes used can vary from nomination to nomination within a particular state.

Informal nomination procedures

In most informal systems, the PCA national group or equivalent has either not been established or is defunct and the nomination decision is made directly by government. In some cases the group is functioning but automatically validates the nomination decision of the foreign ministry. In states that use informal procedures, the selection process is most vulnerable to politicization because the group does not operate independently or at all, contrary to the ICJ Statute. This also affects ICC nominations made under the ICJ procedure. A former ICJ judge suggested that in some cases the PCA national group system can fail to function in the way intended: 'The process is heavily political. Nomination by

[146] Coalition for the International Criminal Court, *Recommended Criteria for States Parties to Nominate and Elect Judges to the ICC* (October 2008), para 6.

[147] Rome Statute, Article 36(4)(a). Paragraph 6 of ASP Resolution 6 further elaborates on the required content of this statement. For example, see Assembly of States Parties, *Election of judges to Fill Three Judicial Vacancies of the International Criminal Court (continued)*, ICC-ASP/7/33/Add.1.

[148] An Advisory Committee on Nominations is provided for by the Statute (Article 36(4)(c)) that might be able to perform a screening function in this regard, but it has not been set up. See the discussion on this issue in Chapter 5.

national groups has not worked; it is meant to be insulated from governments. But governments do make nominations. The national group system is largely ineffective.'[149]

In one African state, a number of interviewees were unaware of the function of the national group under the ICJ Statute and could not confirm whether the group existed or not.[150] A lawyer in a GRULAC state described an informal system used for both ICJ and ICC nominations as 'very direct and personal and not very institutional-like, [more] a friendship thing'.[151] An African interviewee said that in the developing world, institutions like the PCA national group are 'stagnant organizations and it is only the central government who is taking the lead in this respect'.[152] Across different regions, a range of examples were given of government entities being solely responsible for ICJ and ICC nominations:[153]

- In an Eastern European state, ICJ nominations are made internally by the State Secretary, and departments within the Ministry of Foreign Affairs as well as the Minister for Foreign Affairs.[154]
- In an African state, nominations are decided upon by the President alone, with some informal consultation with the universities and the Ministry of Foreign Affairs and the Ministry of Justice.
- In another state, a national judge who was well known to the government was selected directly for the ICC by the President after some minimal outside consultation of a cross-departmental committee in which the Ministry of Justice is the lead department.[155]
- In a WEOG state, the ICC nomination process was conducted entirely by the Ministry of Foreign Affairs, without the involvement of the PCA national group or the Ministry of Justice.[156]
- In an Eastern European state, 'the Ministry of Justice is responsible for the [ICC] nomination and the Ministry of Foreign Affairs deals with campaigning. The Cabinet of Ministers gives the final approval to the candidate'.[157]

149 F47, 5.

150 Note that some interviewees said that the group had been involved in previous nominations and had engaged in a confidential process of assessing the experience and ability of various potential candidates (F38, 2). Others said that nominations were made by the government alone. This difference may be explained by the fact that apparently the PCA national group is composed of civil servants, so is, in effect a government committee.

151 T52, 9.

152 T48, 9.

153 Note that there was some inconsistency in accounts of nomination processes, emblematic of the fact that the procedures lack transparency and only involve a very small number of participants. In some cases, interviewees contradicted one another or simply did not know how a decision was or would be made and could only hypothesize.

154 T1, 4. Note that the PCA national group was apparently also consulted in relation to at least one nomination. However, it appears that the group was simply asked whether it dissented to the nomination of the government-chosen candidate.

155 F40; F46, 1.

156 T39, 11.

157 T7, 2.

According to a number of interviewees, some of these purely government-driven nomination procedures are in fact quite detailed and involve gathering and considering the curricula vitae of a number of potential candidates and discussion of their relative merit. In the case of the ICC, they may reflect the substance of the national judicial selection process, in accordance with the Rome Statute.

In some informal systems, there may be a PCA national group or other national selection process that does play a role in nominations for the ICC, but it is either stacked with government representatives or possesses such close government sympathies that it automatically validates any nomination decision made by the government. A former government lawyer stated, in relation to another state: 'I have no doubt whatsoever it's a sham, really. It is actually the government and their friends and they've just been clothed in the garment of membership of the PCA national group, for the purposes of making a politically convenient nomination. But it's still better than having an overtly political nomination.'[158] In these circumstances, 'the main function of the national group is only to nominate the national candidate after the Government decides on a candidate'.[159] Another interviewee from the same state noted that, 'nomination is seen as a political appointment and is done within government'.[160] PCA national group members can also be motivated to rubberstamp government decisions by their own judicial ambitions: 'Some people on national groups behave in the way they do because they want to be elected themselves.'[161]

In essence, informal nomination procedures are more susceptible to political influence because they lack mechanisms to promote independence, transparency and objectivity. They provide more exclusive access to political insiders and are more likely to be closed to outsiders, increasing the likelihood that candidates are selected for reasons of 'personal ambitions and personal contacts',[162] rather than merit. Interviewees reported cases of serving diplomats directly seeking their own nomination to the ICC.[163] 'If the Permanent Representative in New York says there's an election coming up and he says "I propose that I would like to stand for this judicial office, will you back me?" He is likely to get the backing of the government.'[164] In states using procedures of this nature, the PCA national group (if one has been established) is side-lined and there is no independent body involved in identifying and selecting candidates.

Semi-structured nomination procedures

Semi-structured systems include those in which the PCA national group or other ICC selection body appears to be operating independently by considering potential candidates suggested by the state, and even proposing additional candidates, but ultimately accepts state suggestions as to the most 'appropriate' candidate.

[158] T35, 7. [159] F33, 3. [160] F7, 1. [161] F21, 1. [162] F1, 2.
[163] T39, 9. [164] T36, 4.

These national groups attempt to make some independent input but are highly pragmatic about who has the final decision, in other words, they prioritize harmony and consensus in the nomination process. A former ICJ candidate said that, in his view, 'in many countries, the formal system is completely artificial compared to what takes place'.[165] In these systems, 'the institutionalization and the structures are not strong enough so there is a tendency that whatever is considered important is pushed up'[166] and the group becomes 'absorbed in the various machinations of the Foreign Affairs department'.[167]

A number of the PCA national groups examined operate in an ad hoc manner which may make them more susceptible to greater government influence or control over their decisions. A WEOG PCA national group member said in his group 'there are no institutionalized relationships or procedures. If one day I am replaced in the national group, I don't know how my successor will behave.'[168] These groups often conduct meetings by telephone or email without any set procedures,[169] and many may not even make a record of their discussions.

The close relationship between the candidate pool and the government decision-makers, and the need to start campaigning early, often means that there have been preliminary discussions, and even a decision made as to which candidate the government is willing to support. In one case, a foreign minister called a potential candidate to suggest that he should become a candidate before the PCA national group was involved.[170] Similarly, with regard to a nomination from an African country, one interviewee said that 'the candidacy came out and the lobbying began before anyone even thought of the national group'.[171]

In many of the states studied, interviewees reported that the government considers that the PCA national group is there to be 'consulted', but that it does not have the final decision. In one GRULAC state, the PCA national group 'gives its opinion regarding the background and prospects of a proposed candidate'.[172] In a WEOG state, 'the PCA national group was consulted, but the foreign office had chosen the candidate, it was a *fait accompli*'.[173] One PCA national group member from a WEOG state thought this consultation should take the form of a more open negotiation: 'In the group we were a little bit annoyed with the government because the government indicated that we should propose a particular candidate. In our view the procedure was to have prior consultations, not to have the proposal.'[174]

165 T61, 1. 166 T61, 9. 167 T17, 13. 168 T44, 22.

169 Eagleton has noted how the impermanence of the PCA national groups or groups established by states that are not PCA members (and the fact that the latter are established on an ad hoc basis and there is no obligation to provide their names to the UN) might impact upon how independently they can conduct the task of making nominations: C. Eagleton, 'Choice of Judges for the International Court of Justice' American Journal of International Law 47(3) (1953) 462–3.

170 T44, 7. 171 T61, 5. 172 T58, 10. 173 T77–80, 3.

174 T39, 7. This PCA national group member also suggested that if the government recommended names (which it appears it frequently did) 'it doesn't mean we will decide, yes, we support them, but we will take it into consideration within the group'.

By contrast, there rarely seems to have been a history of conflict between the PCA national group and the state. This consensus may be due to the fact there is often unanimity about the suitability of a candidate, based on objective reasons. However, in many cases, it appeared that the PCA national group was anticipating the government's expectations and falling into line. In one WEOG state, 'Prior to the nomination we have consultations with the government because without the support of the government it is not possible to succeed in the [elections].'[175] It was also suggested that, in some cases, these prior negotiations or consultations have been used to sound out potential PCA national group choices, particularly regarding the selection of PCA national group members themselves. One interviewee noted with regard to a WEOG PCA national group: 'The national group does not work in a real way, it does not come and make proposals and press the Ministry to nominate. It just goes along with what the Ministry decides. It could have a very positive effect with just a small change in the way they operate.'[176]

In some extreme cases, the PCA national group is completely ignored. In one state, the PCA national group was asked to recommend an ICC candidate. It proposed a candidate to the foreign ministry but was overridden 'most likely by the Presidency, or at least from outside the Ministry',[177] and the candidate was replaced by one who had been nominated exclusively for domestic political reasons. One interviewee commented that 'the heads of the ministries who are active and very close to the government are the ones that can make the proposal and there is no regulated procedure'.[178] In another state in the same region, a name was proposed by the PCA national group which 'sat on the [foreign affairs ministry] Director General's desk for six months because the Director had someone else in mind who did not have the support of the national group'.[179]

PCA national groups operating in a passive manner generally do not consult outside bodies as recommended by Article 6 of the ICJ Statute, although there may be informal discussions. A WEOG PCA national group member said that in relation to ICJ nominations his group 'does not consult with outsiders, except academics on occasion, but we would certainly not consult the national judicial appointments body because they do not know the candidates who would be appropriate for the Court'.[180] In relatively informal and closed systems such as this one, 'if you have friends in the Ministry you can press for a candidate, or on the contrary press to veto a candidate'.[181] In one case, it was said that a senior diplomat had pressed for the nomination of a particular candidate because of his

175 T39, 1. 176 F12, 2. 177 T53, 4. 178 T53, 8. 179 T4, 16–17.
180 T39, 8–9.
181 T40, 1. Note that some interviewees also spoke of cases of the informal role of sitting ICJ judges in calling potential candidates and encouraging them to seek nomination to the Court: T61, 5 and later, also making recommendations to their states as to which candidates the state should vote for: T77–80, 7. The latter interviewee said that he considered it to be appropriate for judges to have an input into the process 'as there is a lot of criticism about the way candidates for judgeships are chosen, and the judge doesn't really follow any party or political line': T77–80, 7.

advanced age, in order to 'keep the horizon open'[182] for his own nomination. A former ICC candidate, who had previously held a senior position in one of the Ministries and was nominated without regard to the PCA national group, said that 'there was no open competition',[183] although there had been some minimal consultation with Supreme Court judges.[184]

In relation to ICC nominations, there is also often an important dynamic between the Ministry of Foreign Affairs and the Ministry of Justice as to the selection of a candidate, mainly because the Ministry of Justice will often have jurisdiction over the implementation of the Rome Statute. This relationship can edge out any views of the PCA national group or other selection body; for example, in an Eastern European state a former candidate said: 'Both the Ministry of Justice and the Ministry of Foreign Affairs are involved in ICC nominations. There are some consultations with the PCA national group, but frankly, it's mainly the two ministries between which the discussions and co-operation are more in place and intensive.'[185] A PCA national group member from the same state said that he 'wouldn't expect anybody to be nominated without the agreement of the Minister of Justice, but the final word is with the Ministry of Foreign Affairs'.[186] An interviewee from a WEOG state described the tension between the Ministry of Foreign Affairs and Ministry of Justice with both considering that they should have the final decision on ICC nominations,[187] although the final decision is made by the Ministry of Foreign Affairs.[188]

The picture that emerges for semi-structured procedures is that PCA national groups often have the appearance of operating independently but frequently just provide their imprimatur to a predetermined government choice.

Structured nomination procedures

A very small number of states have adopted more structured nomination procedures, which have two main features. First, there is a PCA national group, or equivalent, comprised of a diverse range of members (usually including representatives from the judiciary, academia, private practice and government); second, practices and expectations have developed as to the independent role and conduct of the group. These procedures are generally more transparent, open, and merit-based than is the norm and they seek to minimize the impact of political considerations in the nomination process. More structured ICC nomination processes that draw on highest courts' nomination processes usually also have these hallmarks, and in some cases operate in accordance with predetermined procedures.

A notable feature of PCA groups in more structured processes is that they are more autonomous and have procedures that draw a larger group of potential

[182] T40, 2. [183] T32, 5. [184] T34, 9. [185] T34, 8. [186] T34, 9.
[187] T77–80, 2. [188] T77–80, 1.

candidates into the nomination process.[189] In general, governments also appear to adopt a more deferential approach towards them. In these systems, the PCA national group is normally asked to propose a candidate or candidates. Where states have looked to identify candidates early in order to start informal soundings and lobbying, they have sought the early decision of the PCA national group, sometimes years prior to the formal nomination process. If the government has a candidate in mind, it may indicate this to the group. If the group has concerns about any candidate favoured by the government, it 'would be listened to, and whether its views would be influential would depend on the reason for the concerns'.[190] It was said in relation to the same PCA national group that 'Because of the independence of all the members of the group, they wouldn't have pushed somebody who they didn't think was deserving of being pushed simply because that's what the government wanted.'[191]

In another state, the foreign ministry 'never sought to exert any influence over whom the national group considered or chose',[192] only providing information to the group where either they wanted it, 'or [it was] felt it would be good for them to have'.[193] During one nomination process, this information included a long list of potential candidates, including 'the usual suspects of public international law but also there might have been names on the list that would not immediately have come to the minds of the group. It was a long list and not exclusive, but sought to make the group think more widely.'[194]

In some states, there is an understanding that the government can only choose to support or reject a candidate selected by the PCA national group, and not pressure the PCA to substitute their own candidate. In one of these systems, 'the Ministry of Foreign Affairs always follows their advice, but there could also be political considerations which may mean they take forward the nomination or not, but there must be an agreement on the candidate with the PCA'.[195] In this state, an informal practice was developed by one PCA national group: 'The national group asked not to know what the views of the government are regarding any particular candidate so it can make its own decision. But none of these processes have been institutionalized.'[196]

PCA national groups in these systems also conduct consultations as recommended by Article 6 of the ICJ Statute; for example, since 1960, the national group of the United States has consulted widely with a range of bodies at the

[189] This does not necessarily change the result of the nomination process, but at least it introduces a larger number of candidates into the decision-making process who may otherwise be excluded.

[190] T22, 6.

[191] T22, 15.

[192] T35, 3.

[193] T35, 4.

[194] F48, 2.

[195] T10, 6.

[196] F29, 2. Another interviewee in this state said that 'sometimes the candidate is produced by the Ministry and sometimes the name is suggested by another area of the executive, and the candidate is proposed to the members of the Permanent Court of Arbitration, for their approval': T53, 1–2. It was also suggested by another interviewee that sometimes the candidate is chosen by the Ministry and approved by the President, and then the name is put to the PCA national group: T58, 5.

domestic level to seek suggestions as to potential candidates.[197] An outside observer suggested that this approach could be adopted more widely:

I think the time has come in which PCA national groups ought to be [consulting], and there's quite a lot of good experience in the USA. They have an institutionalized system of consultation. They have their own, quite vigorous discussions about whom they should nominate and they do not always select the obvious candidate.[198]

Another PCA national group also consults widely as to the suitability of ICC candidates, for example, it 'consulted with four law schools, the legal profession, and civil society. And there was a great debate within civil society about who should be nominated.'[199] The group published a call for nominations and it was distributed to the bar councils, law associations and human rights lawyers groups. Applicants applied and three were short-listed. There was no interview. One candidate was selected and the PCA national group then consulted with the Constitutional Court, who approved the proposed candidate, and it was then sent to and approved by the President.[200] Another PCA national group consults with its Constitutional Court, Court of Appeal and universities.[201]

In these systems, the use of political levers by potential candidates is actively discouraged, as seeking allies who could push the nomination in the foreign ministry would probably have a negative effect because the 'PCA group would view that as interference…as it's not a political process. It's an anti-political process.'[202] Nonetheless, even in the most structured systems the government can refuse to support a candidate nominated by the PCA national group, as any decision of the group 'is not binding upon the government, but you would expect that quite often they would follow the advice, but it is not certain. The government makes its own decision.'[203] Even so, it is harder to dismiss the conclusions of an independent committee that has engaged in a transparent selection process. One WEOG PCA national group member said, 'I certainly don't think I had any sense that we were putting up a suggestion which might be rejected'[204] and it was considered that any complaint made by the foreign ministry would need to be rather serious for the PCA to revisit the proposal and 'would not be a question of whether the candidate was perceived as "pro" government or not'.[205]

The US PCA national group has, quite publicly, twice nominated candidates (Philip Jessup in 1960 and Richard Baxter in 1978) who were not favoured by the government.[206] In both circumstances, the PCA national group resisted pressure to nominate the government's preferred candidate and the government

[197] See also F47. Since 2000 the US PCA national group has consulted with ASIL, ABA, AAA, ILA US branch and leading law school deans. It had been done since 1960 (as explained by Richard Baxter) 'but was never done as transparently' according to one interviewee: T72, 5. L. F. Damrosch, 'The Election of Thomas Buergenthal to the International Court of Justice', op. cit., 581 and R. R. Baxter, 'The Procedures Employed in Connection with the United States Nominations for the International Court in 1960', op. cit., 445–6. The group has also been innovative in its interviewing of potential ICJ candidates.

[198] T35, 17.

[199] T82, 4.

[200] F13, 1.

[201] F19, 2.

[202] T72, 6.

[203] T13, 2.

[204] T73–5, 10.

[205] F2, 1–2.

[206] K. Keith, 'International Court of Justice: Reflections on the Electoral Process' *Chinese Journal of International Law* 9(1) (2010) 49–80, at 53.

eventually agreed to carry the candidature through to election. More recently, the renomination of sitting judge Thomas Buergenthal is unlikely to have found much support with the government of the day, but was not interfered with. In the United Kingdom, there was some publicly expressed opposition within the government to the nomination of Sir Hersch Lauterpacht 'but the legal adviser said that it was not their nomination to make'.[207] However, the government does not always capitulate. In at least one case, an independently nominated candidate was rejected by his state, received no support in campaigning, and was not elected.

Formal nomination procedures therefore depend on an independent approach by national group members, coupled with deference on the part of the foreign ministry. National groups using these procedures operate in a largely independent and transparent manner. They expand the scope of candidates considered for the court and appear to reduce the possibility of individuals within government using their connections to obtain a direct nomination. As Lori Fisler Damrosch has noted in relation to the US procedures: 'In the absence of such procedures, nominations could well have been more politicized and less professional. The discipline of requiring the nominations to be made by the national group has surely contributed, in no small measure, to the quality of the nominations made.'[208]

Equally, a small number of states have established more structured and independent nomination procedures for the ICC. These procedures have increased the numbers of candidates considered for the ICC, aligned the criteria for the court with the criteria used to select judges for the highest national courts, and injected transparency and accountability into the process. The ICC nomination procedure of the United Kingdom is a publicly known example. An ICC selection panel was established by the Foreign and Commonwealth Office and the Lord Chancellor's Department under the 'procedure for appointments to the highest judicial offices', although it deviated significantly from the procedure used at that time for senior appointments. There was a strong view in government that the United Kingdom 'should be nominating someone whom they would in any event have considered for a senior position of this kind domestically'.[209] A public advertisement[210] seeking applications was published approximately nine months before nominations would need to be made.[211] The procedure was as follows:

> Advertisements inviting candidates with the necessary qualifications to apply appeared twice in both The Times and the Scotsman (in April and May). A selection panel then

[207] F48, 2. See also P. Sands, 'Global Governance and the International Judiciary: Choosing our Judges' *Current Legal Problems* 56 (2003) 481–504.

[208] L. F. Damrosch, 'Ensuring the Best Bench: Ways of Selecting Judges: Commentary by Professor Lori Fisler Damrosch', op. cit., 194.

[209] T45, 7.

[210] It is notable that the UK adopted open advertised selection processes for the ECtHR and ICC prior to the establishment of the domestic Judicial Appointments Commission that then extended open advertising to mid-level and senior domestic judicial roles.

[211] Interviewees said that the decision to advertise was motivated by the fact that selection procedures for the European Court of Human Rights are advertised and 'it was thought that we could not do less than that': F32, 2.

sifted the applications received and interviewed a number of candidates on 27 June. The panel members were Sir Hayden Phillips (Permanent Under Secretary, Lord Chancellor's Department), Lord Cullen (Lord President of the Court of Session), Lord Justice Simon Brown, Joanna Foster (Chairman of Lloyds/TSB Foundation and Chair of Equal Opportunities Commission) and Mr Michael Wood (Legal Adviser, Foreign and Commonwealth Office).[212]

A close observer suggested that 'The United Kingdom comes out of this extremely well because the process was open, there was a proper competition, and there was an appropriately high level interview panel for this job. It was the equivalent of the kind of procedure that they now have in mind for senior judicial appointments.'[213]

In a GRULAC state, after the Ministry of Foreign Affairs had taken the decision to nominate an ICC candidate, an ad hoc selection committee was established by Cabinet on the instigation of the Attorney General. The committee, set up under the ICJ procedure as an equivalent PCA 'national group', comprised two legal practitioners (one of whom was appointed Chair of the Committee), an academic and a former diplomat, with a representative of the Ministry of Foreign Affairs sitting as a non-voting secretary. The members of the committee, according to a Ministry of Foreign Affairs interviewee, were 'eminent, independent-minded persons'.[214] They decided its procedure and the criteria for the candidate search, and met three times in total. Advertisements were published in the local press, seeking candidates who were required to meet criteria that included 'at least ten years' experience at the Bar, judicial experience, integrity, judicial skills and further abilities e.g. languages',[215] and those 'likely to be nominated would possess high moral character, impartiality and integrity, and also possess the qualification for appointment to the highest judicial offices of [the state], namely professional competence, experience and temperament'.[216]

Applicants were then short-listed based on the above criteria, without interviews. The committee then ranked the short-listed candidates and the first name was recommended in a report to Cabinet, sent via the Attorney General. The Cabinet could reject the recommendations but it would 'have to have very grave concerns . . . which would be unlikely because it would be difficult not to trust the judgement of the committee'.[217]

Another example was an African state that followed more closely its own national appointments procedure, requiring that candidates 'have been a practising advocate for more than ten years, of good character, have sufficient

[212] Foreign and Commonwealth Office, 'Press Release—UK Candidate for International Criminal Court Judge Confirmed (02/10/2003)', 2 October 2003, available at: <http://www.fco.gov.uk/resources/en/press-release/2003/10/fco_npr_310702_iccjudgeukcand> (accessed 11 December 2008).

[213] T45, 1.

[214] T25, 3.

[215] T25, 5.

[216] T27, 2.

[217] T25, 6–7.

background in criminal law'.[218] The nomination decision was taken by the Judicial Services Commission and approved by the Ministry of Foreign Affairs. An Eastern European state adopted a different approach which involved the participation of the legislature: 'the procedure used for the highest judicial functions was applied to ICC nominations *mutatis mutandis*'.[219] In the domestic procedure, 'the Council of Judges would first nominate a candidate and then the Parliament would have to approve the decision'.[220] However, for ICC nominations, the 'Minister of Justice performed the role of the Council of Judges'.[221]

Overall, the three broad categories of approach to ICJ and ICC nominations reflect the sharply different views on the role of government in the decision-making process. The majority of the states studied used informal or semi-structured procedures. These processes were marked by their lack of transparency and accountability and a stronger likelihood of being informed by extraneous political considerations. The resulting selection pool was small, there was limited outside input into the selection process, and political factors, rather than the individual selection criteria, could determine nominations.

The nomination of non-nationals for the ICJ

One further aspect of the ICJ nomination process is needed to complete the picture: the nomination of non-nationals. PCA national groups may nominate up to four candidates for each triennial election to the ICJ,[222] including a maximum of two nominees of the same nationality as the national group.[223] This procedure permits PCA national groups to nominate candidates who are not nominated by their own governments ('primary nominations') or to indicate their support for candidates who have already been nominated ('supporting nominations'). Political considerations are also a strong theme here, particularly in supporting nominations, as states exercise significant control over who is selected and have autonomy to decide who they will vote for.

Primary nominations have been used to nominate candidates who have not been nominated by their own states.[224] According to a WEOG diplomat, these nominations can ensure that excellent candidates are not lost: 'If the national

218 F15, 1. 219 T6, 3. 220 T15, 1. 221 T6, 3.

222 ICJ Statute, Article 5(2).

223 ICJ Statute, Article 5(2). The practice among states is that no more than one national candidate is nominated in an election. However, note that in earlier elections, some states nominated more than one national candidate: C. Harland, 'Special Report: International Court of Justice Elections: A Report on the First Fifty Years' *Canadian Yearbook of International Law* 34 (1996) 303–68.

224 The possible reasons for this are varied and may include: a change in domestic political circumstances, insufficient merit or another candidate that has been deemed more meritorious, personal animosities, lack of political leverage required to secured sufficient votes, arrangements made at bilateral or regional level not to propose a candidate in a particular election, or an unwillingness to run an election campaign.

group felt that there was a promising candidate who didn't carry enormous clout and would not be nominated, it considered it ought to be helping to secure the election of that person, for the good health of the court and international law.'[225]

A nomination by a foreign PCA national group may also potentially motivate the candidate's own state to nominate him or her. An interviewee from a GRULAC state suggested that 'if you are nominated by a national group of another country first you can put pressure on your country to nominate you'.[226] Two notable candidates have successfully obtained an ICJ seat via this route: Jose Maria Ruda (an Argentinian, nominated first by Belgium), elected in 1972, and Christopher Weeramantry (a Sri Lankan, nominated first by New Zealand), elected in 1990. Both had failed to secure nomination by their own states, ostensibly for domestic political reasons.[227]

Such nominations are usually conducted independently by national groups. However, they can be highly controversial where the state of the candidate concerned has decided to nominate another candidate. An example of this was the nomination of Georges Abi-Saab, an Egyptian, by Belgium in 2001, which was withdrawn after Egypt announced it would nominate Nabil Elaraby. Nominating 'alternative' candidates is generally considered an 'imposition by a foreign power'.[228] Recounting such an incident, a WEOG diplomat said, 'we were very cross about that, because it brought no value to the process and had something slightly mischievous about it'.[229]

The highly political context of the election process also limits the utility of these nominations, and appears to be reducing their frequency. In the increasingly demanding lobbying and vote-trading process, candidates without the active support of their government will be extremely unlikely to win, except in extraordinary circumstances. It also appears that candidates who do not receive the nominations of their states may be regarded as slightly suspect. As one interviewee put it, 'If he is so good, why doesn't his country nominate him?'[230] However, given the political and practical barriers facing potential candidates in many of the nomination processes, there may be good reasons why well-qualified individuals have not been nominated by their state. The trend away from the use of primary nominations may therefore cut off one route by which good candidates who are passed over by their governments can still find their way onto the bench.

In contrast, PCA national groups make more frequent 'supporting nominations' of candidates who have already been nominated by their states. These nominations emerge from a web of requests for support that are sent at the diplomatic level or between national groups and are usually strongly influenced by

[225] T35, 6. [226] F21, 1.

[227] Another example from the ITLOS context is that of David Anderson, a UK national who was nominated by France in the elections to the ITLOS, because the UK had not ratified the Convention in time to be entitled to submit the nomination. He was elected.

[228] T48, 10–11. [229] T35, 6. [230] T51, 7.

political considerations. As with national nominations, there is a wide range of different practices and different degrees of government influence over these decisions. One WEOG PCA national group seeks 'views'[231] from its foreign ministry and in an Eastern European state 'the government consults with the national group and expresses a view because a decision on support is not free of politics'.[232] In the majority of states studied, the foreign ministry makes the final decision because the nomination 'must be approved from the political side'.[233] In a minority, the process was 'more collaborative process than national nominations'[234] and 'the decision is finally with the national group'.[235] One WEOG diplomat noted that 'when our national committee nominated a foreign candidate we weren't even asked because he was not a government nomination, he was a nomination of the national group'.[236]

The types of political considerations that might be taken into account in such nominations include bilateral arrangements and regional political factors. There may be some consultation with the foreign ministry to align the supporting nominations with any vote trading arrangements that have been entered into, or could be entered into, by the state. Supporting nominations can form part of valuable mutual support arrangements, as a former WEOG diplomat explained: 'If a serious close partner had said, "can we have a pact for mutual support?" And that includes nominating one another's candidates; one would have been foolish and also rather rude to brush it aside.'[237]

But this can lead to conflicts. One PCA national group was said to have 'resigned in protest'[238] when it was told that it could not make a supporting nomination because the government had committed itself to another candidate: 'The government refused to back down and said that if a foreign government presents an ass, they would support that.'[239] Clearly, a government can vote as it wishes, 'but for a nomination, it has to have a decision with the stamp and the signatures of the four members [of the PCA national group], or at least three of the four'.[240] For this reason, if the PCA national group refuses, 'the government cannot really do anything about it'.[241] In this circumstance, the group might nominate its preferred candidate or not make any nominations at all.

The value and impact of supporting nominations is the subject of debate. Some diplomats are not impressed by long lists of nominations, nor do they think it is an indication of quality of support. Another interviewee said he felt that 'the PCA national groups are people recognized in the field and their support does imply a certain value-judgement on their part'.[242] Such nominations 'give a

[231] T41, 1. [232] F1, 2. [233] T50, 12. [234] T35, 5. [235] T9, 2–3.

[236] T16, 2. Note that the Canadian PCA national group has consulted widely on previous supporting nominations: M. D. Copithorne, 'The Permanent Court of Arbitration and the Election of Members of the International Court of Justice' *Canadian Yearbook of International Law* 16 (1978) 320–1. [237] T35, 5.

[238] Transcript on file with authours. [239] ibid. [240] ibid.

[241] ibid. [242] T77–80, 12–13.

certain advantage from the beginning, as the more nominations a candidate has, the better it looks'.[243]

E. Conclusion

The picture which emerges from this review of ICJ and ICC nomination processes across a range of states is one of considerable diversity of approach. This is manifested in the balance between politicization and independence as well as in the composition of the national groups and the processes they adopt. In relation to the ICJ nominations—and the ICC for states that decide to adopt the ICJ procedure—it appears that most states studied do not act in accordance with the spirit, nor even at times the letter, of the ICJ Statute.[244] In those instances where ICC nominations are made through national procedures, the picture is even more confused and it is often unclear what, if any, process is being followed. The result is a fragmented, inconsistent and highly variable approach to ICJ and ICC nominations. Some candidates may be selected through a transparent and consultative process that focuses on merit, whilst their competitors may have emerged because they were the best friend of the minister, or they were the minister him or herself. There does not appear to be a markedly 'purer' approach taken to ICC nominations, even though the court was established much more recently than the ICJ and is generally perceived to be less overtly political than the ICJ, if for no other reason than that it is has been established outside the UN apparatus.

It is clearly unrealistic to expect states to be entirely dispassionate about who will be nominated under their name for election to the ICJ and ICC. In an election-based system where the nominations process is operating in a broader political context, it is not surprising that states seek to protect and promote their interests. However, the fact that the judicial elections are part of the wider international governance structure does not mean that the nominations processes need to be shrouded in mystery or carried out in a way which means that talented outsiders will have no realistic prospect of being nominated. If the judicial selection procedures of the ICJ and the ICC are to produce judges who can claim legitimacy and command public confidence, as well as meeting the selection criteria, greater attention needs to be paid to the need to remove overt or crude politicization. Nor does this proposal require states to move into uncharted waters. The research findings show that there are a number of examples of states making nominations through open and transparent processes. These states are more likely to prioritize selection on merit, even whilst acknowledging the legitimate interest of the

[243] T3, 1.

[244] Concerns about this have been expressed as early as 1953: C. Eagleton, 'Choice of Judges for the International Court of Justice', op. cit., 463.

government in the process of nomination. Unfortunately, there is little evidence to date that these more rigorous, formal and open processes are widely viewed as a benchmark to be followed by other states. Nevertheless, there is at the very least some awareness that these practices exist, and evidence of increasing interest in what they may have to offer in terms of 'good practice' to other states in this field.

The findings on nominations are not unique to the ICC and ICJ. An Interights review of the process to the European Court of Human Rights in 2003 raised many of the same concerns:

> The current system of appointments provides wide discretion to States with respect to their nomination systems. In practice, internal processes vary greatly, but are often inadequate, politicized and so opaque that they are barely understood, even by some of the judges appointed by them. There is no meaningful review of these procedures at the international level, and no effective safeguards against arbitrariness.[245]

The need for safeguards against arbitrariness and some form of minimum standards would seem to be equally urgently required in relation to the ICC and ICJ.

[245] L. Limbach et al, *Judicial Independence: Law and Practice of Appointments to the European Court of Human Rights* (London: INTERIGHTS, May 2003) 27. Similarly, a recent report by the Committee on Legal Affairs and Human Rights of the Council of Europe Parliamentary Assembly on the nomination processes for judges to the European Court of Human Rights claimed that: 'the national selection procedures for candidates to the Strasbourg Court have important consequences for the overall quality, efficacy and authority of the Court'. The report went on to stress that the national nomination procedures were important because of their impact on the independence and perceived independence of the Court. Committee on Legal Affairs and Human Rights, Parliamentary Assembly, *Nomination of candidates and election of judges to the European Court of Human Rights,* Doc. 11767, 1 December 2008, available at: <http://assembly.coe.int/Main.asp?link=/Documents/WorkingDocs/Doc08/EDOC11767.htm> (last accessed 2 December 2008) at para 3.

4

The Election Process

A. Introduction

Once ICJ and ICC candidates emerge from the national nomination processes, they are presented for election by the states which are, respectively, for the ICJ, members of the UN General Assembly and Security Council and, for the ICC, the Assembly of States Parties (ASP).[1] The governing statutes of the ICJ and the ICC provide little by way of guidance as to the conduct of the elections and virtually nothing is known publicly about the internal mechanics of the election processes.[2] This chapter seeks to shed light on the way in which election rules are

[1] The ASP is a non-UN entity that is the management oversight and 'legislative' body of the ICC: <http://www.icc-cpi.int/Menus/ASP/>.

[2] The focus of the literature has mainly been on regional representation and discussion of the voting in actual elections and generally does not discuss the practice and impact of regional groups, campaigning and vote-trading. A sample of the literature includes J. L. Simpson, 'The 1960 Elections to the International Court of Justice' *British Yearbook of International Law* 37 (1961) 527–35; S. Rosenne, 'The Composition of the Court' in L. Gross. *The Future of the International Court of Justice*, vol. I (Dobbs Ferry, NY: Oceana Publications, 1976) 377–441; S. Rosenne, 'Elections of Members of the International Court of Justice: Late Nominations and Withdrawals of Candidacies' *American Journal of International Law* 70(3) (1976) 543–9; E. McWhinney, 'Law, Politics and "Regionalism" in the Nomination and Election of World Court Judges' *Syracuse Journal of International Law and Commerce* 31(1) (1986) 1–28; E. G. Lee and E. McWhinney, 'The 1987 Elections to the International Court of Justice' *Canadian Yearbook of International Law* 25 (1987) 379–88; E. McWhinney and S. April, 'The 1990 Triennial Elections to the International Court of Justice and the 1989 Casual Election' *Canadian Yearbook of International Law* 28 (1990) 403–16; E. McWhinney, 'The Contemporary International Court as Independent, and as Representative Tribunal' in *Judicial Settlement of International Disputes: Jurisdiction, Justiciability, and Judical Law-making on the Contemporary International Court* (Dordrecht: Martinus Nijhoff, 1991) 91–121; N. Blokker and S. Muller, 'The 1996 Elections to the International Court of Justice: New Tendencies in the New Post Cold-War Era?' *International and Comparative Law Quarterly* 47(1) (January 1998) 211–23; D. R. Robinson, 'The Role of Politics in the Election and the Work of Judges of the International Court of Justice' *American Society of International Law Proceedings* 97 (2003) 277–82; S. Rosenne, *Rosenne's The World Court: What It Is and How It Works*, Legal Aspects of International Organization Series No. 41, edited by Terry D. Gill (6th rev. edn, Leiden: Martinus Nijhoff, 2003); S. Rosenne, *The Law and Practice of the International Court, 1920–2005*, vol. I: *The Court and the United Nations* (4th edn, The Hague: Martinus Nijhoff, 2006) and O. Eldar, 'Vote-Trading in International Institutions' *European Journal of International Law* 19(1) (2008) 3–41. For a useful overview of the elections to the ICJ from 1946 to 1996, see C. Harland, 'Special Report: International Court of Justice Elections: A Report on the First Fifty Years' *Canadian Yearbook of International Law* 34 (1996) 303–68.

applied in practice and to identify other variables that will influence the outcome of the elections.

Anecdotal evidence provides strong support for the view that political influences play a significant role in the election processes. While some efforts were made in negotiation of the ICC Statute to reduce the potential for politicization of judicial selection procedures, in the light of experience in other international courts, this seems to have had a very limited impact thus far. The picture that emerges from the interviews confirms pre-existing anecdotal evidence, and highlights the important, if not central, role played by political factors that are unrelated to the merits of any candidate. Despite attempts to reduce the role of politics in the ICC election process, the journey of ICJ and ICC candidates from nomination to election is strikingly similar. Many individuals who participate in the ICC process believe it to be even more politicized than other international judicial elections.

It is clear that the election processes of both courts resemble more closely other political elections in international organizations than they do typical judicial selection processes at the national level. The elections are preceded by months or years of intense negotiations, campaigning and vote-trading. Some interviewees noted that in relation to the ICJ political considerations have increasingly come to affect voting and election strategy decisions. Others identified a sharp increase in vote-trading and election campaigning in recent years, alongside a growing role for regional groups in determining which candidates will run, or be supported. According to some, this has coincided with a diminution in the importance accorded to the individual selection criteria.

These findings need to be seen against the wider context of the system for the UN elections. The ICJ is but one organ of the UN organizational complex. The fact that its members are judges rather than politicians or diplomats seems to have relatively little impact on the character of the election process. Although the ICC election process is formally outside the UN system, it has been heavily influenced by the essentially political system used to elect the members of other UN bodies,[3] and this similarity was a factor noted in many interviews. While many interviewees expressed the view that judicial elections were qualitatively different in principle from elections to other political offices, they acknowledged that, in practice, no clear distinction is made within the UN community between the requirements of a judicial and a non-judicial post. Indeed, it would appear that in many cases, the former are traded and lobbied for like any other political position in the UN system.

[3] M-B. Miguel, *Votes in the UN General Assembly*, Nijhoff Law Specials, vol. 35 (The Hague: Kluwer Law International, 1998); see also O. Eldar, 'Vote-Trading in International Institutions', ibid. See also the UN General Assembly website on elections at: <http://www.un.org/ga/63/elections/index.shtml> (Accessed 28 April 2010). See also the non-UN website that discusses elections to different UN bodies: <http://www.unelections.org/>.

Three principal aspects of the election processes of the two courts emerged from the interview data as factors which shape the essentially political nature of the system: first, the role of some UN regional groups in endorsing candidates or negotiating for their withdrawal; second, the practice of campaigning and lobbying; and third, the role of vote-trading or 'mutual support' arrangements. These activities are not sequential; they take place simultaneously throughout the pre-election phase, which can extend for well over a year in advance of the election. The importance of these three interrelated processes is increased by the fact that the judicial elections are conducted in a 'hothouse' environment with limited independent information available about candidates and no objective screening mechanism. The fact that states who appear (or may appear) as parties before the ICJ also nominate and elect its judges entrenches practices that promote deep-seated political interests. This can discourage states from questioning existing practices, or from provoking political tensions. In this context, merit risks being sidelined. Nonetheless, practice varies, as there is evidence to indicate that a number of states *do* place considerable emphasis on the merits of candidates, devoting considerable time and effort to the assessment of their qualities and experiences. There is also evidence that some states will not vote for candidates they consider to be inadequately qualified. Finally, the mechanics of the voting process itself may have an impact on which candidates are elected—for example, candidates who have the support of the permanent five members of the UN Security Council are more likely to win ICJ seats.

B. ICJ and ICC election rules

ICJ judges are elected by the UN General Assembly and the Security Council voting simultaneously but 'independently of one another'.[4] Judges are elected for a nine-year term and can stand for re-election. Elections are staggered, with five judges being elected every three years, although 'casual' vacancies can arise at any time because of the death or resignation of a judge.[5] Candidates are elected when they obtain an absolute majority of votes in both the General Assembly and the Security Council.[6] If seats remain to be filled, a second and, if necessary, a third round of elections may be held.[7]

[4] ICJ Statute, Article 8.

[5] The election rules apply equally to casual vacancies: ICJ Statute, Article 14.

[6] ICJ Statute, Article 10(1). An absolute majority is ninety-seven votes in the General Assembly and eight votes in the Security Council, respectively: United Nations General Assembly and Security Council, *Election of five members of the International Court of Justice. Memorandum by the Secretary-General*, UN Doc. A/63/186-S/2008/502, paras 8–9. This document also sets out the procedural rules in relation to independent General Assembly and Security Council voting and general voting procedure.

[7] ICJ Statute, Article 11. Article 12 establishes a procedure that is to be used if all seats are not filled after the third meeting.

As to how states should exercise their votes, Article 9 of the ICJ Statute provides that:

> [a]t every election, the electors shall bear in mind not only that the persons to be elected should individually possess the qualifications required, but also that in the body as a whole the representation of the main forms of civilization and of the principal legal systems of the world should be assured.[8]

This latter requirement is deemed to be met by states by voting in accordance with the convention of equitable geographical distribution.[9] Therefore, states are expected to vote with equal regard to individual merit and the need for overall regional representation on the court.[10] As noted in Chapter 2, the requirement in Article 9 is taken to be fulfilled by the convention of equitable geographical distribution of seats on the court, combined with the convention that the five permanent members of the Security Council are represented on the court.

The rules governing the election process for the ICC differ significantly from those of the ICJ. The Rome Statute incorporates more detailed and complex voting rules for the election of ICC judges. They are elected by secret ballot during a meeting of the ASP,[11] and the candidates who obtain the highest number of votes and a two-thirds majority of the state parties present and voting are elected.[12] The quorum is an absolute majority of state parties.[13] Successive ballots may be held if there are seats that remain vacant.[14] In the first elections in 2003, thirty-three ballots were required to elect the first eighteen judges of the court.[15] In addition to the requirements for the representation of the principal legal systems of the world and equitable geographical representation for ICJ judges, state parties electing judges to the ICC must also ensure fair representation of female and male judges,[16] and consider the need for judges with particular legal expertise, including in relation to the issues of violence against women and children.[17]

A resolution of the ASP further entrenches these directives and establishes minimum thresholds for the overall composition of the bench by imposing on states a range of mandatory minimum voting requirements.[18] In accordance

[8] ICJ Statute, Article 9. [9] See Chapter 2.

[10] C. F. Amerasinghe, 'Judges of the International Court of Justice—Election and Qualifications' *Leiden Journal of International Law* 14(2) (2001) 335–48.

[11] See: <http://www.icc-cpi.int/Menus/ASP/> (Accessed 28 April 2010).

[12] Rome Statute, Article 36(6)(a); Assembly of States Parties, *Procedure for the Nomination and Election of Judges of the International Criminal Court*, ICC-ASP/3/Res.6, para 16.

[13] Rome Statute, Article 112(7)(a); ASP Resolution 6, paras 15 and 16.

[14] Rome Statute, Article 36(6)(b).

[15] See the results at the website of the first session of the Assembly of States Parties: <http://untreaty.un.org/cod/icc/asp/aspfra.htm> (Accessed 18 March 2010).

[16] Rome Statute, Article 36(8)(a).

[17] ibid. [18] ASP Resolution 6, paras 20–25.

with these requirements, states parties must cast the number of votes required to ensure that there are at least:

- nine judges from List A, that is, candidates with 'competence in criminal law and procedure, and the necessary relevant experience, whether as judge, prosecutor, advocate or in other similar capacity, in criminal proceedings';[19]
- five judges from List B, that is, candidates with 'established competence in relevant areas of international law such as international humanitarian law and the law of human rights, and extensive experience in a professional legal capacity which is of relevance to the judicial work of the Court';[20]
- three judges from the Western Europe and Other States group (WEOG), Africa, Latin American and Caribbean States group (GRULAC) and two each from Eastern Europe and Asia;[21] and
- six judges of each gender.[22]

The precise voting requirements for each election are calculated in accordance with the number of judges remaining on the court who meet the above criteria.[23] In the case of regional and gender factors, the voting requirements may also be reduced in accordance with established formulae if there are less than double the number of candidates as the minimum voting requirement for a regional group or less than eleven candidates for either gender—and the requirements may be removed if there is only one candidate meeting the criteria.[24] In practice, this means that if there are, for example, five female judges left on the court, only one will be required to be elected. However, if there is only one female candidate nominated, this requirement will no longer apply. The minimum voting requirements are adjusted between ballots (if there are multiple voting rounds) until they can no longer be met (ie there are insufficient candidates to enable states to cast the required votes). At this point, regional and gender voting requirements cease to apply. Furthermore, after a fourth ballot, all regional and gender voting requirements no longer apply. The voting requirements regarding List A and B are to be applied until they are fulfilled.[25]

The ICC has triennial elections to fill the six seats that become vacant every three years on a staggered basis. It also has elections for casual vacancies that come about through resignation or death. Minimum voting requirements also

[19] Rome Statute, Article 36(3)(b)(i) and ASP Resolution 6, para 20(a). See also the requirements set down in the Statute itself: Rome Statute, Article 36(5).

[20] Rome Statute, Article 36(3)(b)(ii) and ASP Resolution 6, para 20(a). See also the requirements set down in the Statute itself in Article 36(5).

[21] ASP Resolution 6, para 20(b). This leaves five seats as 'floating seats' that can be allocated to candidates from any region.

[22] ASP Resolution 6, para 20(c).

[23] See ASP Resolution 6, para 20(a)–(c).

[24] ASP Resolution 6, para 20(b) and (c). The calculation of the minimum voting requirements applying to a particular election are provided in Appendix 2 of the ASP Note Verbale announcing the election: for example, Assembly of States Parties, *Nomination and Election of Judges, Note Verbale of 13 May 2009*, ICC-ASP/8/S/20.

[25] ASP Resolution 6, para 21.

apply to casual vacancies, to the extent they are not met by the sitting judges.[26] ICC judges are elected for a nine-year term and cannot be re-elected.[27]

Given the various (albeit different) requirements for geographical, legal system and gender representation in the two courts, it is important to ask what effect these formal provisions have on the actual voting practices of states. Some interviewees were of the view that the rules of the courts regarding the overall composition of the bench detract from the principle of selecting candidates on the basis of merit. Some also felt that the more structured ICC approach limited the possibilities of electing the best judges.[28] Others believed that the representation requirements were not political and sought to achieve legitimate objectives of a more representative and diverse court.[29] These rules can be regarded as an 'essential part of the "buy-in" for an international court'and represent an acceptable balance between selection on merit alone and a composition which broadly reflects the international community. In the ICJ context, in which the convention of equitable geographical distribution applies regardless of the number of candidates nominated, a more problematic question is whether the convention encourages a sense that seats 'belong' to a certain regional group which could lead that group to put forward the same number of candidates as there are seats (often referred to as 'clean slates').

The degree to which the rules or conventions surrounding elections might restrict the election of the most highly qualified candidates and lead to politically motivated choices ultimately depends on the practices of regional groups in subsequently seeking the withdrawal of candidates, and also the surrounding election practices of states. While the formal rules provide a broad framework for the elections, it is these practices which shape the election processes and determine the ultimate result.

C. The role of the UN regional groups

A central feature of the equitable geographical distribution rules and conventions of both the ICJ and the ICC is the practice of 'reserving' seats on the

[26] Rome Statute, Article 37(1) and ASP Resolution 6, para 27.

[27] Rome Statute, Article 36(9)(a), except as provided by Articles 36(9)(c) and 37(2).

[28] However, it might be said that as the ICC has provision for 'floating' seats, it offers some flexibility to choose good candidates without regard to which region they come from. The possibility of extending the nomination period discussed in Chapter 3, combined with the adjustment of the minimum voting requirements depending on the number of nominations made also go some way to reducing the likelihood that a candidate is selected purely because he or she meets the underrepresented criteria. However, in the first elections, there were criticisms of the quality of some of the female candidates elected: see C. Stephen, 'Women Judges Dominate World's New War Crimes Court' *Guardian* 9 February 2003, available at: <http://www.guardian.co.uk/world/2003/feb/09/warcrimes> (accessed 12 November 2008).

[29] T35, 18.

bench for candidates from each of the five UN regional groups.[30] These regional groups of states, organized for the purposes of UN elections, often consider the 'regional seats' as their own, and to varying degrees determine who will take up the seats in a given election, even to the extent of depriving voting states of any real choice between viable candidates. Just as these regional groups often play a vital role in the nominations process, so they strongly influence the decision-making at the election stage.[31] They can perform two main roles at any stage in the election process: first, by endorsing a candidate; and second, by negotiating the withdrawal of other candidates. Both manoeuvres can reduce competition and increase the chances of the remaining candidate or candidates being elected. Thus a candidate from a region may run uncontested. According to many interviewees, endorsements and withdrawals are almost invariably based on political considerations, not merit.

Endorsement

The practice of endorsing candidates for the ICJ and the ICC appears to be limited to the African regional group, and to some extent the GRULAC group.[32] It is unclear why some regional groups endorse candidates and others do not—indeed, whether it is a consequence or a cause of greater internal coordination between members of a regional group. Some regional groups have a strong organization behind them, providing a forum for greater regional cooperation. In the case of the African group, the endorsement decision is taken by the Executive Council of the African Union (AU), based on a report by the Ministerial Committee on Candidatures.[33] AU members are bound to follow the decision of the Council, therefore binding those members of the African group who are also members of the AU. GRULAC endorsement decisions are made during the regional group meetings, which are mostly held in New York on a monthly basis.

[30] See the discussion in Chapter 2. As mentioned earlier, in the ICC context this involves a minimum number of seats for each regional group and a number of 'floating seats' that may be allocated to any regional group. Note, as discussed above, if a clean slate is put forward in terms of regional or gender requirements, those requirements will no longer apply. As a result, according to one interviewee, the ICC is a 'compromise between completely free elections and regional quotas': T3, 9.

[31] See Chapter 3 for a discussion of the role of regional groups in the nomination process.

[32] GRULAC endorsement appears to be more informal and based more on negotiation than a formal endorsement decision. Furthermore, GRULAC does not do this in every election, it depends on the candidates: F29, 1.

[33] See, for example, the endorsement of Dr Abdulqawi A. Yusuf for the 2008 ICJ elections: Africa Union Executive Council, 'Decision on African Candidatures for Posts within the International System', EX.CL/Dec.405 (XII), in *Executive Council, Twelfth Ordinary Council, 25–28 January 2008, Addis Ababa, Ethiopia*, EX.CL/DEC.378—414 (XII), EX.CL/Decl.1 (XII), available at: <http://www.africa-union.org/root/au/Conferences/2008/january/summit/docs/decisions/Executive_Decisions_378-414.pdf> (accessed 28 April 2010) para5.

Endorsement is intended to act as a form of pre-selection, binding all members of the regional group to vote for the candidate and ensuring a strong core of support. Being endorsed may be vital to a candidate's prospects of success. One African diplomat noted that 'if you get the endorsement of the African Union, most probably you'll get the support of the fifty-three African states, and if you have them, you are almost there'.[34] But discipline is not perfect and in some UN elections cases have been noted 'where the number of votes obtained by an endorsed candidate is less than the number of members of the AU'.[35] Where a group endorses a candidate it also hopes that states in other regions will recognize that endorsement and will add their own vote.[36] In some cases, the expectation is that once a candidate is endorsed, other members of the regional group will not compete with the endorsed candidate, leaving a 'clean slate'. This does not always happen, although even if other regional candidates do contest the election, the endorsed candidate is often in a strong position.

It appears that most endorsement decisions are 'not determined by merit'.[37] One interviewee noted that an endorsement can lead to 'more able candidates being squeezed out at an early stage' because of political factors,[38] such as the dominance of a particular state or arguments as to rotation, or that a certain state is due its 'turn' on the court. An African former ICJ candidate claimed that the endorsement process was 'not very rational'. Nor does it appear that decisions on endorsement are always taken with any particular scrutiny of the nature or quality of the candidate. In one case, a sitting judge apparently told the AU it should endorse a particular candidate, which it duly did without any further discussion.[39] It was also noted that the AU only considers nominations made up to a certain date, excluding later candidates nominated before the UN deadline. Furthermore, the AU reportedly will not consider candidates of member states who owe contributions to the AU.[40] One interviewee considered that 'it's wrong in principle that the AU should concern itself with such matters',[41] and argued that endorsement is an illegitimate political process which had no place in the election of international judges.

Other political groupings or organizations may also endorse particular candidates, resulting in members of those organizations pledging their vote to the endorsed candidate; for example, in the ICC elections, CARICOM has endorsed candidates.[42] This form of endorsement tends to give candidates a higher base

[34] T5, 3. [35] T62, 9.

[36] It does not appear that states will trade votes on a regional basis. Endorsement operates more as a lobbying tool.

[37] T5,6. [38] T35, 18.

[39] T82, 1. [40] ibid, 2. [41] ibid.

[42] Blocs of votes of CARICOM members have also been traded in other elections, in order to obtain votes for the CARICOM-endorsed candidate. Within GRULAC, CARICOM has also traded its votes in an ICC election in exchange for support from the wider GRULAC group. More informally, some candidates have been supported as 'sub-regional' candidates, for example, candidates of Canada, Australia and New Zealand (CANZ) and the Nordic states, to build

level of votes than non-endorsed candidates and some measure of political weight. Similar practices occur in the League of Arab States, where again, it was suggested, endorsement decisions are 'rarely a question of choosing the fittest or the most apt to fill the position'.[43]

Negotiations on withdrawal of candidates

Within regional groups there may also be multilateral or bilateral negotiations resulting in the withdrawal of candidates prior to the elections,[44] or states may decide unilaterally to withdraw their candidates. Such 'trimming' of the field is usually as a result of political factors and lacks transparency. It may result in a strong candidate being excluded from the race, a dramatic reduction in competition, or even a 'clean slate'. These negotiations appear most likely to happen in the African and GRULAC groups but can also take place between states in other regional groups.

An Eastern European PCA national group member described the ICJ process in simple terms: 'Members of regional groups bargain with each other, saying "I will drop this candidature if you drop yours" to get another seat. It is an elaborate process that has been in place already for decades.'[45] In the African group, if there are two candidates for an election: 'there will be a recommendation that they sit together and try to work it out. They always discourage the submission of more than one name although it does happen.'[46] Even during the election rounds, states 'come under pressure from the regional group to withdraw so the election does not go into endless run-offs'.[47] A GRULAC diplomat told one interviewee in the midst of an ICC election that 'we're caucusing tomorrow morning to sit together and decide who will be elected'.[48]

A range of arguments is used by states to encourage other candidates to withdraw, often relating to representation, rotation and sub-regional conventions, whereby states argue that they are entitled to a seat in a particular election.[49] Or they may be based on external factors that are bilateral in character; for example, if a state gave a concession in another context, they may consider that the *quid pro quo* is support for a seat on the ICJ or ICC. Negotiations may also be informed by the preliminary results of campaigning and vote-trading. As might

the support behind a candidate from a weaker sub-region within a regional group (in this case WEOG).

[43] T61, 9.

[44] On more general issues relating to the withdrawal of candidates, see S. Rosenne, 'Elections of Members of the International Court of Justice: Late Nominations and Withdrawals of Candidacies' *American Journal of International Law* 70(3) (1976), 543–9.

[45] T34, 6.

[46] T47, 7.

[47] T36, 3.

[48] T4, 10.

[49] In some regional groups, for example the African group, these arguments are built into the architecture of the system—ICJ seats are notionally allocated between Arab, Anglophone and Francophone Africa.

be expected, more powerful states with greater political leverage are the most successful in these negotiations. More generally, negotiations necessitate open dialogue, coordination between members of a regional group and a measure of political interdependence. Such pre-conditions exist in the African and GRULAC groups but in the Eastern European, WEOG and Asian groups there is little coordination of this nature and apparently few negotiations regarding withdrawal, meaning that there may be more competition between regional candidates for one seat.

Withdrawal negotiations take place in triennial elections as well as elections for casual vacancies and at the regional and sub-regional levels. When there is a casual vacancy caused by the death or resignation of a candidate, there is a 'principle that has become a kind of practice'[50] that a judge of the same nationality is elected. However, this 'practice' does not always hold and the outcome will depend on the political power of the state holding the seat. After the death of an African ICJ judge, for example, a candidate from the same state was nominated. The state tried to negotiate the withdrawal of a competitor from the same sub-region, on the basis that its candidate should be allowed to serve the remainder of the term and it would make a written commitment not to run again after the completion of the term. In that case, the competitor did not stand down.

States from outside the region may also become involved in the negotiations at a bilateral level. In an ICJ election, an African state was convinced to withdraw its candidate in favour of a candidate nominated by a second state from the same sub-region, under pressure from the President of a third country, a political ally of the second state. After the second candidate resigned some years later, the first state resubmitted its nomination.[51]

Some states also withdraw their candidates after concluding that their chances of being elected are slim 'because nobody wants to be perceived as a loser'.[52] Alternatively, withdrawal may result from a change of political circumstances at the national level, such as a change of government. Withdrawals also take place during the election rounds, in some cases 'once a certain pre-agreed support threshold is surpassed'.[53] Withdrawing states may then negotiate with their supporters to vote for one of the remaining candidates. Once a state decides to withdraw its candidate, the candidate will not be able to continue.

Not all interviewees were critical of these practices by regional groups. Some expressed the view that it is preferable for regional groups to reduce competition as much as possible, in order to avoid embarrassing intra-regional contests, to save face, and to save money on campaigning. Some interviewees from less powerful states thought that reducing competition is a fair way to ensure that such states are represented on the courts, particularly as the odds are stacked against smaller or developing states in the campaigning and vote-trading processes. Nonetheless,

[50] T44, 11. [51] ibid. [52] T12, 8–9. [53] F18, 1.

many highlighted the risks for the integrity of the bench, particularly if withdrawals result in a clean slate or the elimination of equally qualified alternative candidates. In the ICJ, states 'cannot cast a negative vote',[54] so if a clean slate is presented they must elect that candidate.[55] In the ICC, states are not obliged to vote for a 'clean slate', but they may decide to do so in order to retain regional balance. The risk is that if a clean slate is created for political reasons, a weak candidate could reach the bench uncontested.

In sum, the 'divide and conquer' mentality of some regional groups that overlays the regional representation rules of the ICJ and ICC could result in the election of judges who are not the strongest candidates, or in extreme cases do not even meet the individual selection criteria. In this respect, judicial candidatures are like any other political candidatures in the UN system, in that distorting extraneous political considerations can be introduced into the process that are not transparent to the voting states and may have a significant impact on the field of candidates that eventually reach the election. In the following section we consider the 'engine room' of the election process: campaigning.

D. Campaigning

Once the candidate pool is confirmed, candidates compete against each other both within and across regions. A key component of this process is campaigning, a collection of practices and activities that have developed around ICJ and ICC elections that can be traced from state capital to UN headquarters. The nature and level of campaigning may vary according to the state concerned. In general, one might expect a candidate to be available at some stage at UN headquarters in New York to meet with staff from Permanent Missions of other states, but in many instances far more extensive campaigns are waged. The effectiveness of the campaigning depends predominantly on the level and timing of activity, the extent of government support and the degree of financial outlay and political influence behind the candidate—factors which inevitably throw up significant barriers to entry for candidates from small or developing countries.[56] Campaigning can also provide uneven levels of information on candidates and can be subject to 'much spin' and manipulation.

[54] T14, 4.

[55] Unless a state refused to use all of its votes or abstain; but it would be difficult to imagine circumstances where states leave a seat on the court vacant. One interviewee appeared to contemplate this possibility, acknowledging that clean slates are 'useful but there is no guarantee because each candidate must still obtain the requisite majority of votes'; T2, 7. Alternatively, in the ICJ states could always elect a candidate from another regional group, but this would go against the equitable geographical distribution convention.

[56] Although it might be said that this disadvantage is slightly mitigated by the existence of the regional representation rules or conventions, which increases the chances of candidates from such states being elected.

The growing importance of campaigning

In recent years, campaigning has taken on a more central role in the election process, both in the ICJ and in the ICC, with the running of an active and wide-ranging campaign being seen as the bedrock of election success. Indeed, some argued that the effect of a well-run campaign can be so powerful that—combined with vote-trading—it can result in states voting for 'a lesser candidate',[57] so that almost 'any candidate could get through if politics are at play'.[58]

Campaigns are expensive, however, and require significant government commitment. A WEOG diplomat noted that one effect of the central role of campaigning is that in the ICJ small states have 'got to have everything going in their favour. Big powers can probably still win even if they are not politically favoured by the majority, provided they are prepared to lobby and pull all the levers they are capable of.'[59] Therefore, for a small or developing country to win a seat, it must lobby hard to redress its disadvantage. Yet this is difficult for 'small countries who can't afford the glossy brochure, let alone trips around the world and all the rest that's building up around campaigning'.[60] Regional representation requirements,[61] and forms of regional cooperation, may in some circumstances assist in addressing some of these disadvantages by providing the possibility of building a body of support for a particular campaign.

Campaigning has become such an important part of the process that even some P5 states that are in a virtually unassailable position in ICJ elections[62] feel that they must engage in it,[63] the United Kingdom and France for instance. Views differ as to the extent to which other P5 members campaign. Interviewees said variously that United States only 'rarely'[64] campaigns, that it is 'quite active',[65] that it 'only campaigns for a couple of days',[66] or that it 'does not campaign at all'.[67] It was also said that Russia and China do not campaign,[68] or that they campaign to a lesser extent than the UK or France.[69] An Eastern European diplomat expressed the view that the fact that Russia and China do not campaign 'suggests a sense of entitlement', adding that 'at least they could pretend they care about what we think about their candidates'.[70]

57 T19, 13. 58 T20, 2. 59 T19, 15.

60 T11, 12. Estimates of costs vary. One international judge said he had heard that some 'spend $300,000 or half a million' on their ICJ campaigns: T81, 5–6. However, another interviewee estimated that another major ICJ campaign cost less than one tenth of this amount: T23, 4.

61 See Chapter 3.

62 There is no P5 convention in the ICC although the UK and France have been consistently represented on the ICC since its inception and campaigned for their candidates. The other P5 members are not parties to the Rome Statute.

63 Some interviewees traced this to the losses of the UK and the US seats in the ITLOS and the ILC respectively, which might imply that the P5 convention was not as secure as it once had been: see further in Chapter 2. Another interviewee thought that the change of stance was needed 'particularly as the number of states and competition for seats increased' (T35, 14). 64 T3, 3–4.

65 F47, 4. 66 T72, 14. 67 T11, 9. 68 T6, 13. 69 T11, 9.

70 T6, 13.

The campaigning process

Campaigning involves a broad range of activities that take place across a wide variety of locations. The exact role of the candidates themselves varies between states and individual candidates and views differ as to whether active campaigning is appropriate for prospective judges or, in the case of the ICJ, for sitting judges who are seeking re-election. Some candidates themselves are extremely uncomfortable with their involvement in these processes and believe it may deter high-quality candidates from standing.

One interviewee thought that campaigning for the ICC, at least for the first elections, was 'more intense'[71] than for the ICJ, although both are seen as 'extremely important elections in which quite a lot of energy is invested'.[72] A WEOG diplomat also believed 'there was a lot more campaigning activity for the ICC than the ICJ'.[73] However, as to the nature of the campaigning activities, another diplomat said that he didn't think 'there was essentially any difference'.[74] The interviewees did not identify any regional differences in the way states campaign. In addition to the overarching importance of the effect of power and wealth disparities between large/developed states and small/developing states, timing and government support emerged as two key issues in the campaigning process.

For a number of interviewees, timing was 'the issue that counts the most'.[75] The campaigning period now often extends far beyond the formal nomination period prior to elections. For recent ICJ elections, a few states conducted their campaigns for more than two years. Anecdotally, it appears that ICC campaigns have generally been shorter, at around one year or less. An early start 'prevents commitments from going elsewhere'[76] and ensures candidates make an early impression. One WEOG diplomat said that 'states who regard their chances as less clear-cut will try to sell the election in advance'[77] and other interviewees referred to cases in the ICJ and ICC where they felt that good candidates were severely disadvantaged by a late start. However, not all shared this view as one GRULAC diplomat stated that, at least for her state, 'to be early does not compensate for other shortcomings'.[78] Some states do not start their campaigns until the formal nomination period or even until days before the election, possibly because of limited resources or a lack of engagement by the state concerned. Small or developing states have less capacity to engage in extended campaigns, and may have to rely more, for example, on 'high profile' Permanent Representatives in New York who have become well known on specific political issues.

71 T25, 10. This interviewee suggested that the campaigning for the first ICC election was 'more intense, being the first election to the ICC, because you wanted to bring as many member states in the community on board as possible'.

72 T3, 3.

73 ibid, 12.

74 T5, 12.

75 T15, 4.

76 T23, 9.

77 T35, 14.

78 T10, 17.

Active and high-level government support for a campaign was identified by a number of candidates as a crucial element for a successful campaign. One unsuccessful ICC candidate felt that support often depended on the domestic political connections of the candidate: 'If a foreign ministry person would have been the nominee, I'm sure that the two missions in The Hague and New York would have done it much, much better.'[79] Another interviewee noted that 'legal advisers of the Ministries of Foreign Affairs are a very important lobby and they help each other to get on the ICJ'.[80] Candidates who are, or have been, Permanent Representatives are also in a very strong position as they can organize their own campaigns.

It was felt that candidates from smaller states might have easier access to heads of state and an ICJ candidate was said to have benefited from the direct involvement of the head of state in his campaign. In the case of another ICJ campaign, it was noted that the Prime Minister, Foreign Minister and other ministers raised the subject of the candidate whenever they met officials of another government: 'They had to lobby on every occasion.'[81]

For some candidates, obtaining a base level of support could be a challenge due to a change of government, a refusal to support a candidate nominated by the PCA national group, or because the candidate comes from a 'failed state'. However, at least one example was cited of a candidate to the ICJ with a strong international profile who was elected after endorsement by the African Union, despite a limited campaign conducted by his country's Permanent Mission to the United Nations in New York. Yet in the case of another ICJ candidate the refusal of the government to support the campaign was fatal because 'other delegations would not support the candidate unless they received a letter from the capital endorsing the candidate'.[82]

In addition, states may also band together to campaign jointly for the candidate under a sub-regional banner: for example, Canada, Australia and New Zealand (known as CANZ) came together to lobby for Judge Kenneth Keith for the ICJ, as a 'force multiplier'[83] to make up for the gaps in New Zealand's diplomatic coverage in certain regions of the world. Likewise, in the ICC, the Finnish candidate Judge Erkki Kourula received support as a 'Nordic' candidate in the 2003 and 2006 elections.

Campaigning outside New York

The traditional bedrock of any campaign involves the foreign ministry sending *notes verbales* to the foreign ministries of other states (via its embassies in those

[79] T32, 14. [80] T40, 4. [81] T23, 7.

[82] T82, 3. This is also the reason why primary non-national nominations are becoming less common: as campaigning assumes greater importance, candidates who are nominated by states other than their own will not usually receive the level of support needed to mount a successful campaign. [83] T11, 6.

states, if it has them) seeking support. These are later followed up in New York by the Permanent Mission. In some states the Permanent Mission initiates the process by sending memoranda to other missions.

Beyond this practice, one GRULAC diplomat identified 'three levels of campaigning: in capitals, at embassies in the capital of the campaigning state, and in New York'.[84] Normally, there will be visits to embassies in capital (and possibly also functions for ambassadors) and diplomatic contacts in capital cities in which the nominating state has embassies. However, smaller states may have more limited overseas representation and will rely more heavily on *notes verbales* and lobbying through their Permanent Mission in New York,[85] but will lack the advantage of face-to-face contact. In some states, the PCA national group members may also take a limited role in writing letters to other states, seeking their support and attending any in-country functions.

A few states have toured their ICJ or ICC candidates to meet foreign ministry officials in capitals, particularly to cover regions where they do not have diplomatic representation or where they would like to develop a support base. Some consider that this is the future of campaigning for international judicial posts. The archetypical example of this more 'extensive campaign' is New Zealand's campaign for Judge Kenneth Keith for the ICJ in 2005, considered by many interviewees to set a benchmark for modern ICJ campaigns. The campaign was conducted over a period of at least two years and included visits to more than thirty capitals and three visits to the General Assembly, in 2003, 2004 and 2005.[86] In the ICC context, interviewees mentioned the campaigns of South Korea for Judge Sang-Hyun Song in 2003 and 2006. Other states have used this technique on a more limited scale, for example by piggy-backing on overseas visits made by the candidate in his or her other capacities. Candidate visits to capitals are seen as 'probably the most effective technique', as many states are flattered to have a visit from an ICJ candidate, 'but probably the most costly'.[87]

Some campaigns also involve lobbying of states through a range of political, interest-group and geographically based organizations; for example, candidates have met with lawyers' organizations, regional political organizations, international political groups (for example the Alliance of Small Island States, the Non-Aligned Movement, G77) to seek votes. In the ICC context, one state also leveraged the support of other states by seeking the support of domestic NGOs that were 'well accepted'[88] by those states. This strategy has been used by some smaller or developing states to cut across various potential support groups to build votes. In a recent ICJ election, a candidate sought to meet with some of the sitting

[84] T10, 12.

[85] Permanent Missions are listed in the 'Blue Book', available at <http://missions.un.int/protocol/bluebook.html> (Accessed 28 April 2010).

[86] T60, 13.

[87] T10, 14.

[88] T6, 5.

judges 'and really campaigned and wanted them to talk to their national groups and their foreign ministries'.[89]

Electioneering in New York

Most of the hard-edged lobbying for the ICJ and ICC elections takes place in New York. The direct involvement of the candidate in these processes varies greatly, but most candidates go to New York and are presented to delegations by their Permanent Missions. Candidates are expected to take an active role in presenting their candidacies by conducting seminars and attending social events. The first ICC elections were held in New York and the practice has continued for subsequent elections, even though the court is located in The Hague.[90] A WEOG diplomat thought that 'more ICC lobbying will be done in the future in The Hague, because obviously more knowledge will be accumulated in the embassies there and the court itself is there'.[91]

In the meantime, however, the ICC and ICJ campaigns have inhabited the same political space in New York and are influenced by the same atmosphere. This has the effect of tying the elections for both courts into the more general schema of UN elections, with the attendant campaigning and vote-trading. One foreign ministry legal adviser noted the increasing professionalization of the election process, which 'has become way more developed in the last fifteen years. There are now people in New York who do nothing but elections. So these judicial elections are regarded as yet another election by most countries.'[92]

This new breed of election professionals is supported by the UN election database, known as CandiWeb, that centralizes all data on elections and candidates.[93] Most larger states coordinate their campaigns through a civil servant in their capital and election officers in New York. However, not all missions have dedicated election officers. Smaller or developing states might have one person in the mission with some responsibility for elections (combined with other duties) but some missions do not have anyone at all. The level of staffing on the ground in New

89 T77–80, 6.

90 The election of judges for two vacancies on the ICC in November 2009 was scheduled to be held at the meeting of the Assembly of States Parties in The Hague.

91 F13, 12. One ICC candidate said that he had been sent to The Hague to meet with delegations and participate in a reception during a session of the Assembly of States Parties: T32, 7.

92 T18, 6.

93 The UN delegate website states that 'Candiweb is a collaborative website that allows for sharing of information on elections and candidatures within the main bodies of the United Nations. It is intended to simplify and provide updated information to elections officers and other interested members of the Permanent and Observer Missions': <http://www.un.int/wcm/content/site/portal/cache/offonce/home/pid/6409>. It is only accessible by password. The United Nations Institute for Training and Research (UNITAR) has also conducted workshops for elections officers, providing information on election rules and procedures, campaigning and regional endorsements: see <http://www.unitarny.org/en/electionunorgans.html> (Accessed 28 April 2010).

York and the experience of that staff can have significant impact on the size and success of the campaign.

There are three main types of activities in New York: meetings with the candidate at the Permanent Missions; official functions and receptions; and lobbying in the Indonesian Lounge or the Delegates' Lounge at UN headquarters. The scope of campaigning in New York may also depend on the international profile of the candidates and whether there is a need for their 'exposure to be increased',[94] though it is clear that candidates must make an appearance in New York and 'campaign actively'[95] because 'the ones who do not have fewer chances'.[96] Even if 'there is a good candidate, but they do not lobby enough in New York, they will not win'.[97] However, in some cases, a state cannot afford to pay for the visit of the candidate and all lobbying is conducted by the mission staff, or candidates have to pay their own way.

Meetings at the Permanent Missions are the foundation of the New York lobbying process. Usually, the candidate is accompanied by staff from the mission[98] and meets with the Permanent Representative or other mission staff and the election officer (if any). If a candidate has personal relationships with diplomats in New York this can be extremely useful in the election because then 'people know the candidate', which eases the discussion in the meeting.[99] These meetings usually involve the candidates setting out their experience and general views about the court, but do not address issues relating to current or potential matters before the court. The mission staff from the campaigning state may explain why a judge from their state should be elected to the court (for example, arguments about representation of different groups, sub-regional conventions, rotation, etc). There was also some recognition that in both the ICJ and ICC elections some states will choose to run 'dirty' campaigns, involving the 'denigration of other candidates'.[100]

Mission staff usually ask the candidate questions, based on their curriculum vitae and other campaign materials. The rigour of this process varies significantly from state to state. Some missions adopt a 'screening' approach and ensure that legal advisers are involved in the interviewing process, supported by election officers who gather information. They see these meetings as an opportunity to assess merit and test the candidates' capability and proficiency in their discipline, so that 'they can make their mind up'.[101] One WEOG diplomat described these meetings as 'an important part of our intelligence gathering';[102] another said it was 'extremely informative to meet the candidate in person'.[103] Some missions

[94] T18, 4. [95] T9, 3. [96] T13, 7. [97] T15, 6.

[98] It was noted in relation to the ICJ elections that it is 'necessary' for the Permanent Representative to be involved in lobbying if the candidate is going to be successful: T19,7.

[99] T47, 7. [100] T18, 8.

[101] T5, 5. Although some interviewees did note that 'the people that run for these posts are usually not unknowns and people running for the ICJ are well known international scholars, judges, diplomats, so we usually have knowledge of their previous activities': T16, 3. [102] T11, 7.

[103] T3, 7.

take the process very seriously: one meeting was described by an ICC candidate as an 'interrogation'.[104] A former ICC candidate felt that most missions were genuinely trying to assess the candidate's merit: 'except in one or two instances, there was a real sense of a worthwhile process in terms of getting to know the candidates'.[105] Some interviewees suggested that this 'screening' approach is less rigorous for ICJ judges because most missions already know the candidates or are at least familiar with their work.

Some mission staff also ask their colleagues from other missions about candidates and undertake proactive investigations,[106] including through the courts and other 'informal channels'.[107] The outcome of these investigations can be significant: one state reversed their decision to vote for a candidate when they met him and found that 'he was not well versed in matters of international criminal law'.[108] Other missions ask 'very shallow'[109] questions and simply seem to accept the information provided by the candidate. Some interviewees believe this is due to the fact that most mission staff do not have legal backgrounds, and also to a lack of engagement by missions because the final decision is invariably taken in the capital on political grounds. During these meetings, the diplomats will also discuss possible vote-trading deals, even in the presence of the candidate. The mission will then send a note of its views to the foreign ministry. There may be multiple follow-up meetings between the diplomats as part of a 'continuous process' of confirming support.[110]

In addition to meetings at Permanent Missions, many campaigning states also host functions and other events. Functions might include 'breakfast seminars, with a question and answer session'[111] (which one diplomat said were 'annoying because candidates are so paranoid about saying something politically naïve or prejudicial that they give remarkably safe answers'),[112] seminars on specific legal issues to be presented by the candidate, lunches and dinners with Permanent Representatives, drinks receptions and parties. One ICJ candidate had what he described as 'a very good election party in the UN building, a week or so before the election'.[113] The information conveyed during these events is usually quite informal. Interviewees indicated that the circuit of events is enthusiastically attended by mission staff, and other candidates use them as lobbying opportunities for their own campaigns in the same or other elections.

In the ICC context, campaigning has also included participation by some candidates in panels and questionnaires organized by NGOs in which they have answered questions on their experience, their views about the court and also substantive legal issues.[114] In the first elections, some NGOs were involved in lob-

[104] T32, 15. [105] T45, 4.

[106] One diplomat said she might 'Google some additional information': T13, 4.

[107] T6, 9. [108] T5, 6. [109] T6, 5. [110] T18, 9 and T5, 9. [111] T10, 14.

[112] T11, 13. [113] T60, 13.

[114] They were conducted by the Lawyers Committee on Human Rights (now Human Rights First) and the Coalition for the International Criminal Court and the results were posted on the

bying for or against particular candidates, but now the NGOs (particularly the Coalition for the International Criminal Court) do not adopt views on particular candidates.[115] Nevertheless, some interviewees felt that it was inappropriate for NGOs to be adopting any type of 'screening' role in ICC elections, particularly as they were more focused on 'substantive legal issues and how candidates lined up on particular issues',[116] and would filter information through their own 'perfectly appropriate [but] vested interests'.[117] Not all candidates felt it was appropriate for judicial candidates to participate in panels and questionnaires which one ICC judge described as 'competitive tendering'.[118] Others welcomed the involvement of NGOs and felt that it improved 'transparency'[119] and injected useful and sufficiently independent information into the election process by highlighting 'huge differences between the candidates'.[120]

In the run-up to the election, focus turns to lobbying in the Indonesian Lounge and the Delegates' Lounge at the UN headquarters, the epicentre of diplomatic activity. Some candidates lobby there prior to the election process, during other sessions of the General Assembly and Security Council, which they may also attend. However, most converge on the UN in the weeks and days leading up to the ICJ and ICC elections. Former candidates for the ICJ and ICC explained that they had spent days in these rooms 'meeting people all day'.[121] The staff sent to interview candidates range very broadly, from Permanent Representatives to unpaid interns and the approach taken to these meetings varies greatly, with some taking a rigorous approach to questioning and others remaining largely passive. One ICC candidate described being 'interviewed by interns and some interviewers who said they did not feel qualified to ask me questions'.[122] Of course, some candidates are already well known by many in the electorate: some (from diplomatic/government background) because they have already achieved a high profile in the UN as Permanent Representatives, or are members of the UN General Assembly Sixth Committee; others (from legal practice and academia) because they may be well-known practitioners in the field or the author of leading textbooks on international law. It was widely recognized that being 'known'—having an existing good reputation—was a significant factor.

internet. See: <http://www.humanrightsfirst.org/international_justice/icc/election/elections.htm> and <http://www.iccnow.org/?mod=electionjudges> (Accessed 28 April 2010).

[115] Coalition for the International Criminal Court, 'CICC Recommended Criteria for States Parties to Nominate and Elect Judges to the ICC', available at: <http://www.iccnow.org/documents/CICC_Judicial_Nomination_Election_Criteria_FINAL.pdf> (accessed 3 October 2008).

[116] T45, 4.

[117] ibid, 6.

[118] ibid, 5.

[119] T76, 8. This interviewee also thought that the involvement of NGOs was an important aspect of engaging civil society in the work of the court.

[120] T13, 15.

[121] T18, 9.

[122] T27, 3.

The long journey from nomination to election continues into the voting chamber. Lobbying reaches fever pitch on the day of the election. In one ICJ election, an interviewee observed 'fifteen or twenty very eager junior diplomats getting at every person in the General Assembly hall, asking, "do you know about Mr X and how great he is?" '[123] One ICJ candidate's promotional material included a pop-up card in English and French that was put on each delegate's desk; it included information about the candidate and the nominations he had received from PCA national groups, and a glossy brochure which offered information on the regional distribution of the seats and the voting process. Last-minute meetings are held in the UN cafés and hallways, deals are cut and reciprocal arrangements are confirmed.

The appropriateness of campaigning in judicial elections

In light of the importance that interviewees attached to the process of campaigning and the uneven access of different candidates to the resources and influences necessary to campaign successfully, serious questions are raised as to whether such campaigning is an appropriate means of identifying the best qualified candidates. Some felt strongly that campaigning should not be used in elections to international judicial posts and that the level of involvement required of candidates could be damaging to the integrity of individual candidates and to the courts in general: 'The ICC election process is fundamentally flawed. The practice of lobbying that is carried on for the appointment of a judge leads one to feel that bias is either apparent or in fact exists.'[124]

While one interviewee indicated that the questions asked of campaigning candidates do not stray into 'contemporary and politically contentious issues',[125] others described their concern that active involvement in lobbying could potentially lead to the perception or reality that candidates are being asked to 'make assurances'[126] and divulge their views on matters that may come before the court. One former legal adviser commented that efforts had been made to ensure that candidates are not directly involved in the vote-trading side of lobbying as this would 'overstep the mark'.[127] Not all UN missions follow this approach, however: an ICC candidate described how she had been approached by mission staff and presented with a vote-trade proposal for her to convey to her government, something that she considered 'highly inappropriate'.[128] The apparent practice of candidates asking sitting judges to lobby their states on their behalf would also appear to draw them into the political process of campaigning. A former ICJ judge felt that the process, particularly at UN headquarters, is like 'an election for a local council'[129] rather than a high-level judicial election.

[123] T77–80, 8. [124] T27, 4–5. [125] T11, 14. [126] T9, 4.
[127] T35, 14. [128] F13, 2. [129] T47, 12.

From a personal perspective, some candidates described the activity of campaigning as 'an affront',[130] 'humiliating and highly embarrassing',[131] and a 'completely bizarre experience'.[132] However, a WEOG diplomat pointed out that views about the process differ according to whether a candidate's background is from a civil or common law jurisdiction. He suggested that common law judges 'have a tradition of being reserved and a bit aloof' whereas 'Civil law judges operate in a more interactive legal system and have more of a public role so perhaps campaigning comes more naturally to civil law judges.'[133] This categorization might well have some general truth but it did not appear to hold true in all cases. One international judge from a common law country felt that campaigning was an 'immensely interesting experience';[134] another interviewee reported that a judge from a civil law country had described 'courtesy visits' as the worst part of the process since he had never anticipated that his career would require him to visit embassies to 'sell himself'.[135]

Campaigning is also a major time commitment that can be problematic for candidates with successful and demanding careers—arguably exactly the sort of high-quality candidates that the courts would wish to attract. Some interviewees believed that the demands of campaigning deterred good candidates of this kind.

Campaigning by ICJ judges seeking re-election

In relation to the issue of campaigning, and more generally, many interviewees expressed concerns regarding the potential re-election of ICJ judges. A number of interviewees claimed that the problems of campaigning were compounded when candidates are sitting ICJ judges seeking re-election,[136] though the campaigns of most sitting judges were described by some as low-key. Sitting judges might personally write to PCA national groups seeking supportive nominations but their campaigns are limited in scope, focusing on New York. At the same time, one interviewee said that some judges seeking re-election 'had spent a couple of weeks in New York just to run a campaign'.[137] Some missions apparently ask sitting judges 'what is going on in the court and how he sees the organization and whether there is anything that needs to be developed'.[138] Candidates seeking re-election are generally seen to be at an advantage as 'they are in and the others are out'[139] so overall campaigning is considered to be less necessary.

The possibility of re-election could compromise judges' actual or perceived independence as they may be consciously or subconsciously influenced by their desire to obtain the support of states for re-election,[140] and, as one judge described

130 T11, 7. 131 T27, 6 and 13. 132 T45, 3. 133 T11, 7. 134 T45, 3.
135 F43, 1. 136 Provided for by ICJ Statute, Article 13(1). 137 T77–80, 6.
138 T13, 3. 139 T31, 10.
140 And the support of their own state in order to be nominated again.

it, to 'write an opinion to the outside world'.[141] One interviewee referred to a situation where an ICJ judge whose dissenting opinion had favoured a particular state received strong support from that state for his re-election (although it was not suggested that the judge was seeking such support in writing his decision). A former judge claimed that on a number of occasions he had perceived 'colleagues thinking about how something would be received in the General Assembly'.[142] Conversely, judges from less powerful states who 'stick their necks out' may not be re-elected, with all that implies for their purported independence.[143] The process of lobbying and campaigning required of ICJ candidates, however low-key, was seen by some to contribute to this actual or perceived lack of independence and to be inimical to the role of a sitting judge.[144] A number of interviewees felt that a single term of nine or twelve years, which would be appropriate to address these concerns whilst providing for the continuity of the work of the Court.[145] If such a change was not possible, it was felt by some that sitting judges should at least set themselves aside from the lobbying process.[146]

On the other hand, in some cases, re-election might be preferable to leaving a judge dependent on his or her state for a post-bench career.[147] As one interviewee put it, a judge seeking re-election will 'rely on *all* states rather than just *one*'. Re-election was also thought to support the continuity of the court, and those who supported re-election generally felt that concerns regarding the independence of judges and their involvement in lobbying and campaigning were overplayed.

Overall, the evidence suggests that the very nature of the campaigning process builds in disadvantages for certain candidates and militates against a level playing field in which a contest is played out on the basis of merit. Reports of the meetings held between candidates and Permanent Missions suggest that merit is not without relevance to voting decisions. However, those candidates who are known at the international level and whose states are able to conduct large, well-timed and well-supported campaigns are clearly at an advantage. In the blur of meetings and slick campaign functions, merit is likely to be relegated to a second

141 T77–80, 10. 142 F47, 5. 143 F6, 2.

144 This may be of particular concern in light of the duration of contemporary campaigns for seats on the ICJ.

145 It was also felt by some that re-election leads to judges serving multiple terms when they are 'well past it': T35, 15. Re-election can also limit representation on the court, and a number of interviewees suggested that seats should rotate to other states after a certain number of terms (for example, two terms).

146 Two interviewees suggested that, in the absence of an amendment to the Statute, the General Assembly could pass a resolution expressing the view that a judge who has served a full term should not stand again: F47, 5, F48.

147 This was considered to be more problematic as there is a trend towards younger ICJ judges. It was noted in relation to another court that a judge who had delivered unfavourable decisions against his own state was denied a pension and became a refugee, suggesting there are real potential costs for former international judges. However these are not problems that are fully resolved by allowing re-election.

or third level of consideration—if it remains relevant at all. The highly politicized nature of the process and the involvement of candidates in the campaign process also raised concerns about its impact on the integrity of judges and the courts. It is against this background that another issue of great significance arises, namely the securing of vote-trading agreements or reciprocals.

E. Vote-trading

At the core of the campaigning process is the negotiation of vote-trading agreements, referred to as 'reciprocals' or 'mutual support agreements', by which a state will vote for a candidate in exchange for a vote in the same or another election (for the same or another body), or in exchange for other benefits or inducements.[148] In the ICJ and ICC most votes are based on reciprocals, and states now feel a need to conclude them if they want to enhance the prospects for their candidate. As the following section will show, these agreements are largely motivated by political considerations rather than merit.

Votes traded and the role of merit

Vote-trading is the main lobbying strategy used by states to secure votes. In practice, few states treat judicial elections as qualitatively different to other individual or state candidatures, even if they view them as different in principle. Therefore, whether a candidate meets the selection criteria is often not the main consideration in decisions about reciprocals. The evidence suggests that states trade votes for bodies both within and outside the UN system, as well as for other benefits. Votes in ICJ, ICC and other judicial elections are included in this process.[149]

The fact that the ICC is included amongst the institutions involved in vote-trading will be surprising to many. When the ICC was being created, many participants in the process sought to ensure that the new court would be kept out of this bargaining process. Before the first elections, for example, the President of the ASP Bureau, HRH Prince Zeid Ra'ad Zeid Al-Hussein, appealed to states to 'refrain from entering into reciprocal agreements of exchange of support in respect of the election of judges of the Court… [i]n order to ensure the integrity of the electoral process'.[150] Nonetheless, vote-trading took place from the

148 S. Rosenne, *Rosenne's The World Court: What It Is and How It Works*, op. cit., 67.

149 O. Eldar, 'Vote-Trading in International Institutions', op. cit., 23–7.

150 Assembly of States Parties to the Rome Statute of the International Criminal Court, *First session, New York, 3–10 September 2002, Official Records*, ICC-ASP/1/3, para 27. See also Assembly of States Parties, Assembly of States Parties, *First Session (First and Second Resumptions), New York, 3–7 February and 21–23 April 2003, Official Records*, ICC-ASP/1/3/Add.1, para 16. With regard to NGO activity on this issue, see, Human Rights Watch, 'Letter to H.E. Mr. Christian Wenaweser, President of the Assembly of States Parties' (19 December 2008), available at: <http://www.iccnow.org/documents/HRW_ASP_Bureau_letter_ on_election_of_judges_19_Dec_08.pdf> (accessed

outset, following the ICJ practice. One WEOG diplomat said that he thought 'fewer reciprocals were concluded for the first ICC elections than other elections due to the goodwill surrounding it. But if I had to look into a crystal ball, I'd say that the gloss will wear and the ICC will become an election much like any other.' [151]

A number of interviewees said they thought this was already the case in the first elections. In 2008 the Coalition for the International Criminal Court (CICC) responded to concerns about this issue by setting out some recommendations to the states parties for the 2009 nomination and election process. It argued that amongst the practices adopted in the first ICC elections, 'Among the most objectionable is the practice of making reciprocal agreements between governments in exchange for votes. The CICC strenuously appeals to State Parties of the Rome Statute of the ICC to renounce this practice in ICC elections.'[152] Many of the interviewees shared similarly critical views of the practice of vote-trading and reciprocal agreements, with one GRULAC diplomat referring to the system as 'the multilateral bazaar'.[153]

Reciprocals, it seems, have always played some role in ICJ elections, but in earlier years they were usually concealed. One former foreign ministry official who became an international judge said that: 'They were always hidden for the sake of appearances, at least. You would write a letter supporting somebody then a week later they would write supporting your candidate, whereas now it is unabashed.'[154] Votes are traded for a wide range of international candidatures, with states usually requiring some equivalence between the votes that are being traded, as one WEOG diplomat explained: 'if the first reciprocal offer is a for b, and we don't consider them equivalent, we might go back with what about a for b and c'.[155]

Normally, a seat on the ICJ or ICC is seen as equivalent to major political positions such as a non-permanent seat on the UN Security Council. Lesser candidatures, for example, for the Commission on the Limits of the Continental Shelf and expert positions on the UN human rights treaty bodies, or positions within regional organizations, can be combined to 'equal' an ICJ or ICC vote. Some states will only vote-trade judicial candidatures with other judicial candidatures. Reciprocals may be concluded between states from the same regional group (and, in this case, may include positive votes or even agreements not to run in later elections), or with outside states. Normally, they are concluded as early as possible in the campaigning process, and candidates who

10 May 2009). This letter calls on the Bureau to issue a *note verbale* discouraging states from vote-trading and also asks the Bureau to monitor the completeness of the supporting statements accompanying nominations, and seek further information from states as required.

[151] T11, 16–17. See also B. N. Schiff, *Building the International Criminal Court* (Cambridge: Cambridge University Press, 2008) 107.

[152] Coalition for the International Court, *Recommended Criteria for States Parties to Nominate and Elect Judges to the ICC*, October 2008, para 20.

[153] T12, 7. [154] T81, 6. [155] T11, 10.

come late or 'sit back and do nothing might find that their candidate's chances are diminished'.[156] Reciprocals can include agreements to vote in future elections, including elections for individual or judicial candidatures for which candidates have not yet been announced. States may also conclude reciprocals in relation to the possible multiple voting rounds of the elections, for example, they may have an agreement that a state will vote for them if a third round of voting is required. States that are campaigning for 'sub-regional' candidates can also offer a bloc of votes in exchange for a vote for their candidate.

It is not only votes that are traded: some states may suggest the possibility of support for international development aid or projects in exchange for votes, or expect support from existing aid recipients. One interviewee who was part of a delegation in the first ICC elections told us that the practice of vote-trading in exchange for aid was more prevalent in the ICC than the ICJ elections.[157] Another confirmed that in the ICC elections 'votes can be traded against promises of development assistance'.[158] In the ICJ context, a diplomat from a developing African state, while expressing a personal commitment to selection on merit, acknowledged that his government would be 'stupid'[159] not to support candidates from states that provide it with development aid and that deciding on these votes is a 'political and economic process'.[160] Another WEOG diplomat explained that 'Some of the European countries have huge connections in terms of trade and aid and when they are lobbying for support, the person who they are lobbying is not unconscious of these connections.'[161]

In this way, votes are used as a 'quid pro quo'.[162] Small states, by becoming promoters of various initiatives at the UN, for example, peace-building or reconstruction, have 'become popular in other ways'[163] and increased their profile in elections. Some states even go even further, to the extent that 'foreign policy decisions might be affected by the interests of the ICJ campaign',[164] or they may also offer 'cross-pledges to some other electoral or foreign policy issue'[165] in exchange for votes. Most of the inducements referred to by interviewees were in the form of development aid or other, unspecified, bilateral (state-to-state) assistance. However, one interviewee (although not directly corroborated by others) told us that cars were promised to those who voted for a particular candidate in an ICC election.[166] It is not clear from the interviews how widespread the provision of bilateral assistance or other forms of inducement are in judicial elections, but one interviewee suggested that such practices were common in relation to elections to the Security Council. As a diplomat put it: 'Security Council campaigns are incredibly expensive, partially because you need some money to coerce votes.'[167]

156 T35, 14–15. 157 F32, 2. 158 F20, 2. 159 T5, 5.
160 ibid, 7–8. 161 T19, 12. 162 T2, 7. 163 T6, 14–15.
164 T23, 7. 165 T35, 14–15. 166 T24, 12. 167 T11, 8.

Occasionally the inducements offered are less direct and will be built into campaigning activities. In Security Council and ILC elections there are, apparently, some states that pay for diplomats to go on 'lavish trips'[168] to visit their capitals and attend campaign meetings. One interviewee thought that this amounted to 'political bribery'.[169] At a more diffuse level, states may feel compelled to vote for a particular candidate to guarantee his or her state's contribution to the budget of the court. In one case at the ICC, a number of diplomats present during the election process said that they thought this was the reason a particular candidate had been elected, combined with the political standing of the candidate's state and the effectiveness of its campaigning. One interviewee pointedly described this as 'a sort of international blackmail, because no-one wanted to vote against that country'.[170]

It is apparent that reciprocals are not principally—or indeed, often at all—based on an assessment of the merit of the candidate, even where the elections involve individual expert candidatures or judicial candidatures that have specific individual criteria.[171] Most states conclude reciprocals based on the actual or desired bilateral relations with the offering state and the attractiveness of the offer. Merit is relatively low on the agenda, if it is there at all. As a former international judge explained:

> If you're lobbying for a judicial appointment you point out that the candidate is well qualified. But the objective of the people you are speaking to is to get Ruritania on this or a Ruritanian on that and if they can achieve that result they get [an advantage] back home—however much you stress judicial appointments are different, it only washes to a certain extent.[172]

As this is a political process, campaigning states with significant economic and political leverage have an advantage.[173] They have the bilateral relationships and the membership of a wide range of international and regional organizations and economic power, in order to obtain a high number of votes. This is a problem for smaller, less powerful, developing or politically unfavoured states that, according to one unsuccessful ICC candidate, 'have nothing to offer and bear no gifts'.[174] A candidate for the ICJ in 2008, Senator Miriam Defensor Santiago, publicly criticized what she perceived to be a 'power game', in which 'developed states tend to vote for countries where they have interests to protect such as foreign

[168] T14, 10.

[169] T14, 11. Another interviewee said that 'developed countries may also help least developed countries to attend international meetings (particularly those where votes are cast) which can secure the support of some African countries': F1, 2.

[170] T24, 12.

[171] One WEOG PCA national group member said that 'elections are a political compromise between the individual and the state because there are many posts to fill in the UN': T44, 7.

[172] T36, 2–3.

[173] One interviewee said that a state may have particular leverage when it is a non-permanent member of the Security Council: T32, 13.

[174] T27, 24.

investments, use of natural resources and a big export market . . . As a developing state, we have no such cards to play.'[175]

It is apparent that the system is highly politicized, entirely lacking in transparency and, according to one ICC candidate, 'inappropriate for the appointment of a judge'.[176] Vote-trading, according to one interviewee, 'has got to proportions that is potentially seriously damaging to the UN and its institutions'.[177]

Some states believe that judicial positions should be treated differently, particularly for courts of such importance as the ICJ and ICC.[178] However, they accept the political reality that one must trade votes in order to get votes. But they will only trade votes for candidates they believe to be 'exceptionally well-qualified'.[179] A Nordic diplomat explained: 'In principle we have to become confident that the candidate is qualified, and then how any support is expressed depends on the relations we have with this particular country.'[180] An ICC judge thought that most states took this approach in the first ICC elections and that 'missions did try to focus on the personal qualities of the candidates and I think there was a real sense that they were in the business of electing judges, rather than civil servants or other administrators'.[181] One state that takes this approach waits until the last couple of weeks before the election to make its decision, 'so all the candidates are on the table'.[182]

But, of course, politics are not entirely excised from this process. This interviewee suggested that in her state there is an initial filtering on political grounds before merit is considered: '[The department] will then consider the offers from a political point of view, and if some are not acceptable, they would exclude them. The requests are then passed to the PCA national group that will decide which candidates are technically stronger and we will work on the agreements with the stronger candidates.'[183] Another interview confirmed that some states will not vote for certain states, regardless of the offer. They will tell these states 'it would be good if you vote for us, but we cannot enter into an agreement'.[184]

In such cases, where states maintain a primary focus on merit, there is more likelihood of ensuring the integrity of the individual selection criteria. However this may be at a potential cost to the individual state. In a system where most states are playing a political game, a state that puts merit first will be at a disadvantage in securing the election of its own candidates. As one WEOG diplomat put it: 'you've got to be out in the field, but you've got to behave in a decent way, it's a very difficult balance to strike'.[185]

175 M. Lim Ubac, 'Santiago Blames "Power Game"' *Philippine Daily Inquirer* 8 November 2008, available at: <http://globalnation.inquirer.net/news/breakingnews/view/20081108-171051/Sant> (accessed 12 November 2008).

176 T27, 14.

177 T19, 13.

178 Some states also refuse to conclude reciprocals for certain state candidatures, such as the Human Rights Council, because of their particular subject matter: T15, 5.

179 T11, 4.

180 T13, 8.

181 T45, 9.

182 T10, 12.

183 ibid, 18.

184 T16, 4.

185 T35, 14–15.

Some small states do not vote-trade due to their special political circumstances, as a diplomat from a small state explained: 'We don't have many strong bilateral relations and we don't participate in contested elections so we don't feel obliged to countries to look at candidatures in a favourable manner. This gives us the certain luxury of being able to consider candidatures on the basis of merit.'[186] Some states that otherwise vote-trade may also decide to vote for a candidate unilaterally and 'build political capital',[187] because they believes the candidate is particularly strong or because of their special political relationship with the campaigning state (for example, if they are from the same regional group).

Moreover, not all powerful states engage in reciprocals. Those that don't, however, may suffer in terms of their representation on international bodies.[188] An interviewee explained why one such state was not represented in a significant UN institution: 'I spoke to a European ambassador and he said "we didn't vote for him because [the state] would not enter into a reciprocal arrangement with us."'[189] Some states that had earlier refused to trade votes have changed their practice over the last decade or so because they had recognized that without such trading their chances of representation was reduced.[190]

In sum, the interview evidence suggests strongly that most states conclude mutual support arrangements for judicial candidatures on reciprocal political grounds that often do not take into account issues of qualifications. Some states only do so on the basis of merit, but this can place them at a disadvantage in the international election system.

Reliability of vote-trading arrangements

As the ICJ and ICC elections are held by secret ballot, a state can never be sure which states voted for its candidate. Do states therefore always honour the reciprocals they have entered into with other states? A Nordic diplomat cited a 'lie factor of between 20–30%',[191] a figure that was confirmed by a number of other diplomats. One WEOG diplomat claimed that the reliability of reciprocals has increased recently because 'it was getting to a ridiculous level and nobody believed a reciprocal when they saw it, which was to everybody's detriment'.[192] This has led to a formalization of the process and reliability has increased because 'many states now require reciprocals to be in writing and send confirmations to both the capital and Permanent Mission of the state concerned',[193] and because 'more information is now shared between Missions'.[194] It is common for states that

[186] T3, 6. [187] T10, 20.

[188] T11, 13. The interviewee thought this explained why the US candidate Michael Matheson was not elected to the ILC in 2006. [189] T82, 8.

[190] T36, 2. F2, 3 [191] T16, 15. [192] T11, 10–11. [193] ibid, 11.

[194] T14, 17–18.

have voted for candidates under reciprocals to write after the elections, sending their congratulations and pointing out that they did vote for the candidate.[195]

The picture is made more complex by the fact that some states will conclude reciprocals for particular election rounds, that is to say, they will undertake to vote for the candidate in the first round but not in subsequent rounds (if the candidate is not elected in the first). Sometimes the exact nature of the support is not specified. A diplomat from a state that only concludes reciprocals on the basis of the merit of the candidate said that the state would 'pledge support and maintain it throughout',[196] whilst other states may renege on reciprocals after the first round and cut new deals. If a supported candidate fails to secure support, a mission may seek instructions as to which candidate to vote for, or it may agree its own reciprocal.

The political basis of vote-trading undoubtedly introduces a note of uncertainty. This, in addition to the lack of focus on merit, may be a drawback for the election system in that states that are uncertain about which agreements will be honoured are more likely to try to make other agreements to insure against their failure. Paradoxically, a degree of uncertainty may also benefit well-qualified candidates by opening up space for states to change their minds and undercut these arrangements where a state is persuaded that a particular candidate is exceptional and worth supporting. Nonetheless, the ideal result in terms of the selection of the most able candidates would be for states to agree to vote for candidates only if they believed they had sufficient merit, on the basis of the formal selection criteria and an objective assessment of the candidates' qualifications and abilities. On the whole, the trading of votes threatens the primacy of the individual criteria in both the ICJ and ICC election processes. It enhances the role of extraneous political considerations in the process to the overall detriment of the quality of the bench and the legitimacy of the courts. It is clear that many states—though not all—consider judicial positions as just another international pawn. Although some have explicitly rejected this approach, they increasingly appear to be swimming against the tide of international practice.

F. The voting process

The preceding sections have considered the three central aspects of the election process: the role of regional groups, campaigning and vote-trading. This section brings together these factors to consider how states make their voting decisions and the impact of the formal voting processes on the composition of the ICJ and ICC.

[195] F45, 1. [196] T10, 11.

Decisions on voting

The voting process is meant to inject an element of competition and choice into the process and so ensure that the most highly qualified candidates are ultimately selected. However, it is apparent that a range of additional considerations apply in the decision-making process. In the majority of states, the final voting decision is made by the foreign ministry in the state capital. In some states it is a ministerial decision and in at least one state an interviewee confirmed that 'even the Head of State takes an interest'.[197] Some Permanent Representatives from smaller states have significant discretion over whom the state votes for, and campaigning states focus greater efforts on these missions.[198]

The range of factors influencing the voting decisions of states depends on the particular state and its priorities. Relevant factors may include the views of the ministry as to the importance of judicial candidatures, the merit of the particular candidate, the relative power of the state and any political benefits it hopes to obtain (for example, candidatures, international aid or bilateral relationships with particular states). These variables are also affected by the relative position of the campaigning state; in particular, whether there is a relationship between the two states (which may include historical ties, bilateral relations and common membership of various groupings or organizations). In addition, the political position of the state will be relevant, as will the extent and quality of its campaign, whether the candidate has been endorsed by a regional group or other political groups and the reciprocal arrangements that have been secured, or any previous reciprocals that are outstanding. To varying degrees, states will also consider any preferences they have for candidates with particular backgrounds, how well the candidate is known, equitable geographical representation considerations (and in the ICC context, the need to meet the minimum voting requirements), and factors such as the representation of different legal systems and gender.

One WEOG diplomat pointed out that 'votes will also be influenced by broader political considerations'[199] so that 'the candidate sometimes suffers the consequences of the country's policies':[200] for example, if a state's foreign policy is unpopular internationally its candidate may not be elected, no matter how meritorious. Campaigning and vote-trading may help to address this to some extent, but much depends on the political importance of the issue. Conversely, the general standing of a candidate's state can have a positive impact: if a state is the 'darling' of the international community because of its recent successful transition to democracy, for example, its candidate may be more likely to be elected.

[197] T12, 1–2.

[198] One interviewee from a GRULAC state said that 'a third or a fourth of delegations have this authority': T12, 7. One candidate said that he had secured pledges of support directly from Permanent Representatives because he had attended the same Cambridge college as one of them and could quote something in the mother tongue of the other: T81, 6.

[199] T19, 15. [200] T2, 8.

While some states pay more attention to the merit of the candidates in their voting decisions, it is clear that none can afford to ignore completely the political implications of its decision.

The sources of information on candidates include the curriculum vitae submitted with the candidate's nomination (and in the case of the ICC, the supporting statement accompanying the nomination), any articles or other writings circulated by the Permanent Mission in New York, and any campaigning material. The process of scrutinizing the candidates involves looking at what is there and 'also what is not there', as curricula vitae in particular 'only point to the positive and are selective'.[201] An African diplomat felt that the 'information for the ICC candidates was more explicit and detailed than that provided for ICJ candidates'.[202] An Eastern European diplomat agreed, noting that 'the ICC was actually very transparent compared to the ICJ'.[203] According to a WEOG diplomat, this was because the required supporting statement to be submitted with the nomination created 'an incentive to bring forward more information'.[204] For the ICC, states may also consider any reports published by NGOs. States may also contact their embassies to find out whether they have views on the candidates and they may share information and opinions on candidates with their close regional partners 'as a force multiplier in intelligence gathering'.[205] Some states consult with their PCA national groups. Legal advisers might also gather information about candidates at the informal meeting of legal advisers held every year before the General Assembly session each October.

Permanent Missions will send back reports on the candidates they have met. However, a GRULAC diplomat noted that, in her state, reports from New York 'have a relatively minor impact' on the final decision.[206] In some states, the decision as to who to vote for is taken in the state capital and the individuals making the voting decision will not normally have met the candidate. They will therefore lack the immediacy of any positive or negative impression made during meetings with mission staff in New York, even if this is conveyed to the capital in writing, meaning that it may be easier for political considerations to sway the final voting decision. However, it may also mean that a state is less influenced by campaigning and can focus on the merit (or otherwise) of the candidate.

As reciprocals are negotiated there will be a 'constant ebb and flow'[207] of information between the capital and the Permanent Mission. The time frame for final voting decisions varies significantly. One WEOG Permanent Mission

[201] T3, 7.

[202] T5, 12. However, the interviewee went on to note that he attributed this in part to the fact that a number of ICJ candidates were running for re-election and 'these are people you know'.

[203] T6, 9. [204] T3, 11. [205] T11, 6.

[206] T10, 12–13. Note that one interviewee said that 'votes can also be determined by the fact that two diplomats work well together in the Sixth Committee. This may have a greater impact than instructions from capital and lobbying because the personalities at play matter': T62, 8.

[207] T11, 10.

legal adviser said that 'we receive voting instructions six months before the elections',[208] whilst a GRULAC Permanent Mission elections officer said that instructions may come in only a matter of weeks before the elections. The extent of the voting instructions also varies: they may cover all rounds, the first round only or certain subsequent voting rounds.[209] If the selected candidate fails or is losing votes over the voting rounds, the mission may 'seek instructions [to vote for] for someone else' between voting rounds,[210] or may have autonomy to make a decision itself.

All the political factors involved in the campaigning process coalesce in the final voting decision. Given that voting decisions are, in most cases, primarily motivated by political considerations, a key question is how these various voting decisions are carried through to the election. The next two sections will consider the impact of the formal voting structures and political voting bodies for the ICJ and ICC, focusing on a selection of issues that may determine whether the decision is driven by considerations of merit.

The mechanics of the ICJ voting process

Both the structure and timing of the ICJ voting process may have an impact on whether well-qualified candidates are selected. The dual architecture of an ICJ voting process that requires votes from an absolute majority of members of the UN Security Council and the UN General Assembly 'voting independently'[211] was intended to ensure both the representation of the P5 on the court but also a measure of control by the General Assembly.[212] In order to be elected, candidates must obtain an absolute majority of votes in the General Assembly (currently 97 votes) and the Security Council (8 votes).[213] For the purpose of voting in ICJ elections, 'no distinction is made between permanent and non-permanent members of the Council'; therefore the P5 members do not have a veto.[214]

Yet, according to most interviewees, the dominance of the Security Council ensures the continued representation of the P5 on the court, and

[208] ibid, 8.

[209] Some voting instructions are even more tactical—setting out how the mission should vote in various potential scenarios: T16, 3.

[210] T47, 14.

[211] ICJ Statute, Article 8. It was noted by one interviewee that it appears that 'some states don't use all their votes in ICJ elections': T18, 10. This might draw out an election and increase the level of lobbying.

[212] M. O. Hudson, *The Permanent Court of International Justice, 1920–1942: a treatise* (New York: The Macmillan Company, 1943) para 140.

[213] United Nations General Assembly and Security Council, *Election of Five Members of the International Court of Justice. Memorandum by the Secretary-General*, UN Doc. A/63/186-S/2008/502, paras 8–9.

[214] ICJ Statute, Article 10(2). Article 27(3) of the UN Charter regarding the P5 veto for non-procedural matters does not apply to elections to the ICJ: 'Decisions of the Security Council on all other matters shall be made by an affirmative vote of nine members including the concurring votes of the permanent members…'

also affords the P5 considerable control over who else is elected. 'The permanent five tend always to vote for each other's candidates, it's solidarity. So in order to get a majority, it's only a simple majority, there's no veto of course for this type of vote, you only need to get three from the remaining ten and you've got eight.'[215] Thus to try to vote for another candidate and push out a P5 candidate would be 'really very gratuitous in the election system we now have'.[216] Also it could be politically impossible: interviewees said that they had observed that some P5 members, particularly the United Kingdom and the United States, had adopted a practice of retiring judges between triennial elections to the court, triggering a casual vacancy for which only a candidate from that country was nominated. This way, 'they are not competed against',[217] making 'it much easier to guarantee election for their candidates',[218] and shielding 'their' seat from challenge.[219] However, this did not happen in the most recent election.

The support of the P5 was described as a 'very potent factor',[220] because 'it can influence the non-permanent members of the Security Council'.[221] Theoretically, a candidate could be elected by eight of the non-permanent members, but in practice it appears that the P5 have considerable influence over the voting decisions of the non-permanent members. Their influence is such that the support of the P5 is effectively needed in order to obtain a seat on the court. Obtaining the requisite Security Council vote is 'strategically important and is a separate focus for campaigning'.[222] This drives down standards, as noted by one diplomat: 'I don't need the criteria. I just need to learn how it works in New York to get the Security Council'.[223] A GRULAC diplomat pointed out that as a consequence, 'you would be very, very brave to put forward a candidate that you know will generate rejection from the P5 because you would probably not get him elected'.[224]

If a campaigning state is itself on the Security Council as a non-permanent member it may 'have extra leverage over the election because its vote will count for more'.[225] This influence spills over into the General Assembly. Even though the two chambers are meant to vote independently of one another, in practice there is extensive communication between them during the voting process. According to some diplomats, the General Assembly will generally listen to the

[215] T36, 3. [216] T17, 7. [217] F34. [218] T14, 4.

[219] Note that the ICJ elections in 2008, according to an interviewee, 'was the first time since 1973 that the UK has had a candidate in a triennial election' (F48, 3). Clearly, there is nothing to stop another state from nominating a candidate for a casual vacancy caused by the retirement of a P5 judge, but this would be considered a highly unfriendly act.

[220] T35, 17. [221] T5, 9. [222] T18, 7–8. [223] T65, 19. [224] T10, 21.

[225] T9, 3. See also B. Fassbender, 'Chapter I. Organization of the Court: Article 9' in Andreas Zimmerman et al (eds), *The Statute of the International Court of Justice: A Commentary* (Oxford: Oxford University Press, 2006) 270.

voting pattern in the Security Council and will be influenced by it.[226] Another interviewee said that 'the fact that someone is over the top in the Council influences some waverers who will then switch'.[227] In effect, this gives the P5 a 'disproportionate say'[228] in the composition of the court. One diplomat referred to a situation where he believed the Security Council was influenced by the voting tendency in the General Assembly 'and reversed its position'.[229] Other interviewees also thought this was the case in some elections.

The timing of the elections, it was believed, could also lead to increased politicization of the process. Some interviewees reiterated the recommendations of the Institut de Droit International that the elections should be clearly separated from the elections for other UN organs and should be conducted as early as possible in the UN General Assembly session, immediately after the end of the general debate.[230] Conducting the elections later in the session increases last-minute lobbying and deal-making. However, considering the current practice of extensive pre-election campaigning of candidates in New York and throughout the world, this may have little impact on the current system.

The mechanics of the ICC voting process

Although the election of ICC judges takes place at UN headquarters in New York, and is therefore drawn into the electioneering and vote-trading industry of UN elections, the Assembly of States Parties (ASP) is not a UN body. It is comprised of the states parties to the Rome Statute and some non-voting observer states and organizations. The P5 members that are party to the Rome Statute do not have any privileged position in the ASP. States parties must meet the minimum voting requirements (to the extent they apply) in order for their ballots to be valid. To obtain a seat, candidates must win the votes of two thirds of the states present and voting.[231] A number of interviewees criticized these rules as 'too complex and complicated'[232] and said that they preferred the ICJ procedure because 'you come, boom, boom, boom and you vote'.[233] Others were less critical, as one diplomat explained: 'it's not difficult when you understand it and I think it's fair'.[234]

There was criticism of the number of voting rounds in the first ICC elections: thirty-three rounds of voting were conducted before the bench was fully

[226] The Institut de Droit International has recommended that measures should be taken to prevent such communications between voting rounds: Institut de Droit International, *La Composition de la Cour Internationale de Justice, Session de Sienne—1952*, Resolution, 24 April 1952, para 2.

[227] T36, 3. However, Rosenne says that this influence has declined since the 1960s: see S. Rosenne, *The Law and Practice of the International Court, 1920–2005*, vol. I: *The Court and the United Nations* (4th edn, The Hague: Martinus Nijhoff, 2006) 395.

[228] T59, 14.

[229] T47, 5. See also S. Rosenne, *Rosenne's The World Court: What It Is and How It Works*, op. cit., 47.

[230] ibid, para 1.

[231] As noted, a quorum is an absolute majority of all states parties.

[232] T5, 11.

[233] ibid.

[234] T7, 9.

elected.[235] One diplomat said that the problem was not caused by the rules, 'but by the two-thirds majority, which is a very high threshold'.[236] Whatever the cause, a number of rounds in which votes are spread thinly due to the voting rules or the threshold required may encourage last-minute politicking on the floor of the UN to break a deadlock, which could force out meritorious candidates from less politically savvy or less powerful states.[237] Multiple rounds will also mean that voters will be free to change their voting preferences (based on reciprocals or other deals) in order to end the election, and may be more susceptible to political deals. However, as noted in the section on regional groups, there are also incentives for states to stay in the election, because they could win one of the five free or 'floating' seats that are not allocated to any particular regional group.

G. Conclusion

The picture that is emerging is of an ever more highly politicized electoral process. Attempts to protect the ICC from being subsumed into the wider UN election system have largely failed, and the ICJ and ICC election systems have become part of the broader landscape of political elections, which are generally not afforded special consideration for the fact that they are high-level judicial vacancies. It is clear that a candidate's success depends to a considerable extent on a state's political influence in its regional group, its commitment to campaigning and its willingness and that of other states to engage in vote-trading. Political and economic leverage are crucial, and states that do not have them are at a distinct disadvantage. Although many interviewees declared a personal commitment to merit-based selection, and some states do prioritize considerations of merit, in practice extraneous factors, taken together, almost invariably outweigh the individual merit of the candidate. One unsuccessful ICC candidate summarized the process: 'I don't think I lost because I am bad and had I won, it would not have been because I am good.'[238]

While the evidence leads unequivocally to the conclusion that merit is not the main driving factor in the election processes, it does not automatically follow from this that the consequence is the election of low-calibre candidates. The interview evidence showed a range of different views about the effect of the

[235] Some interviewees considered that this was just because the whole bench was being elected in the first elections and that this number of voting rounds would not be likely in subsequent elections. This was borne out by the 2006, 2008 and 2009 elections.

[236] T3, 10. It is also contributed to by the high number of candidates in ICC elections (at least in the first elections) and the way the regional allocation of seats is structured.

[237] Some states may stubbornly stay in the race for political reasons. One interviewee said that his government was reluctant to withdraw a candidate even though the candidate was not polling well in the election rounds because 'they are just interested in national interest and selling the candidature here and now': T6, 5.

[238] T32. 14.

politicization on the outcome of the judicial elections. While many interviewees were troubled by the increasing dominance of extraneous political considerations and the greater power which this gives to larger and wealthier states, others were less concerned by politicization and saw it as an inevitable result of election by states. It was also generally accepted by interviewees that the overall bench requirements for the ICJ and ICC serve useful functions in ensuring representation and diversity. In this regard, the ICC minimum voting requirements can be considered to be an improvement as they ensure diversity across regional groups, gender and expertise. The interviews suggested that any shortcomings in terms of merit and representation are not caused by the rules and the way they are structured. In fact, these rules seem to have relatively little impact on the politicization of the final result. Rather, it is the broad range of political factors that weigh on the election processes and the context in which they operate that determines the result.

Despite this politicized context, some felt that the processes had produced 'good results'[239] and that there are 'good people on the Court who are the locomotive of the Court and they can bring out the best in what is available',[240] whilst others said that most ICJ candidates were 'fairly okay'[241] and 'most of the people who get through tend to have the right credentials'.[242] Others were less sanguine and believed that it was quite possible under the current system for an inadequately qualified candidate—or even a wholly unqualified candidate—selected through a highly politicized or inadequate national selection process, to be elected.

Such concerns are compounded by the problems identified earlier regarding the national nomination processes. If these processes were impeccably conducted, with a stronger emphasis on the selection of the best qualified candidates so that all the candidates in the election pool had passed through a rigorous merit-based filtering process, it might be less problematic if political factors played a dominant role in the actual election process. Concerns raised about the election process are therefore real and serious: they raise questions about the competence, legitimacy and independence of the courts, and the prospects for the future development of the international rule of law. Where a court has been established by states, it is inevitable that there will be a measure of politicization surrounding its structure and constitution. Nor is this necessarily unhealthy. However, the increasingly overt politicization described by interviewees is not necessary, nor is it inevitable, even if it is endemic in the way that international elections are currently conducted.

[239] T3, 8. [240] T35. [241] T3, 1.

[242] T18, 13. See also N. Blokker and S. Muller, 'The 1996 Elections to the International Court of Justice: New Tendencies in the New Post Cold-War Era?' *International and Comparative Law Quarterly* 47(1) (January 1998) 223.

These concerns are not reserved for the ICC and ICJ and have been raised in relation to other courts. A 2003 Interights report on the selection process to the European Court of Human Rights noted that:

The election at the Parliamentary Assembly is commonly characterized by lobbying on the part of governments, who frequently 'parade' preferred candidates around Strasbourg to enhance their chances of election. On occasion, candidates themselves electioneer to secure votes. While such lobbying is far from unique to the European context, and reflects the realities of an otherwise inadequate appointment procedure, it has a detrimental effect on the independence, and the perception of independence, of the judge ultimately elected.[243]

Despite such criticisms by highly respected international commentators, it is clear that states are not yet ready to contemplate relinquishing power over judicial elections to non-state bodies or screening bodies. Most consider that states should still be the exclusive—or primary—actors in this process. Nonetheless, there are a number of developments across a range of international courts and tribunals, at least at the regional level, to suggest that moves can be made towards a greater focus on merit in international judicial appointments. A number of these trends are discussed in the next chapter. In the ICJ and ICC contexts, it may be that for the meantime it is a question of a gradual move towards merit-based selection processes through peer influence. However, there are changes underway at the international level that will place ever-increasing pressure on states to address the shortcomings in the election processes.

[243] J. Limbach et al, *Judicial Independence: Law and Practice of Appointments to the European Court of Human Rights* (London: INTERIGHTS, May 2003) 24.

5

Trends and Reforms

A. Introduction

Proposals for reform of the selection processes of the international judiciary command considerable support in certain quarters, but face real political hurdles. For this reason, reforms to date have been uneven, making it difficult to identify clear trends. In some courts, such as the ICJ, very little change has occurred. In others, such as the European Court of Human Rights (ECtHR), considerable efforts have been made in recent years to improve the processes. Some of the most notable developments have arisen in the new courts, in particular the Caribbean Court of Justice (CCJ), the African Court on Human and Peoples' Rights (ACHPR) and the new UN administrative justice tribunals. Despite the very disparate nature of the developments, it is possible to discern two tiers of principles at play, which underpin—explicitly or implicitly—recent trends. The first tier concerns the higher-level concepts of independence, professional competence and integrity that are constant across all international courts. Below this layer is an emerging second tier that seeks to operationalize these requirements, including principles of transparency, non-politicization, merit, diversity, and representation. The second tier is highly contextual, depending on the function, institutional framework and political context of the particular court.

In order to place developments in the ICJ and ICC in the wider context of the international judiciary, interviewees were asked for their views on the merits of recent changes and potential future reforms in other courts. The following analysis reviews their responses in the light of developments in judicial selection processes in different parts of the international court system. Responses tended to fall into the following four main categories: (1) transparency; (2) independence and non-politicization; (3) competence and merit; and (4) diversity and representation.

B. Transparency

The need for greater transparency in international judicial selection procedures has been a common refrain for some years. This key concept is generally regarded as playing a role in bolstering the independence and non-politicization of selection procedures, and in promoting the prioritization of merit as well as greater diversity and representation. In 2003, for example, the human rights group Interights commented in a report on the selection process to the ECtHR that:

> Without the effective implementation of 'objective and transparent criteria based on proper professional qualification' there is the very real possibility that the judges selected will not have the requisite skills and abilities to discharge their mandate.[1]

In addition to enhancing the qualities of the judges selected, transparency is also seen as a means of widening the pool of potential candidates and opening the process to a range of outside institutions and the broader public, facilitating awareness of the courts and dialogue on potential reform. Yet despite the strong rhetorical support for transparency in judicial selection amongst political and legal actors alike, in practice there is considerable resistance to reforms which might open up the selection processes to greater scrutiny. Inevitably, such increased transparency would threaten the closed world of nominations and elections described in the previous chapters by opening the process to institutions and individuals who would otherwise be seen as outsiders. While this might widen the candidate pool and so increase competition for posts and the potential quality of those selected, it is also seen as posing a threat to those vested interests which currently exert a strong hold on the selection processes.

This tension between transparency and support for the status quo was evident in the interviews. In relation to the ICJ and ICC, interviewees generally recognized that states 'now need to be very transparent about nominations'.[2] The importance of transparency was linked to the first tier principle of independence, since the process 'must be open to public scrutiny'[3] because in the 'absence of a clearly independent nomination process, one remains vulnerable to the lurking question of judicial independence'.[4] Openness was felt to be essential to ensure that 'all people of competence have an equal chance'[5] and to eradicate 'arbitrariness'.[6] One PCA national group member thought that transparency required the advertising of posts, the use of more effective consultation and setting out clear procedures in advance.[7] However, several of those interviewed took the approach that 'if it ain't broke don't fix it', arguing that 'so far, the process hasn't appointed the wrong people, so that's an argument in its favour, even though it's not transparent'.[8] There was concern that increasing democratization would not necessarily lead to the appointment of better judges. One interviewee recognized the potential political barriers to change, noting that it was a question of 'selling governments the idea that a transparent process means an independent candidate which is good thing for them'.[9]

[1] J. Limbach et al, *Judicial Independence: Law and Practice of Appointments to the European Court of Human Rights* (London: INTERIGHTS, May 2003). [2] T23, 9.
[3] T27, 5. [4] T28, 5. [5] T29, 7. [6] T65, 14. [7] T39, 11.
[8] T73–75, 10. [9] T56, 8.

Despite these reservations, the evidence from other international courts indicates a growing recognition in recent years of the need for more openness. References to the importance of transparency are found in most recent proposals for reform and in the governing rules or guidelines for newly established courts. ECtHR nominations, for example, must now be made through a 'fair, transparent and consistent national selection procedure'[10] in order 'to maintain the efficiency and authority of the Court'.[11] Similarly, the African Union has endorsed guidelines for the ACHPR that recommend that states '[e]mploy a transparent and impartial national selection procedure in order to create public trust in the integrity of the nomination process'.[12] In courts other than the ICJ and ICC, requirements have been introduced to advertise judicial vacancies, consult with particular individuals or institutions during the nomination process, produce template curricula vitae for candidates and publish information about the nomination procedure. Uniquely, the Council of Europe Parliamentary Assembly requires states nominating candidates to the ECtHR to 'describe the manner in which they were selected'.[13] Similarly, nominations to the ICC must be accompanied by a supporting statement setting out how the candidate meets the individual criteria.[14]

There is no requirement, however, that this statement include details of the nomination process used,[15] nor is it mandatory to publish reasons for the selection of the particular candidate or the rejection of others. This last issue is particularly controversial, and has been the subject of criticism in relation to some courts.[16] Yet in practice the publication of reasons would be a radical step, and one which has not been adopted at national level in even the most

[10] 'In the absence of a real choice among the candidates submitted by a state party to the Convention, the Assembly shall reject lists submitted to it. In addition, in the absence of a fair, transparent and consistent national selection procedure, the Assembly may reject such lists': Council of Europe Parliamentary Assembly, Recommendation 1646 (2009), *Nomination of candidates and election of judges to the European Court of Human Rights*, available at: <http://www.assembly.coe.int/Main.asp?link=/Documents/AdoptedText/ta09/ERES1646.htm> (accessed 26 April 2009), para 2. See the section on gender below, in particular the rejection of lists that do not include a female candidate.

[11] Parliamentary Assembly of the Council of Europe, Committee on Legal Affairs and Human Rights, 'Report: Nomination of candidates and election of judges to the European Court of Human Rights', 1 December 2008, Doc. 11767, available at: <http://www.assembly.coe.int/Main.asp?link=/Documents/WorkingDocs/Doc08/EDOC11767.htm> (accessed 18 September 2009), summary.

[12] Note Verbale, Commission of the African Union, 5 April 2004, Reference BC/OLC/66.5/8/Vol.V, ('ACHPR Guidelines'), para 5.

[13] Council of Europe Parliamentary Assembly, Recommendation 1646 (2009), *Nomination of candidates and election of judges to the European Court of Human Rights*, op. cit., para 4.2. Transparency could also be improved by states publishing in advance the procedure that will be followed in selecting candidates.

[14] See Chapter 3.

[15] Rome Statute, Article 36(4)(a). Paragraph 6 of ASP Resolution 6 further elaborates on the required content of this statement: Assembly of States Parties, *Procedure for the nomination and election of judges of the International Criminal Court*, ICC-ASP/3/Res.6 (ASP Resolution 6).

[16] J. Limbach et al, *Judicial Independence: Law and Practice of Appointments to the European Court of Human Rights*, op.cit.

forward-looking processes. The appointment of judges to the South African Constitutional Court, for example, includes interviews before the Judicial and Legal Services Commission which are held in public and widely covered in the media. Yet it was decided when the new system was established that the need for confidentiality, both to protect the candidates' privacy and to guarantee the commission's freedom to discuss candidates frankly, meant that their deliberations would not be published and no reasons for the selection or rejection of candidates would be given.[17] It is also likely that a requirement to provide reasons for a nomination could be circumvented by states by producing anodyne statements, as has sometimes been the case with ICC supporting statements.

There is acknowledged potential for international courts to make more use of the national selection systems as a way of increasing transparency. Some interviewees felt that the incorporation of nomination processes into the national system might be beneficial where a more open system was used to select national judges; for example, where a judicial appointment commission has been established to select judges on the basis of merit in accordance with set selection criteria. Such commissions have been deliberately established to ensure greater openness, increase diversity and prioritize selection on merit,[18] and in some cases the interviewing of candidates by the commission is held in public.[19] Other developments include the use of parliamentary selection or screening procedures for appointments to the higher courts.[20] Even if not adopted wholesale, elements of these national systems could be applied by states in developing their nomination processes for the international courts. Some interviewees, however, had concerns about the use of national processes, commenting that if a national selection procedure was more public, this could discourage potential applicants.[21]

Advertising

Only a handful of states publicly advertise international judicial vacancies,[22] although the interview data indicated that more states are considering taking this step. Only the Parliamentary Assembly of the Council of the Europe, the body that elects judges to the ECtHR, has imposed a requirement that states

[17] See K. Malleson, 'Assessing the Performance of the South African Judicial Service Commission' *South African Law Journal* 116 (1)(1999) part 1.

[18] See K. Malleson, 'Creating a Judicial Appointments Commission: Which Model Works Best?' *Public Law* (Spring 2004)102–21.

[19] See n 17 above.

[20] See K. Malleson, 'Parliamentary scrutiny of Supreme Court nominees: A view from the UK' *Osgoode Hall Law Journal* 44(3), (Fall 2006)557–64.

[21] T36, 9.

[22] For example, the UK has advertised for candidates for judicial vacancies at the ICC, ECtHR and ECJ.

'issue public and open calls for candidatures'[23] through the 'specialized press'[24] because it 'helps contribute in particular to the fairness and transparency of the selection procedure, making all potential candidates aware of this vacancy'.[25] Advertisements are also used by selection committees, such as those for the CCJ and the UN and European administrative tribunals.

Some interviewees were surprised to learn that international judicial vacancies were open to application in certain states and expressed mixed views as to whether advertising would be a useful practice for the ICJ and ICC. One interviewee, referring to the International Tribunal for the Law of the Sea (ITLOS), said: 'It is not the kind of position for which one would invite nominations by advertisement. There are not many persons out there who would be qualified, and so the ministry felt competent to identify those nationals who can meet and satisfy the criteria for appointment.'[26]

For some senior appointments, such as for the ICJ, 'the virtues of advertisement can be exaggerated, because the chances of anybody cropping up in response to an advertisement that one wouldn't have thought of would be absolutely absurd'.[27] However, in cases where there was not a clearly defined group who would be appropriate for the position in question, advertising for senior roles could make sense: 'What you want is an international criminal lawyer, and I wouldn't really recognize a breed of international criminal lawyer. There are various people who participate in international tribunals, but I just don't regard that as a genus. Whereas I certainly do regard an international lawyer as a genus.'[28]

[23] Council of Europe Parliamentary Assembly, Recommendation 1646 (2009), *Nomination of candidates and election of judges to the European Court of Human Rights*, op. cit., para 4.1.

[24] Council of Europe Parliamentary Assembly, Recommendation 1649 (2004), *Candidates for the European Court of Human Rights*, available at: <http://www.assembly.coe.int//main.asp?link=http://assembly.coe.int/Documents/AdoptedText/TA04/EREC1649.htm> (accessed 20 November 2008), para 19. The Parliamentary Assembly requested the Committee of Ministers to invite states to advertise (and also comply with other nomination procedural requirements in addition to the individual criteria in Article 21(1) of the European Convention on Human Rights). The Committee of Ministers refused because it considered that advertising is merely one of a number of ways of ensuring transparency and fairness: Council of Europe Committee of Ministers, *Candidates for the European Court of Human Rights Parliamentary Assembly Recommendation (Reply adopted by the Committee of Ministers on 20 April 2005 at the 924th meeting of the Ministers' Deputies)* 1649 (2004), CM/AS(2005)Rec.1649 (22 April 2005), available at: <http://www.wcd.coe.int/ViewDoc.jsp?id=849699&BackColorInternet=9999CC&BackColorIntranet=FFBB55&BackColorLogged=FFAC75> (accessed 26 April 2009). See also Council of Europe Parliamentary Assembly, Recommendation 1429 (1999), *National procedures for nominating candidates for election to the European Court of Human Rights*, available at: <http://www.assembly.coe.int/Main.asp?link=/Documents/AdoptedText/ta99/EREC1429.htm> (accessed 26 April 2009), para 6.

[25] Parliamentary Assembly of the Council of Europe, Committee on Legal Affairs and Human Rights, 'Report: Nomination of candidates and election of judges to the European Court of Human Rights', op. cit., para 18.

[26] T25, 9.

[27] T73–5, 3.

[28] ibid, 4.

Advertising could also increase the prevalence of candidates 'lobbying'[29] to be nominated. However, some interviewees felt that in most circumstances, advertising could be valuable:

You may be on a selection panel and have a sense of who you would like to see make the applications, is it then sufficient that the members of a selection panel go out and invite people? Because while it maybe a small society, one cannot expect that five, six people on a selection panel have full knowledge of all the potential candidates.[30]

A related suggestion was that states should 'advertise' the reasons for a nomination decision in the print media as a useful way of making the nomination process more transparent and promoting merit.[31] An alternative approach to open advertising could be for professional organizations, such as the International Bar Association, to distribute information to potential candidates, asking them to make direct contact with their national authorities.[32]

Consultation

For nominations to the ICJ, ECtHR and ACHPR, states are recommended to consult with a range of individuals and institutions at the national level. As noted, Article 6 of the ICJ Statute provides that:

Before making these nominations, each national group is recommended to consult its highest court of justice, its legal faculties and schools of law, and its national academies and national sections of international academies devoted to the study of law.

In relation to the ECtHR, the Parliamentary Assembly recommends that states 'consult their national parliaments when drawing up the lists so as to ensure the transparency of the national selection procedure'.[33] The guidelines of the ACHPR recommend that: 'State Parties should encourage the participation of civil society, including Judicial and other State bodies, bar associations, academic and human rights organizations and women's groups, in the process of selection of nominees.'[34]

From the interview data it is clear that few PCA national groups consult as recommended by Article 6 of the ICJ Statute,[35] although there was agreement that they and other selection bodies should consult more effectively and widely

[29] T65, 13. [30] T28, 15. [31] T56, 7. [32] T3, 15–16.

[33] Council of Europe Parliamentary Assembly, Recommendation 1429 (1999), *National procedures for nominating candidates for election to the European Court of Human Rights*, op.cit., para 7. See also the recommendation: 'the Assembly also urges the governments of member states to notify their parliaments and their appropriate committees of their procedures and timetables when drawing up lists of candidates for the Court': Council of Europe Parliamentary Assembly, Recommendation 1649 (2004), *Candidates for the European Court of Human Rights*, op. cit., para 20.

[34] ACHPR Guidelines, para 5. [35] See Chapter 3.

with outside experts.[36] Some suggested that greater consultation would open up the pool of potential candidates[37] and ensure wider and more informed discussion of the relative merits of different candidates. It would also ensure a greater sense of 'ownership' over the nomination process. In some states there is already a strong recognition that this is important, according to an ICC judge: 'serious governments like European governments are now fully aware that they cannot adopt purely political decisions but that they have to be open to listening to ideas coming from different bodies and organs within their countries'.[38]

A WEOG interviewee felt the time had come to open up the nomination process: 'I think that there is scope for the national group to be less tightly private, and secretive about its operations, and if they had asked me during my time, would it be a good thing to start a process of discreet, wider consultation, I would have said, yes, why not?'[39] Others believed that consultation should include the bodies mentioned in Article 6 of the ICJ Statute, as well as bar associations, law societies and lower judges working in fields related to the particular court. Some PCA national groups, notably those of the USA, are known to consult in this manner. In relation to human rights courts and the ICC, consultation might also be opened to non-governmental organizations, as is recommended for nominations to the ACHPR.[40]

Other interviewees felt that consultation was neither desirable nor feasible, and that the absence of consultation was accepted as a 'fact of life' in the process.[41] In some states where the PCA national group is comprised of a range of individuals from different branches of law and politics it was thought that wider consultation would be superfluous because the process was already taking place inside the national group. Concerns were expressed that introducing new people and processes into the system would promote new, unwanted political influences into the nomination process,[42] or that there would be government opposition to demands for wider consultation because 'it is not practised in our part of the world. It is only centralized at a very high level and they don't care about what the people would say.'[43]

The frequency of references to the presence of political barriers to greater openness highlights the fact that significant political will is required to enhance transparency. In the ECtHR, the fact that the Parliamentary Assembly is a cross-partisan body consisting of national parliamentarians has meant that it has been possible to criticize and impose requirements on the nomination process. At the ACHPR, the court is politically significant as the first African regional human rights court. Indeed, that both are human rights courts may also partly

[36] T39, 12. [37] T52, 25. [38] T76, 9. [39] T35, 17.
[40] T76, 3–4. See also ACHPR Guidelines, 3. [41] T77–80, 4.
[42] As one interviewee noted, it may not be a good idea to remove the nomination process entirely from the political sphere, because if academics, for example, are to be the ones who select candidates, 'academic life is really full of jealousies and hierarchies. So, I'm not convinced that better people would just come out at the top of all that'. (T77–80, 8) [43] T48, 9.

explain these developments, as there are likely to be higher expectations for such courts that the selection processes will be transparent.

There are also questions as how effective these developments have been in improving transparency: ten years of calls to states to improve the transparency of their ECtHR nomination processes have resulted in some positive change, but 'there is still significant variance as concerns fairness, transparency and consistency'.[44] Similarly, the first nominations to the ACHPR were criticized by non-governmental organizations for lacking transparency and failing to produce a sufficiently large pool of adequately qualified candidates.[45] Across the international courts, there appears to be significant resistance to measures that would increase transparency. In the ICJ and ICC contexts, apart from a few states that have adopted more open procedures, there appears to be little appetite for addressing transparency at an institutional level.

C. Independence and non-politicization

Overt politicization of international nominations is seen as a concern in relation to several international courts; consequently, some developments across the international court system have sought to reduce politicization by increasing the independence of judicial selection procedures. An independent selection procedure does not necessarily guarantee transparency, proper regard for merit, or an entirely apolitical decision, although it diminishes the government monopoly of control. As independence increases, more institutional and procedural constraints are often imposed on selection bodies which may help to make the selection process more consistent and transparent, enhancing merit-based selection. In many court systems, the link between independence in the selection process and independence of the bench is regarded as a given. In the ECtHR context, it has been said that selection procedures

> 'have a direct impact on the independence and impartiality of the judges, which is required in order to ensure public confidence in the independence of any judicial

[44] Parliamentary Assembly of the Council of Europe, Committee on Legal Affairs and Human Rights, 'Report: Nomination of candidates and election of judges to the European Court of Human Rights', op. cit., para 40.

[45] C. A. Odinkalu, 'How the Judges of the African Court Emerged', 30 January 2006, available at: <http://www.allafrica.com/stories/200601310508.html> (accessed 12 July 2006) and Coalition for an Effective African Court on Human and Peoples' Rights, 'The Election of Judges to the African Court on Human and Peoples' Rights', document submitted to the Assembly of Heads of State and Government, the Executive Council and the Permanent Representatives Committee of the African Union Mid-term Summit in Khartoum, the Sudan, from 16–25 January 2006 (n.d.), on file with authors.

institution. Nomination procedures must be and be seen to be in conformity with international standards guaranteeing judicial independence.'[46]

A number of interviewees agreed that independent selection procedures are essential to ensure that the best candidates are selected. However, given that such independence may erode governmental control over nominations, many states will only be willing to countenance more independent processes when there is strong external political pressure and/or an incentive to do so. Selection procedures which are decoupled from the member states, such those used in the CCJ, emerge only in very specific political contexts.

The three main developments with regard to independence have been (1) a movement toward greater independence of PCA national groups; (2) calls to states to establish other independent nomination bodies; and (3), more radically, the establishment of fully-fledged independent selection committees that take the selection process out of state hands completely.

Reinforcing the independence of national nomination bodies

One way to increase the independence of the selection process is to establish independent bodies at the national level which are given the task of making nominations. These bodies would be responsible for identifying and assessing potential candidates and would be able to designate a candidate without governmental interference. The requirement that ICJ nominations should be made by PCA national groups was intended to provide this element of independence.[47] Although it is not clearly stated in the ICJ Statute that PCA national groups must be independent of government, this can be inferred from the fact that the groups were established to act as independent arbitrators in disputes under the auspices of the PCA. Yet it is clear from the interview data that the majority of PCA national groups do not function independently of governmental control.[48]

Many of the interviewees agreed that the PCA groups need greater operating independence in order to properly perform their central role under the ICJ Statute, as the group's independence could be 'a very useful protective hedge against the influence of a government which has a strongly politicized attitude towards international courts'.[49]

> What needs to be done is for the national groups to be given the authority that they are given in the ICJ Statute. Because they are supposed to be an independent group that makes the nomination. The whole purpose, as I understand it, is to remove the political factor from the nomination procedure. But what has happened is that the political factor has got back into the procedure.[50]

[46] Parliamentary Assembly of the Council of Europe, Committee on Legal Affairs and Human Rights, 'Report: Nomination of candidates and election of judges to the European Court of Human Rights', op. cit., para 3. See also para 20.
[47] See Chapter 1.
[48] See Chapter 3.
[49] T35, 6–7.
[50] T82, 8.

Some argued that one means of bolstering the independence of PCA national groups might be to 'publicize the role of the PCA national group amongst judges and lawyers so that their role is better understood and supported'.[51] Independence could also be supported by appointing non-government members and taking steps to ensure that national groups operate within clearer procedures, as is the case with some more 'structured' PCA national groups. Interaction between groups and discussions of their role could also be encouraged. Most important, however, would be a change of attitude on the part of governments to recognize the legal role of the national group under the ICJ and ICC Statutes. There does not currently appear to be widespread interest on the part of states to increase the independence of PCA national groups; general practice errs towards a light-touch advisory role at best, with final decisions taken by government.

Independent national nominations procedures might also be established through the use of the highest national courts nomination procedure in the ICC Statute, or by employing national judicial selection procedures and institutions. In general, the independent national selection committees have a statutory basis, clear procedures and accountability structures, and operate with a high level of independence. One interviewee thought that these procedures could introduce 'ideological issues and interests groups'[52] into international nominations. On the other hand, some national selection procedures can be even more politicized than international selection procedures.

The ECtHR is the only other international court for which independent national selection procedures have been discussed in detail. The Parliamentary Assembly of the Council of Europe has stated that, as a minimum requirement, member states should 'set up—without delay—appropriate national selection procedures to ensure that the authority and credibility of the Court are not put at risk by ad hoc and politicized processes in the nomination of candidates'.[53] This proposal follows an earlier, detailed recommendation by Interights which argued that the Council of Europe should require states to establish an independent body to devise the state's list of candidates:

> The independent body would consist of independent persons including judges and individuals with academic and other experience of international law and human rights.
>
> The independent body would *consult* with interested civil society such as judicial and other State bodies and where possible human rights organizations and national bar associations. It would then shortlist and interview candidates, and forward the names of three nominees to the national government, for transmission to the Council of Europe.

[51] T39, 13. [52] F27, 1.

[53] Council of Europe Parliamentary Assembly, Recommendation 1646 (2009), *Nomination of candidates and election of judges to the European Court of Human*, op. cit., para 5. See also M. O'Boyle, 'On Reforming the Operation of the European Court of Human Rights' *European Human Rights Law Review* 1 (2008) 1–11.

Where, as a result of a thorough procedure, three suitable candidates emerge but there is a hierarchy between them, the independent body should be free to rank the candidates.[54]

Establishing independent national nomination bodies that have a real, determinative role in the selection procedure requires political will that has only been seen in a handful of states. However, the increasing focus on reinforcing the statutory role of the PCA national groups and developments in bolstering independence in national judicial selection procedures is encouraging and might point the way to possible future changes which could increase the level of independence in the selection processes of the ICJ, ICC and other international courts.

International judicial selection committees

For a small number of international courts and tribunals there has been a more far-reaching shift towards independent judicial selection procedures in which the role of governments in nominating or electing judges has been removed or strictly limited. Most notably, the judges of the CCJ are appointed by an independent non-state selection committee; the only committee of its kind at the international level. The staff administrative tribunals of the EU and UN have also recently been established with procedures for the nomination of candidates by international, independent committees. These procedures were established from the inception of the courts and are a product of their particular political contexts and functions.

The Regional Judicial and Legal Services Commission (Caribbean Court of Justice) (RJLSC) of the CCJ is the only non-governmental international judicial selection body. The CCJ is a regional court that has original and appellate jurisdiction,[55] and the Commission was established in response to concerns that the CCJ was intended to replace the Judicial Committee of the Privy Council as the court of final appeal for Commonwealth states in the region. It was felt that there would be doubts about the independence of Caribbean judges appointed by governments,[56] and so an eleven-member Commission was established to

[54] J. Limbach et al, *Judicial Independence: Law and Practice of Appointments to the European Court of Human Rights*, op. cit., 27.

[55] Under its original jurisdiction, the court has the power to interpret and apply the Revised Treaty of Chaguaramas Establishing the Caribbean Community, Including the CARICOM Single Market and Economy (the Treaty) and in its appellate jurisdiction it can act as the final court of appeal from certain decisions (including decisions on domestic constitutional matters) of the Courts of Appeal of the Contracting Parties that have accepted the appellate jurisdiction of the Court: see the Agreement Establishing the Caribbean Court of Justice of 2001, available at: <http://www.caricom.org/jsp/secretariat/legal_instruments/agreement_ccj.pdf> (Accessed 28 April 2010) (CCJ Agreement), Parts II and III.

[56] See K. Malleson, 'Promoting Judicial independence in the International Courts: Lessons from the Caribbean' *International and Comparative Law Quarterly* 58(3) (July 2009), 671–97.

make the appointments. It comprises the President of the Court (as Chair), academics, representatives from judicial and public services commissions of member states and representatives from civil society who were appointed by a range of non-governmental bodies.[57]

The RJLSC determines its own procedure for the appointment of judges to the court. In February 2004 it published advertisements in the regional and international media seeking applications for the first judicial posts. It then conducted interviews with shortlisted candidates, assessing them against the criteria set out in the agreement establishing the court.[58] The first judges were appointed to the court on 19 November 2004. Controversially, the Commission did not appoint a judge from Jamaica, one of the largest member states of CARICOM. Although this attracted some criticism from the legal and political community in Jamaica, it was seen more generally as evidence of the independent nature of the process and the priority given by the Commission to selecting the best candidates irrespective of their origins.[59]

It is also worth noting a second unique feature of the CCJ in relation to its source of funding. The court is financed by a trust fund established originally from funds borrowed on the international money markets by the Caribbean Central Bank, to be repaid by the governments of the region. This means that neither the court nor the RJLSC is dependent on contributions from the member states, and this has contributed significantly to the perceived and actual independence of the court and its selection procedures. It is also interesting to consider the potential value of such a funding structure in election-based courts, as it might reduce pressure on states to elect judges from states that contribute significant amounts to the courts' costs (because of fears that the contributions might be withdrawn).[60]

In addition to the RJLSC, two committees have also recently been established that nominate judges for three specialized staff administrative tribunals: the European Union Civil Service Tribunal (CST), the United Nations Dispute Tribunal (UNDT), and the United Nations Appeals Tribunal (UNAT). These committees seek candidatures and compile a shortlist of candidates. Judges are then appointed or elected by political bodies.

[57] CCJ Agreement, Article 5(1). It should also be noted that in the Caribbean region, particularly in common law countries, the appointment of national judges by a legal services commission is a common model. This has meant a good level of familiarity with making judicial appointments by independent committee, helping the transition of this concept to the international environment. It could be imagined that a similar trajectory could be possible at the international level. If states increasingly adopt national judicial selection committees for national judicial appointments, this may potentially ease the way towards the establishment of international judicial selection committees.

[58] CCJ Agreement, Article IV(10) and Article IV(11).

[59] Interviews conducted by the authors in 2008 with a range of legal, political and civil stakeholders revealed a high degree of confidence in the Commission as having undertaken its tasks in an effective and appropriate manner and appointed competent and independent judges (see n 56 above).

[60] See Chapter 4.

The CST is a judicial body that determines EU staff disputes.[61] Article 3 of the Annex I to the Protocol on the Statute of the Court of Justice provides for the establishment of a committee that the Council of the European Union must consult when appointing judges to the CST, consisting of:

seven persons chosen from among former members of the Court of Justice and the Court of First Instance and lawyers of recognized competence. The committee's membership and operating rules shall be determined by the Council, acting by a qualified majority on a recommendation by the President of the Court of Justice.[62]

The role of the committee is to seek and vet potential candidates who are then forwarded to the Council of the European Union for appointment by that body 'acting unanimously'.[63] In 2005, the Council made a public call for applications for the first appointments to the tribunal and, in the course of a number of meetings on the papers, decided on a list of fourteen candidates.[64] Article 3(4) of the Annex provides that:

The committee shall give an opinion on candidates' suitability to perform the duties of judge at the Civil Service Tribunal. The committee shall append to its opinion a list of candidates having the most suitable high-level experience. Such list shall contain the names of at least twice as many candidates as there are judges to be appointed by the Council.

The seven judges of the tribunal were appointed from this list by the Council, having regard to balanced geographical representation and representation of national legal systems.[65]

The UNDT and UNAT, which began work in July 2009, comprise the United Nation's new two-tier formal system for the administration of justice.[66]

[61] See also H. Cameron, 'Establishment of the European Union Civil Service Tribunal' *The Law and Practice of International Courts and Tribunals* 5 (2)(2006) 273–83.

[62] EC Treaty, Article 225a, Annex I to the Protocol on the Statute of the Court of Justice: Consolidated Versions of the Treaty on European Union and of the Treaty Establishing the European Community, Article 3(2), *Official Journal* C 321E of 29 December 2006 (EC Treaty and Annex).

[63] EC Treaty, Article 225a, Annex, Article 3(2).

[64] Council Decision 2005/151/EC, Euratom, OJ C 47 A, 23.2.2005, 1. The text of the call is in Council Decision 2005/150/EC, Euratom, OJ L 50, 23.2.2005, 8 and states that in addition to the minimum conditions set down in Article 225a of the EC Treaty and the relevant part of Annex 1, 'the committee will be prompted to take into particular consideration candidates' ability to work within a collegiate structure in a multinational, multilingual environment, and also the nature, extent and duration of their experience suitable for the duties to be performed'. Two hundred and forty-three applications were received in response to this call. The committee then met on a number of occasions and presented a list of fourteen candidates to the Council for consideration, from which the Council selected seven judges: Council Decision 2005/557/EC, Euratom, OJ L 197, 28.7.2005, paras 6 and 7.

[65] As required by Article 3(1) of Annex I to the Statute of the Court of Justice: see Council Decision 2005/557/EC, Euratom, OJ L 197, 28.7.2005, para 9.

[66] United Nations General Assembly Resolution 62/228. Administration of justice at the United Nations, UN Doc. A/RES/62/228, para 39.

The tribunals decide internal UN administrative disputes relating to staffing, pensions, and related matters. In terms of composition, the governing statute states that 'no two judges should be of the same nationality, and due regard should be given to geographical distribution and gender balance'.[67] The selection criteria state that: 'A person shall be of high moral character and possess at least ten years of judicial experience in the field of administrative law, or the equivalent, within one or more national jurisdictions'.[68]

The first twelve judges of the UNDT and the UNAT were elected in March 2009 by the General Assembly, on the recommendation of the Internal Justice Council (IJC).[69] The IJC consists of a staff representative, a management representative and two distinguished external jurists, one nominated by the staff and one by management, and is chaired by a distinguished jurist chosen by consensus by the four other members.[70] The IJC made recommendations following a public advertising process, seeking applications from interested individuals. The Council shortlisted the applicants based on established criteria and 'with due regard to geographical distribution'.[71] Shortlisted candidates underwent a two-hour written exam and a 30–45 minute interview. For each shortlisted candidate two referees were asked to provide written references. The Council then consulted with the local bar association of each candidate and the International Bar Association to seek views on their suitability. The Council recommended two candidates for each UNDT vacancy and fifteen candidates for the seven UNAT vacancies.[72] Only the recommended candidates were eligible for election by the General Assembly.

Nomination issues have also been considered in the context of the World Trade Organization (WTO), specifically in relation to the review of the Dispute Settlement Understanding. In relation to the first tier of adjudication in the WTO dispute settlement process, the panels, questions have been raised about the nomination of persons to the panel roster. A Consultative Board reporting to the WTO Director-General in 2004 noted that:

> One serious question regarding the roster idea for first level panels, however, addresses the procedures by which the roster persons will be appointed. There exists considerable worry that the usual diplomatic and political processes might not produce the best calibre individuals the tasks require. Thus, thought is needed about a small apolitical body of experts who would examine applications and produce a list of nominees who meet

[67] Dispute Tribunals Statute, Article 4(2).

[68] Dispute Tribunals Statute, Article 4(3).

[69] United Nations General Assembly Resolution 62/228, op. cit., para 37(a), (b) and 40. See also United Nations General Assembly, *Appointment of the full-time and half-time judges of the United Nations Dispute Tribunal, Memorandum by the Secretary-General*, UN Doc. A/63/700, (3 February 2009).

[70] United Nations General Assembly Resolution 62/228, op. cit., para 36.

[71] ibid, para 37(b).

[72] See also United Nations General Assembly, Report of the Internal Justice Council, UN Doc. A/63/489 (16 October 2008). The report includes the curricula vitae of the shortlisted candidates.

carefully set out criteria. This body could then work with the [Dispute Settlement Body] in finalizing the roster.[73]

These new developments suggest that there are circumstances in which governments may be willing to relinquish some direct control over nominations and elections. However, these cases have arisen in particular circumstances. As one might expect, any proposal for removing the ICJ and ICC nomination and elections from the control of states was not generally supported by interviewees. For some the objections were principled, for others they were pragmatic. A number of interviewees felt that significant reforms were unlikely to succeed, given that they would require amendments to the Statutes of the two courts and changes in state practice. Others were unable to conceive of an international judicial appointment system other than by process of nomination and election by political bodies. As one former legal adviser said:

> It would be lovely to conjure one out of one's fertile imagination, but it has to be election in some kind of body representing the states party or the sponsoring organization. Therefore, it will be an election by a political body, and is likely to turn into a political election. There is just no way around it, unpleasant as the situation is.[74]

In relation to the ICC, it was hypothesized that 'the ASP could introduce some kind of voting machine but opposition to it is huge'.[75] One diplomat said that 'the best way to deal with all of these concerns is to leave it up to states parties',[76] because, according to another interviewee, 'they are accountable'.[77] An interviewee from the Caribbean region commented on the applicability of the CCJ model of selection: 'Although it is a clear-cut and transparent appointment procedure that should be effectively adopted for other international courts, I can see that the wider international community may not be willing to give up their sovereignty to an impartial third party.'[78]

These views are in line with the rejection of the original US proposal for a Nominating Committee 'composed by the Assembly of States Parties' that could be convened at each election to draw up a list of candidates.[79] Nevertheless, the benefits of such a mechanism could be significant. To take away the selection process from direct governmental control would remove the politicking

[73] P. Sutherland et al, *Future of the WTO: Addressing Institutional Challenges in the New Millennium*, Report by the Consultative Board to the Director-General Supachai Panitchpakdi (Geneva: World Trade Organization, 2004) 57. See V. Hughes, 'The WTO Dispute Settlement System—from initiating proceedings to ensuring implementation: what needs improvement?' in G. Sacerdoti, A. Yanovich and J. Bohanes, *The WTO at Ten: The Contribution of the Dispute Settlement System* (Cambridge: WTO/Cambridge University Press, 2006) 193–234, 209. Hughes notes that while the idea of an apolitical body coming up with a list of nominees is 'an interesting one . . . I wonder whether the process for selecting who will be on that body will be any less problematic than choosing who eventually should be on the roster'.

[74] T35, 11.

[75] T35, 12.

[76] T2, 15.

[77] T44, 15.

[78] T27, 3.

[79] M. Rwelamira, 'Composition and Administration of the Court' in R. Lee (ed), *The International Criminal Court: The Making of the Rome Statute: Issues, Negotiations, Results* (The Hague: Kluwer Law International/UNITAR, 1999) 162–3.

and vote-trading which currently plays such a significant role in the electoral processes. Although no committee will be completely apolitical, the move to a more independent system would be likely to enhance the role of merit as the main focus in selection decisions. As has been shown with the selection process for the administrative tribunals, selection committees can take into account representational issues such as geography and gender whilst also focusing on merit.

A number of interviewees could see the value of more independent selection procedures for the ICJ and ICC, while not envisaging a shift from the status quo of state control in the near future, particularly in the ICJ, the jurisdiction of which is dependent upon consent of states parties to disputes. Nonetheless, the trends observed in other courts towards more independent national selection procedures and international selection committees suggest that the tension between independence and political control in the selection processes to the ICJ and ICC may well grow in the near future.

D. Competence and merit

Reforms designed to promote greater transparency and independence in judicial selection processes are not ends in themselves but are intended to increase the likelihood of selecting only the highest quality candidates. In the absence of an independent assessment of candidates' suitability it is more likely that political considerations will prevail. To address this concern, a number of international courts have established or considered procedures aimed at assessing, or facilitating assessment by states of the merit of candidates. The expectation is that procedures which focus on merit are more likely to be transparent and independent and will limit crude political considerations.

A number of courts explicitly recognize that the selection of the highest quality candidates is the determining feature of the selection process. The ACHPR guidelines remind state parties that 'the effective functioning of the Court will... require judges with irreproachable integrity, established competence and experience in the area of human rights'.[80] In relation to the ECtHR, the Parliamentary Assembly has noted that 'shortcomings in the national selection and international nomination procedures can engender the risk that judges are not properly qualified to carry out their mandates, to the detriment of the legitimacy and authority of the Strasbourg Court'.[81] This conclusion was shared by the Interights report on the selection process to the ECtHR, which argued that in order to promote selection on merit all candidates should be formally

[80] ACHPR Guidelines, 1.

[81] Parliamentary Assembly of the Council of Europe, Committee on Legal Affairs and Human Rights, 'Report: Nomination of candidates and election of judges to the European Court of Human Rights', op. cit., para 3.

interviewed by the nominating states and that the Council of Europe should provide states with an interview template.[82] The template would require interview panels to:

A. abide by the criteria for judicial appointments in the Convention and Council of Europe recommendations concerning candidates
B. agree in advance what areas should be covered in the questions
C. ensure that these are relevant to the criteria and do not carry built-in advantages for some candidates (especially in relation to gender, eg family commitments)
D. cover the same areas with each candidate, and
E. mark the candidates' performances on an agreed scale under agreed (and relevant) heads.

These sorts of initiatives were supported by a number of the interviewees in discussing possible improvements to the ICC and ICJ selection processes. Most felt that greater importance should be placed on individual merit.[83] A former international judge said 'I would like merit to be given a higher priority than I fear it is.'[84] Many felt that there is insufficient focus on the selection criteria in national nomination processes, a failure to provide adequate information about candidates to facilitate assessment of their relative merits, and an absence of independent input on the qualities of candidates. In this context, merit was often felt to be sidelined and overshadowed by political considerations.

However, it is clear that, as with transparency and independence, increasing focus on merit might threaten the primacy of state control in the selection process. It is to be expected, therefore, that there will be resistance from many states to changes which seek to reinforce merit-based decision-making. Nevertheless, in a number of international courts, there have been initiatives which seek to do just this, including (1) calls to improve the consistency and rigour of nomination processes; (2) requirements to provide detailed and uniform information about candidates and their eligibility; and (3) the establishment of international screening mechanisms to assess the merit of candidates and either make recommendations or exclude certain candidates from the process. Although each of these developments has arisen in the particular political and institutional circumstances of each court, taken together they indicate an emerging trend towards greater consideration of questions of merit. The following sections consider whether similar developments could be introduced in the context of the ICJ and ICC.

[82] J. Limbach et al, *Judicial Independence: Law and Practice of Appointments to the European Court of Human Rights*, op. cit., 28.

[83] The Institut de Droit International also made recommendations on this issue—suggesting an amendment to the Statute to clarify that in Article 9 primacy should be given to the individual criteria: (from the French) Institut de Droit International, *La Composition de la Cour Internationale de Justice, Session d'Aix-en-Provence—1954*, Resolution 26 avril 1954, para 1.

[84] T36, 4.

Consistency in nomination processes

Consistent nomination and election processes based on pre-determined and rigorous selection methods are generally regarded as being more likely to produce meritorious candidates, improve the independence and transparency of the selection processes, and reduce the likelihood of bias against under-represented groups. In the ECtHR context, the Parliamentary Assembly has argued that established procedures with a formal legal basis are preferable to ad hoc arrangements. Although an established formal procedure 'does not in itself guarantee its substantive fairness, it does help ensure a certain level of consistency and transparency',[85] and a number of interviewees believed that broadly common nomination procedures would be desirable for the ICJ and ICC to ensure internal consistency and allow greater comparability of candidates from different states. Such procedures could include interviews, written examinations, and the taking of written references, drawing on examples from some of the non-state independent selection committee processes.[86] The functioning of PCA national groups could also be more effectively regulated by the creation of uniform selection criteria and methods, which might in turn bolster their independence.

The use of national procedures for selecting judges to the domestic courts, as provided for in the ICC and the ACHPR guidelines, is increasingly regarded as one method for producing a more formal system for the nomination of candidates to the international courts.[87] Drawing on national systems does not, however, ensure greater consistency. The range of processes used to select judges at national level varies a great deal, both between civil law and common law systems and within them. This diversity is not, however, necessarily problematic and could be seen as a strength in that it allows the international courts to reflect the different cultures and procedures of the legal systems and judiciaries of the member states. Provided the national systems each comply with basic standards of openness, fairness and the objective consideration of merit-based qualities, there is no reason for consistency to be taken to require homogeneity.

However, some interviewees questioned whether national judicial selection processes were always best placed to identify the most qualified candidates as the higher courts will tend to select from the cohort of the judiciary or a limited group of senior practitioners, which would exclude the wider pool of candidates who might otherwise be considered eligible to sit on the international courts. Furthermore, national selection institutions will often lack knowledge about international law and may be ill-equipped to select the best candidate for this particular role. An alternative approach to the wholesale adoption of national

[85] Parliamentary Assembly of the Council of Europe, Committee on Legal Affairs and Human Rights, 'Report: Nomination of candidates and election of judges to the European Court of Human Rights', op. cit., para 17.

[86] For example, the IJC used written examinations, interviews and references to assess candidates for the UNDT and UNAT, as discussed above.

[87] See n 34 above.

procedures might therefore be to draw on best practices from the national level in developing and adapting the international selection systems.

Information about candidates

The creation of more independent, structured and consistent selection procedures could help to produce more and improved information about candidates and so facilitate the assessment of the merit of candidates on a comparable basis. Recently, there have been calls for information about candidates to be set out in more standardized formats, an example being the requirement that in making nominations to the ECtHR member states must set out the process by which the candidate was nominated and submit a model curriculum vitae.[88] Similarly, nominations to the ICC must be accompanied by a supporting statement setting out how the candidate meets the individual criteria and 'other supporting documentation', which normally includes a curriculum vitae. These are then posted on the website of the ASP.[89] In the ICJ, curricula vitae are, by convention, submitted with nominations and circulated by the UN prior to the elections.[90] The ACHPR requires states making nominations to provide 'detailed information on the information on political and other associations [of the candidate] relevant to determining questions of both eligibility and incompatibility. In addition, nominees should submit statements indicating how they fulfill the criteria for eligibility contained in the Protocol'.[91]

There appears to be a general trend towards requiring more detailed and uniform information to be provided about candidates. This is evident in both the ICJ and ICC, although it is as yet unclear whether states will agree to increase the scope of the information provided to include information about the nomination process, model curriculum vitae formats and information about prior political activities.

[88] Council of Europe Parliamentary Assembly, Recommendation 1646 (2009) *Nomination of candidates and election of judges to the European Court of Human*, op. cit., para 4.2 and Appendix. However, it has been noted that there are problems with the distribution of this information: 'Members of the Parliamentary Assembly may seek information on the candidates, which is kept in the library, but neither the curricula vitae, nor the report of the Sub-Committee is distributed to voters': J. Limbach et al, *Judicial Independence: Law and Practice of Appointments to the European Court of Human Rights*, op. cit., 24.

[89] Rome Statute, Article 36(4)(a) and ASP Resolution 6, para 8.

[90] See for example United Nations General Assembly, *Curricula vitae of candidates nominated by national groups*, Note by the Secretary-General, UN Doc. A/63/188-S/2008/504.

[91] ACHPR Protocol, Article 18; ACHPR Guidelines, 2. The Guidelines also suggest that states parties should consider the positions of '[A] member of government, a Minister or under-secretary of State, a diplomatic representative, a director of a ministry, or one of his subordinates, or the legal adviser to a foreign office' to be incompatible, drawing on the proposals of the Advisory Committee of Jurists made in relation to the Permanent Court of International Justice: at 2.

Screening mechanisms

Four main screening mechanisms have been established or contemplated for the international courts. The two mechanisms currently in operation are the Sub-Committee on the Election of Judges to the European Court of Human Rights that screens ECtHR candidates and the selection committee for members of the World Trade Organization Appellate Body (WTO AB). The Treaty of Lisbon provides for a screening mechanism for nominations to the ECJ and the Court of First Instance (CFI) to be created. As noted, the Rome Statute makes provision for the establishment of an advisory committee on nominations to the ICC, but the proposal remains dormant and appears to have little support.

The ECtHR Sub-Committee is the longest-standing and most developed of these screening mechanisms.[92] It interviews the three candidates nominated by each member state and ranks them in order of merit. One candidate from the list (often the first ranked candidate) is then elected by the Parliamentary Assembly.[93] Uniquely, the Sub-Committee can also decide to reject lists of candidates if it considers that there is 'no real choice' between the candidates, there is an absence of a 'fair, transparent and consistent national selection procedure', or that the list has failed to meet the gender requirements.[94]

The Sub-Committee has been criticized in the past for being 'at best limited, at worst... fundamentally flawed' because of the lack of human rights and international law expertise of the Sub-Committee members, the cursory nature of the assessment of candidates, the secretiveness of deliberations and the failure to state reasons, and the apparent influence of party politics over ranking decisions.[95] Even though it is considered 'an improvement on the previous system as it guards against the Parliamentary Assembly simply rubber-stamping [rankings by states]... it risks adding an additional level of arbitrariness to the appointments' procedure'.[96] Lord Hoffmann, a former UK Law Lord, has recently criticized the composition of the Sub-Committee in strong terms:

> [it] consists of eighteen members chaired by a Latvian politician, on which the UK representatives are a Labour politician with a trade union background and no legal

[92] It was established in 1997: see Council of Europe Parliamentary Assembly, *Resolution 1082 (1996) on the procedure for examining candidatures for the election of judges to the European Court of Human Rights*, available at: <http://www.assembly.coe.int/Main.asp?link=/Documents/AdoptedText/ta96/ERES1082.htm> (accessed 26 April 2009). It is comprised of eighteen members of the Parliamentary Assembly's Committee on Legal Affairs and Human Rights, appointed by the five political groups of the Parliamentary Assembly, and there is no requirement of legal expertise: J. Limbach et al, *Judicial Independence: Law and Practice of Appointments to the European Court of Human Rights*, op. cit., 21.

[93] J. Limbach et al, *Judicial Independence: Law and Practice of Appointments to the European Court of Human Rights*, op. cit., 24.

[94] Council of Europe Parliamentary Assembly, Recommendation 1646 (2009), *Nomination of candidates and election of judges to the European Court of Human Rights*, op. cit., para 2.

[95] J. Limbach et al, *Judicial Independence: Law and Practice of Appointments to the European Court of Human Rights*, op. cit., 9.

[96] ibid, 21.

qualifications and a Conservative politician who was called to the Bar in 1972 but so far as I know has never practised. They choose from lists of three drawn by the governments of the forty-seven members in a manner which is totally opaque.[97]

Such criticisms are arguably less valid in the light of the very public and rigorous review of the selection process which the Parliamentary Assembly carried out in 2008–9 in an attempt to formalize and improve the procedures. One consequence of the review and subsequent report is that the process by which the names of candidates are scrutinized by the Committee and forwarded to the Parliamentary Assembly has been set out:

The Sub-Committee considers the candidates not only as individuals but also with an eye to a harmonious composition of the Court, taking into account, for example, their professional backgrounds and a gender balance. It formulates a recommendation to the Bureau of the Assembly, which the Bureau forwards to the Assembly members and may decide to declassify (make public).[98]

While it is true that reasons are not given for the Committee's decision in individual cases, the disclosure of such deliberations is not the practice in other judicial selection processes either at national or international level. The need for frank discussion by judicial screening or selecting committees and the fear that if such deliberations were made public candidates would be deterred from applying for judicial office has meant that very little information of this kind is ever revealed.

Criticisms have also been made of the screening committee of the WTO AB, the seven-member dispute resolution body of the WTO.[99] The role of the Selection Committee is to assess candidates nominated by WTO member states,[100] consult with member states as to the candidates who would be politically acceptable

[97] Lord Hoffman, 'The Universality of Human Rights', Judicial Studies Board Annual Lecture, (19 March 2009), available at: <http://www.jsboard.co.uk/downloads/Hoffmann_2009_JSB_Annual_ Lecture_Universality_of_Human_Rights.doc> (accessed 26 April 2009), para 39.

[98] Sub-Committee on the election of Judges to the European Court of Human Rights, *Procedure for electing judges to the European Court of Human Rights*, AS/Jur (2009) 34 (1 July 2009), para 13.

[99] Agreement Establishing the World Trade Organization, available at: <http://www.wto.org/english/docs_e/legal_e/04-wto.pdf> and Annex 2 'Understanding on Rules and Procedures Governing the Settlement of Disputes' available at: <http://www.wto.org/english/docs_e/legal_e/28-dsu.pdf> (DSU). See WT/DSB/1, 19 June 1995, Establishment of the Appellate Body, Recommendations by the Preparatory Committee for the WTO, approved by the Dispute Settlement Body on 10 February 1995. The Committee comprises 'the Director-General, and the Chairpersons of the General Council, the DSB, the Council for Trade in Goods, the Council for Trade in Services and the TRIPS Council': World Trade Organization, press release 'WTO appoints four new Appellate Body members', 27 November 2007, available at: <http://www.wto.int/english/news_e/pres07_e/pr501_e.htm> (accessed 12 December 2008). They are all government representatives: J. Pauwelyn, 'La sélection des juges à l'OMC, et peut-être celle d'un Chinois, mérite plus d'attention' *Le Temps, Economie & Finance* 16 November 2007, available at: <http://www.letemps.ch/Page/Uuid/d4952ece-ac44–11dd-bf59-ad3d6140ad87%7C2> (accessed 22 April 2009).

[100] Note that this includes both a written examination and an interview: J. Pauwelyn, 'La sélection des juges à l'OMC, et peut-être celle d'un Chinois, mérite plus d'attention', op. cit.

and also 'broadly representative'[101] of the WTO membership, and then submit the names of the candidates for appointment by consensus of the WTO Dispute Settlement Body. The main criticism is that the Selection Committee takes an overtly political role in 'consensus building',[102] which may have the effect of distorting considerations of merit. The process is also said to lack transparency.[103]

The Treaty of Lisbon provides for the establishment of a screening panel 'to give an opinion on candidates' suitability to perform the duties of Judge and Advocate-General of the Court of Justice and the General Court [currently named the Court of First Instance] before the governments of the Member States make . . . appointments'.[104] The ECJ and CFI are both full representation courts for which a single candidate is nominated by each member state for appointment by 'common accord of the governments of the Member States'.[105] The screening panel will comprise 'seven persons chosen from among former members of the Court of Justice and the General Court, members of national supreme courts and lawyers of recognized competence, one of whom shall be proposed by the European Parliament'. The role of the panel will be to discourage the nomination of unqualified candidates: if an unqualified candidate is nominated and an adverse opinion is provided, member states are encouraged to refuse to appoint the candidate.[106] Full details of the operation of the panel will be determined by the European Council.[107]

It is perhaps not surprising that the most developed and credible mechanisms (both instituted and proposed) for screening judicial candidates are found in the

[101] Dispute Settlement Understanding, Annex 2, Agreement Establishing World Trade Organization, Article 17(3).

[102] 'In other words, the selection committee will ultimately select and present to the Dispute Settlement Body those candidates who stand the best chance of being appointed by consensus in the Dispute Settlement Body, having been "pre-approved" by WTO Members': T. Broude, '"Judges Shalt Thou Make Thee in All Thy Gates": Reforming Judicial Office in the WTO Dispute Settlement System' Free University of Amsterdam Journal of International and Comparative Law (The Griffin's View) 6(2) (2005) 45.

[103] J. Pauwelyn, 'La sélection des juges à l'OMC, et peut-être celle d'un Chinois, mérite plus d'attention', op. cit.

[104] Treaty of Lisbon, amending the Treaty on European Union and the Treaty establishing the European Community, signed at Lisbon, 13 December 2007, Official Journal C 306 of 17 December 2007 (Treaty of Lisbon). See also consolidated versions of the Treaty on European Union and the Treaty on the Functioning of the European Union, *Official Journal* C 115 of 9 May 2008.

[105] See Articles 221 and 224 of the EC Treaty: Consolidated Versions of the Treaty on European Union and of the Treaty Establishing the European Community, *Official Journal* C 321E of 29 December 2006.

[106] T. Tridimas, 'The European Court of Justice and the Draft Constitution: A Supreme Court for the Union?' in T. Tridimas and P. Nebbia (eds), *European Union Law for the Twenty-First Century: Rethinking the New Legal Order* (Oxford: Hart Publishing; 2004 118).

[107] 'The Council shall adopt a decision establishing the panel's operating rules and a decision appointing its members. It shall act on the initiative of the President of the Court of Justice': Treaty of Lisbon, Article 2, para 209. An identical provision was also found in the unsuccessful Treaty establishing a Constitution for Europe, *Official Journal* C 310 of 16 December 2004.

context of full representation courts, the ECtHR and, prospectively, the ECJ.[108] In these courts, it might be expected that there would be a greater appetite for screening of the nomination decisions of states because each state is entitled to be represented. It should also be noted that the more robust screening mechanism for the ECtHR has emerged within an institutional framework which includes a body independent of member states, the Parliamentary Assembly, which can impose additional requirements on the election of candidates. A former international judge noted that 'screening procedures make more sense in courts like the European Court of Justice where every country is guaranteed a seat, but they are more controversial when there is competition for seats'.[109]

This point may explain why there has been resistance to the establishment of the ICC Advisory Committee on Nominations, which was provided for in the Rome Statute but has not yet been established.[110] The proposal for a committee was put forward by the United Kingdom, which 'wanted to have a better machinery for ICC elections borrowing from what was happening in Strasbourg [for the European Court of Human Rights]'.[111] One interviewee involved in the proposals said it was intended to 'filter out the duds',[112] suggesting that the committee could declare certain candidates unqualified and exclude them from the elections. It appears that the proposal failed because states did not want anyone 'looking over their shoulders'[113] and questioning nominations. Nonetheless, a number of interviewees thought the idea of the committee should be revived and reconsidered, but with a more 'light-touch' recommendatory or ranking role. One former ICC candidate thought it would be more 'important and effective than strengthened consultation at the national level'.[114] However, others were less enthusiastic: 'It would be wrong to have some kind of filtering mechanism, however informal, that separated the candidates from the body of electors. I do believe that the voters should have good information on candidates that they should be receiving without some kind of body deflecting attention away from some candidates and focusing attention on others.'[115] And others foresaw difficulties with the composition of the committee and its establishment.[116]

It was suggested that the ICC Advisory Committee on nominations could perform a range of functions, short of excluding or ranking candidates, such as checking and standardizing information about candidates to facilitate comparisons between them: one former Permanent Representative noted that 'there can be quite a bit of subjectivity in how qualifications are recognized and presented'.[117] It was also proposed that it could gather peer reviews of the candidates to supplement state (and in the ICC context, NGO) investigations as to

[108] With the exception of the Caribbean Court of Justice, which has a full appointments commission and is not a full representation court.
[109] T37, 15.
[110] Rome Statute, Article 36(4)(c).
[111] T35, 12.
[112] F32, 2.
[113] T14, 18.
[114] T32, 18.
[115] T45, 7.
[116] T44, 15. A key issue here is how a committee can be seen to have a mandate or political legitimacy to perform a screening role, but also be independent of states.
[117] T20, 2.

their merit and information provided by states about their candidates. It remains to be seen whether the body of opinion evident from the interviews and elsewhere supporting the idea of some form of screening mechanism will be strong enough to overcome the political resistance from states which, to date, has prevented the institution of such a mechanism.

Although proposals for an equivalent screening process for the ICJ are less developed than for the ICC, similar arguments have been made as to how such a system could help improve the quality of candidates appointed. A report by the Commission on Global Governance in 1995 argued that:

> We would like to see introduced a system of screening of potential members of the Court for both jurisprudential skills and proven objectivity. This practice is already followed in many countries, which have processes for consultation with or even approval by independent national bodies before a person is elevated to high judicial office. Such a system would not affect the involvement of all states through the General Assembly or displace the role of the Security Council in the political act of selection. It would mean judges were chosen from a slate of candidates who all have the required experience, skills, and independence of mind. Both the General Assembly and the Security Council would be free to ask for a further set of candidates.[118]

Asked about the merits of such a proposal, many interviewees felt that a screening mechanism for the ICJ would not be appropriate. One former international judge argued that it would be 'quite invidious because people are known, it's a smaller court and states come before the Court'.[119] There was a sense that there is already sufficient information available about ICJ candidates, who are generally well known to the electorate. In addition, the fact that candidates have been vetted by their PCA national groups made any further scrutiny superfluous. On the other hand, there is in reality a complete absence of objective assessment of candidates, suggesting that some form of screening is needed.

This brief overview of the use of screening mechanisms in the international court system shows that their use to date has been limited and has not been without controversy. Nevertheless, they do add another layer of scrutiny and at least the possibility of some independent assessment of the merit of candidates. This may result in more objective information about candidates being provided to states, which in turn may encourage states to prioritize merit in the election process. It may also lead to the exclusion of poorly qualified candidates. Given that in recent years there have been publicly expressed concerns as to whether certain elected candidates have in fact fulfilled the selection criteria, this issue is not purely academic.

118 Commission on Global Governance, *Our Global Neighbourhood: The Report of the Commission on Global Governance* (Oxford: Oxford University Press, 1995) 315.
119 T35, 18.

E. Diversity and representation

Across international courts, in common with developments at national level, concerns have increasingly been raised about the lack of diversity in the composition of the courts and the potential impact this might have on perceptions of legitimacy in the eyes of court users and the wider public. Of particular concern have been gender diversity, geographical representation, and the representation of different legal systems and languages. This section considers developments across international courts aimed at improving diversity and the representation of certain groups through composition, nomination and election requirements. It also looks at how such measures might interact with considerations of selection on merit.

Gender balance

The lack of gender balance in the international judiciary has been the subject of growing criticism over the last decade,[120] and has been linked to issues of legitimacy and public confidence in the courts. In 2003, an Interights report on the selection process to the ECtHR noted that: 'To command public confidence, the Court should be diverse in its composition. This includes ensuring a visible equality of opportunity for women to be nominated and elected to the bench in Strasbourg.'[121] Academics have also begun to argue that gender representation is as pressing an issue as geographical representation. Sally Kenney's 2002 study of the appointment of women to the European Court of Justice argued, for example, that: 'It is not a big leap from the unquestioned position that someone

[120] See Report of the Fourth World Conference on Women, Beijing, 4–15 September 1995, UN Doc.A/CONF.177/20, 17 October 1995, para 142(b). Resolution adopted by the General Assembly, Improvement of the status of women in the United Nations system, UN Doc.A/RES/56/127, 30 January 2002; Security Council Resolution 1325(2000), 31 October 2000. The activities of the International Association of Women Judges (IAWJ) (<http://www.iawj.org/>) are evidence of the widespread and growing commitment to gender equality on the bench at national, and increasingly, international levels. Academic work on women judges and gender representation at the national level include the special issue, 'Women of the Courts Symposium' in the University of Toledo Law Review 35(4) (2005) and the special issue, 'Gender and Judges' in the International Journal of the Legal Profession 15(1/2) (2008). In relation to the international courts, see H. Charlesworth and C. Chinkin, *The Boundaries of International Law: A feminist analysis* (Manchester: Manchester University Press, 2000); J. Linehan, 'Women and Public International Litigation: Background Paper Prepared for the Project on International Courts and Tribunals' (2001), available at: <http://www.pict-pcti.org/publications/PICT_articles/Women1.pdf> (accessed 20 August 2006); and the work of PICT referred to at <http://www.pict-pcti.org/activities/meetings.html> (Accessed 28 April 2010).

[121] J. Limbach et al, *Judicial Independence: Law and Practice of Appointments to the European Court of Human Rights*, op. cit., 17.

from the UK must be on the Court, to the position that there must be women on the Court.'[122]

Despite growing awareness of the problems created by a lack of gender balance in the courts, the participation of women on 'general' international courts is still low and in some cases non-existent.[123] For example, there have been no female ITLOS judges appointed and only one woman has ever been elected to the ICJ (apart from two ad hoc judges). The retirement of the President of the Court, Rosalyn Higgins, in 2009 left the court without a single female judge. If expressed in terms of female and male 'court years', over the period of the ICJ history, there have been a mere fifteen female years compared to 945 male years. Women have been slightly better represented on regional courts, human rights courts and as *ad litem* judges on the ad hoc criminal tribunals.[124] As at December 2008, there were 236 judges on the main international courts, of which 57 were female (24 per cent).[125]

Across the international court system, a raft of measures have been introduced to try to increase the number of women judges.[126] These range from requirements in the court's governing statute that the need for gender balance be considered to the more radical gender requirements of the ICC, which is the only court that currently has a minimum gender quota.[127] More proactive and formal provisions, such as those of the ICC, tend, not surprisingly, to be found in the more recently created courts which generally have a better gender balance. It is notable, for example, that the ICC is the first international court in which there is now a majority of women on the bench. Similarly, the first twelve judges of the UNDT and the UNAT, elected in March 2009, were made up of seven men and five women.

Relatively formal provisions in relation to gender equality are also found in the ECtHR, enforced through the screening mechanism for nominations to

[122] S. Kenney, 'Breaking the Silence: Gender Mainstreaming and the Composition of the European Court of Justice' *Feminist Legal Studies* 2004, 10(3–4), 269.

[123] D. Terris, C. P. R. Romano and L. Swigart, *The International Judge: An Introduction to the Men and Women Who Decide the World's Cases*, International Courts and Tribunals Series (Oxford: Oxford University Press, 2007) 18–19.

[124] See also J. Linehan, 'Women and Public International Litigation: Background Paper Prepared for the Project on International Courts and Tribunals', op. cit.

[125] The international courts and tribunals included in this survey were ICJ, ICC, ITLOS, European Court of Justice, Court of First Instance, ECHR, Inter-American Court of Human Rights, ICTY, ICTR, WTO Appellate Body and the African Court of Human and Peoples' Rights.

[126] See also the efforts made through the Fourth World Conference on Women in Beijing op.cit., paras 13, 36, 79 and 190; General Assembly, Follow-up to the Fourth World Conference on Women and full implementation of the Beijing Declaration and Platform for Action, UN Doc A/RES/51/69, 12 December 1996, para 27 (promoting women candidates); and also para 74(e) of the Report: J. Linehan, 'Women and Public International Litigation: Background Paper Prepared for the Project on International Courts and Tribunals', op.cit.

[127] See Chapter 2 for details.

the court. These requirements provide that each list of three names nominated by a state should include at least one member of the 'under-represented sex' (defined as the sex which constitutes less than 40 per cent of the bench).[128] The Sub-Committee of the Parliamentary Assembly can reject lists of candidates submitted by member states if they do not include a female candidate, unless the member state can show that it has 'taken all the necessary and appropriate steps to ensure that the list contains a candidate of the under-represented sex, but has not been able to find a candidate of that sex who satisfies the requirements of Article 21 § 1 of the European Convention on Human Rights'.[129] The gender requirement therefore applies unless it would mean that an unqualified candidate would need to be nominated, in which case a state can avail itself of the exception. The Sub-Committee then ranks the lists of three candidates with regard to the overall 'harmonious composition of the Court'.[130]

Significantly, the Parliamentary Assembly has recognized the importance of gender balance in the bodies at national level which nominate or advise the government on nomination and has stated that 'it invites the governments of member states to ensure that the selection bodies/panels (and those advising on selection) are themselves as gender-balanced as possible'.[131] The relatively weak nature of this guidance raises questions about its likely effectiveness. Nevertheless, it at least represents an acknowledgement that gender equality is unlikely to be promoted seriously if the bodies responsible at national level for nomination themselves have very few women amongst their members.

Many of the more recently created courts include in their governing statutes or guidelines some wording which encourages or requires the selection process to

[128] Although the under-represented sex is currently female, it is worth remembering that in a number of European judiciaries there is considerable 'feminization' of the bench and the under-represented sex, at least in the lower ranks, is male.

[129] The Sub-Committee had previously rejected lists simply because they did not have candidates of both genders. Malta sought an Advisory Opinion from the Court regarding this practice: *Advisory Opinion on certain legal questions concerning the lists of candidates submitted with a view to the election of judges to the European Court of Human Rights*, 12 February 2008, available at: <http://www.cmiskp.echr.coe.int/tkp197/view.asp?action=html&documentId=828910&portal=hbkm&source=externalbydocnumber&table=F69A27FD8FB86142BF01C1166DEA398649> (accessed 23 November 2008). The Advisory Opinion prompted the inclusion of the exception: Council of Europe Parliamentary Assembly, Resolution 1627 (2008), *Candidates for the European Court of Human Rights*, available at: <http://www.assembly.coe.int/Main.asp?link=/Documents/AdoptedText/ta08/ERES1627.htm> (accessed 20 November 2008), para 4. See also A. Mowbray, 'The Consideration of Gender in the Process of Appointing Judges to the European Court of Human Rights' *Human Rights Law Review* 8(3) (2008) 549–59.

[130] Parliamentary Assembly of the Council of Europe, Committee on Legal Affairs and Human Rights, 'Report: Nomination of candidates and election of judges to the European Court of Human Rights', op. cit., para 7.

[131] Council of Europe Parliamentary Assembly, Recommendation 1646 (2009), *Nomination of candidates and election of judges to the European Court of Human Rights*, op.cit. para 5.

take account of the need for gender equality or to promote gender balance on the court.[132] The Protocol of the ACHPR, for example, provides that: 'Due consideration shall be given to adequate gender representation in nomination process' and 'in the election of the judges, the Assembly shall ensure that there is adequate gender representation'.[133] The ACHPR guidelines also require that in the slate of up to three candidates which each state can nominate, it 'should ensure that at least one (1) of the candidates they nominate is a female'.[134] This relatively 'light-touch' approach resulted in just two female judges out of eleven on the first bench of the court.[135] The Protocol of the African Court of Justice and Human Rights (ACJHR), the court into which the ACHPR will eventually be merged, also has provisions requiring states to 'take into account gender representation in the nomination process' and, in the election of judges, to 'ensure that there is equitable gender representation'.[136]

Despite the strikingly poor record of gender balance in the ICJ, there is little sense of urgency to institute new rules or practices to promote the appointment of more women to the court.[137] The absence at the ICJ of the equivalent of the Women's Initiatives for Gender Justice, which played such a significant part in securing gender balance in the ICC, is likely to be one reason for the lack of women on the bench. It is clear that without sustained political pressure from NGOs and other civil society groups, gender equality is generally marginalized as an issue in the selection processes of the international courts.[138] It is only through the activities of these groups that the barriers for female candidates, such as assumptions about the desired career path an individual must have pursued, are highlighted. One such barrier is the fact that women have less access

[132] With the exception of the Caribbean Court of Justice, which has no reference to gender balance in its judicial selection provisions.

[133] ACHPR Protocol, Articles 12(2) and 14(3). Also note the provisions relating to nomination of ICTY and ICTR *ad litem* judges that states and permanent observers must nominate candidates 'taking into account the importance of a fair representation of female and male candidates': Article 13 ter(1)(b), Statute of the International Tribunal for the Prosecution of Persons Responsible for Serious Violations of International Humanitarian Law Committed in the Territory of the Former Yugoslavia since 1991, UN. Doc. S/25704 at 36, annex (1993) and S/25704/Add.1 (1993), adopted by Security Council on 25 May 1993, UN. Doc. S/RES/827 (1993); Article 12 ter(1)(b), Statute of the International Tribunal for Rwanda, adopted by S/RES/955, (1994).

[134] ACHPR Guidelines, 2.

[135] C. A. Odinkalu, 'How the Judges of the African Court Emerged', op.cit.

[136] ACJHR Protocol, Articles 5(2) and 7(5).

[137] See Chapter 2. For a review of the political process by which the gender requirements were established in the ICC, see also C. Steains, 'Gender Issues' in R. S. Lee, (ed), *The International Criminal Court: The Making of the Rome Statute: Issues, Negotiations, Results* (The Hague: Kluwer Law International, 1999) 357–90 and L. Chappell, 'The International Criminal Court: A New Arena for Transforming Gender Justice' in S. M. Rai and G. Waylen (eds), *Global Governance: Feminist Perspectives* (Basingstoke: Palgrave Macmillan, 2008) 160–84.

[138] For a review of the role played by the WIGJ in shaping the ICC, see P. Spees, 'Women's Advocacy in the Creation of the International Criminal Court: Changing the Landscape of Justice and Power' *Signs* 28(4) (Summer 2003) 1233–54.

to the 'conduits' to the court, such as the International Law Commission (ILC) and the PCA national groups. Critics of proactive gender initiatives have generally argued that the low number of women in the courts is simply a reflection of the fact that the selection pool of potential female candidates is small because of women's limited access to the higher ranks of the legal profession, the diplomatic corps, academia and the benches of the national courts, and that these factors are changing over time.[139] However, it is also clear that women are often not *seen* to be in the pool because of exclusionary nomination processes that favour male candidates from more traditional international law backgrounds or make assumptions about career paths and candidates' motivations.[140]

In the end, the achievement of a greater gender balance in the international courts—as in all institutions of power—is dependent on the presence of political will to seek out qualified female candidates and nominate them, and for voting states to prioritize gender in choosing between qualified candidates. Reasonable numbers of female judges currently sit on the Inter-American Court of Human Rights and as members of the WTO AB (three out of seven members in each case) even though there are no gender requirements for those courts. The reasons why female candidates are nominated and elected in particular circumstances are complex, but these examples demonstrate that gender balance can be achieved where states choose to nominate female candidates.

Geographical and political representation

In selective representation courts, concerns have been raised about the adequacy of the distribution of seats on a geographical basis. Geographical representation is one important means by which selective representation courts acquire and retain their legitimacy, therefore states expect that they will have the opportunity to have a judge of their nationality on the bench, and, as we have seen from the interview data on nomination and election, they will often fight to get it. Despite the commitment to the notion of judicial independence in government rhetoric on the international courts, there is an equally strong attachment to the concept of 'representation'. This need to ensure that states or regions are guaranteed an adequate presence on the courts is effected through a range of different mechanisms. In the ICJ, the principal judicial organ of the UN, the convention of equitable geographical distribution has led to the allocation of a set number of seats to each of the five UN regional groups. In ITLOS, geographical distribution is determined by a decision of the Meeting of States

[139] See J. Limbach et al, *Judicial Independence: Law and Practice of Appointments to the European Court of Human Rights*, op. cit., 17.

[140] J. Linehan, 'Women and Public International Litigation', Background Paper prepared for the Project on International Courts and Tribunals, op. cit., 4–5.

Parties. In the proposed ACJHR, seats are allocated to the various sub-regional groups in Africa.[141]

In the ICC, another approach has been adopted: the allocation of a minimum number of seats to each of the five UN regional groups. However, in addition, a number of 'floating seats' are allowed for that can be won by candidates from any of the regional groups, with an additional requirement that a minimum number of candidates are nominated from each regional group. The strength of this system is that it increases competition for seats and avoids 'clean slates' whereby only one candidate from a geographical area is put forward. For selection to some other selective representation courts, for example, *ad litem* judges of the ad hoc criminal tribunals, and the ACHPR, there are broader requirements to '[bear] in mind the importance of equitable geographical distribution', or 'ensure that in the Court as a whole there is representation of the main regions of Africa'.[142] The WTO Appellate Body is to be 'broadly representative of the membership of the WTO'.[143] However, some selective representation courts, such as the CCJ and the IACHR, have no geographical representation requirements.

Concerns have been raised about three aspects of geographical representation: (1) the organization of states into regional groups for the purposes of elections; (2) the distribution of seats between those regional groups; and (3), the practices within regional groups, in particular the politicization of the 'allocation' of seats and the dominance of large or wealthy states.[144] In relation to the ICJ, there are also doubts about the fairness or relevance of the P5 convention. Underlying these concerns is a belief by many less powerful states that they are not properly represented on the courts, or that they have little real chance of having a candidate elected. A number of interviewees felt that the five UN regional groups were arbitrary and outdated and work to the disadvantage of smaller and developing states. To address this problem, it was suggested that the UN regional groups should be reorganized into 'more closely knit groups'.[145]

The distribution of seats across regional groups has also been criticized.[146] It has been argued that the allocation of seats does not take into account the increased numbers of African and Asian states with large populations that have joined international courts in recent years, as a result of which Europe is over-represented. This issue has come to a head in relation to ITLOS, where African and Asian states made a joint proposal to the Meeting of States Parties to the

[141] ACJHR Protocol, Article 3(3).

[142] ICTY Statute, Article 13 ter(1)(c); ICTR Statute, Article 12 ter(1)(c)ACHPR Protocol, Article 4(2).

[143] DSU, Article 17(3). Note, however, that since the entry into effect of the WTO dispute settlement system, there have always been Appellate Body members from the US and from the European Communities and, for almost the entire period, a member from Japan. Thus representation in this context does not seem to be limited to a geographical concept.

[144] Note the general criticisms of the adequacy of geographical representation, as discussed in Chapter 2.

[145] F25, 1.

[146] Note the shifts in the regional allocation of seats in the ICJ and ICC over time, as discussed in Chapter 2.

UN Convention on the Law of the Sea, seeking the allocation of a seat held by Western Europe to be rotated between Africa and Asia to reflect the increased number of states from those regions that had joined the tribunal.[147] This development suggests that the issue of geographical distribution of seats is very much a live issue and that states are increasingly willing to challenge the rules on the allocation of seats.

It was also suggested that the existing seats on the ICJ could be reallocated to reflect the size of regional groups (based on population): 'There could be redistribution among the regions, because the Asian group is the biggest group in the UN, and that is not reflected in the number of seats that we have.'[148] As in ITLOS and the ILC,[149] certain seats could be rotated between regions, or 'one of the seats should become our shared seat between Europe and Asia'.[150] Some interviewees suggested that one solution to the problem of representation on the ICJ could be to increase the number of judges on the court. Opinions on the desirability of such a change were divided, with one former ICJ judge arguing against it.[151] Another interviewee objected to the proposal for increasing the seats so as to secure greater representation for Asia on the grounds that the court would become 'unmanageable'. He saw 'an inverse relationship between quantity and quality'.[152]

Conversely, a WEOG diplomat said: 'I have felt for a long time that the ICJ should be totally reorganized. There should be something like twenty-one judges which would provide for better representation of different regional groups and legal systems, because at present we are strained.'[153] Such a reform would require amendment of the Charter, and the approval of the P5 members.[154] As this would open debate as to the legitimacy of the P5 convention and whether, for example, other permanent or non-permanent members should be admitted, it was generally recognized that such reforms are unlikely in the near future. Many noted that any changes to the P5 convention or any structural change to the UN regional groups will depend on wider reform of the UN, particularly the reform of the Security Council, and would require an amendment of the ICJ Statute. Issues of ICJ representation are therefore inextricably tied to fundamental issues of change in the organization as a whole. Those who advocate reform at an institutional level recognize that it would be a long and complicated process. It is acknowledged that the P5 convention could not be reformed at any institutional level without also reopening the question of the number and distribution of seats

[147] In 2009, the states parties to the UNCLOS decided upon a new arrangement for the allocation of seats on the tribunal as follows: five members each from the Group of African States and Group of Asian States, four members from the Group of Latin American and Caribbean States, and three members each from the Group of East European States and Group of Western European and other States (WEOG), and the one remaining seat elected from among the African and Asian Groups and WEOG. Press release, SEA/1920, UN Department of Public Information, 29 June 2009.

[148] T59, 12–13.

[149] T59, 13.

[150] T81, 11.

[151] T31, 9.

[152] T81, 11.

[153] T9, 8.

[154] ICJ Statute, Article 69; UN Charter, Article 108.

on the Security Council: 'it would be ideal not to have it but it is part of wider UN reform which starts with the position of the P5 in the Security Council'.[155]

It is also not clear that all P5 members would be treated the same if there was to be a serious challenge to the convention through reform of the election system or other structural reform. One interviewee suggested that France and the United Kingdom would be the most exposed states if the P5 convention came under threat: 'Britain and France will struggle to hold their places with all these things in time, but I think people will always want to make sure that China and Russia and America are on the Court.'[156]

In the broader context of UN reform, questions have been raised as to whether states will change the status of the P5 on the Security Council and the court or simply increase the number of permanent members and non-permanent members of the Security Council, a move that might have some repercussions for the composition of the ICJ. These proposals prompt a number of political questions as to which states should be accorded permanent membership and institutional questions such as how the ICJ might operate in such changed circumstances. One interviewee expressed his perspective on the likelihood and scope of possible Security Council reform:

> The main problem we are facing now, politically, when we discuss the reform of the UN system is the composition of the Security Council and whether or not there will be more permanent members of the Security Council, and whether those permanent members will have political power. That is why the reform of the Security Council has stopped because there is no agreement, and I don't think there will be an agreement. From the very first day we discussed the question in 1993, my personal opinion was that if there is a reform, it will be in line with the reform of 1965. More non-permanent members, changes in rules, method, procedures, more accountability, but no reforms of the hard structure, the hard core of the Security Council.[157]

If the P5 convention were to be set aside, many interviewees suggested there may be potential consequences for the court. Some felt that to strip members of the P5 of their position on the court might result in a 'downgrading of their engagement in international law'[158] and represent a 'financial risk to the organization'.[159] As a result, altering this aspect of the composition of the court could have far-reaching consequences. The P5 convention may be secure at present, but the interview data suggest that challenges will continue and intensify.

With regard to the practices within some regional groups, in particular, the use of clean slates and the political negotiations surrounding who will nominate a candidate, endorsements and withdrawals, some interviewees argued for a 'rotation of seats within the regional group'.[160] One interviewee also suggested a system of rotation between states in their regional groups, placing 'a limit on the number of terms one country could have' so that 'after maybe two terms,

[155] F18, 1. [156] T18, 7. [157] T58, 12. [158] F48, 3–4. [159] F29, 2.
[160] T13, 10.

then that seat should rotate to another country'.[161] Although this approach might result in greater representation, it might also be at the expense of merit as it would effectively allow the state to appoint a judge even if there was a more highly qualified candidate from the region.

Drawing together the different views expressed in the interviews, it appears that the best way to ensure fair geographical representation combined with the highest quality of judges is to remove the politicized aspects of the election process and encourage open competition within regional groups. The expectation is that this would ensure a more natural rotation of seats within regional groups based on merit, rather than the distorting effects of state power and prestige that plays such a considerable part in intra-regional representation at present.

Legal systems, language and expertise

Across the international courts there have also been attempts to ensure diversity in terms of language, legal system or culture and expertise, so that each particular bench is well equipped to undertake its task and also represents the full range of domestic legal systems. In the contexts of both the ICJ and ICC, it was noted that both have requirements that electors bear in mind, that in the 'body as a whole the representation of the main forms of civilization and of the principal legal systems of the world should be assured' and 'take into account the need... for the representation of the principal legal systems of the world'.[162] These requirements and similar ones in ITLOS[163] are generally understood to be satisfied by equitable geographical distribution or representation. However, some courts have taken the concept of representation of legal systems further; for example, the ACHPR guidelines required that states, in making nominations, 'give preference to candidates with experience in more than one of the principal legal traditions of Africa (Civil Law, Common Law, Islamic Law and Custom and African Customary Law)'.[164]

The appointment of judges to the CCJ by the RJLSC apparently took into account the need for representation of different legal systems by appointing a

161 T59, 13. Amerasinghe also notes that some judges have spent long periods on the bench, and advocates a rotation system: C. F. Amerasinghe, 'Judges of the International Court of Justice—Election and Qualifications' *Leiden Journal of International Law* 14(2) (2001) 346–7.

162 ICJ Statute, Article 9 and Rome Statute, Article 36(8)(a)(i).

163 Articles 2(2) and 3(1) of ITLOS Statute that provide that when electing judges, states must ensure the representation of the principal legal systems of the world and equitable geographical distribution in the composition of the Tribunal as a whole. A. Yankov, 'The International Tribunal for the Law of the Sea and the Comprehensive Dispute Settlement System of the Law of the Sea' in P. C. Rao and R. Khan (eds), *The International Tribunal for the Law of the Sea: Law and Practice* (The Hague: Kluwer Law International, 2001) 42–3.

164 ACHPR Guidelines, 2. See also ACHPR Protocol, Article 14(3) and ACJHR Protocol, Article 7(4).

judge from a state with a Roman-Dutch legal system.[165] However, this could be accounted for by the fact that the CCJ has a small membership and that one of its functions is to act as an appeal court (hence requiring an understanding of domestic law). It is also relevant that the judges were appointed by a selection committee that was not constrained by geographical representation rules.

A number of interviewees expressed concerns about the under-representation of certain legal cultures on the ICJ and ICC, though this issue has not exercised states as much as geographical representation. States could perhaps be encouraged, in making decisions on candidates from particular regions, to consider the overall diversity of legal systems on the bench.

Language diversity can be an extremely important issue with regard to the competence and effectiveness of the judges, particularly where the court has more than one official language.[166] An example of this is the ECtHR where the language skills of the judges have become a particularly problematic and controversial issue. In response to concerns that some recently appointed judges have not had adequate command of both French and English (and in some cases neither), the Parliamentary Assembly has imposed a requirement that 'candidates should possess an active knowledge of one official language of the Council of Europe and a passive knowledge of the other'.[167] At a purely practical level, the need for sufficient language skills in an international court is vital for judges to participate effectively in discussions and reading documents.[168] In more representational terms, the presence of language diversity is also a reflection of the broader diversity of the bench. Put another way, the dominance of one language on an international court suggests that the full range of cultural backgrounds does not have a voice (quite literally) amongst the judges.

Diversity of expertise is another emerging issue in the courts. The ICC has provided for the representation of judges with criminal law and international humanitarian law/human rights experience. This development has been picked up in the ACJHR Protocol that provides for the selection of judges with recognized competence and experience in international law and human rights law. Eight candidates from each of the two categories must be elected to the bench of sixteen judges.[169] Interviewees did not consider this type of requirement to

[165] The Honourable Mr Justice Jacob Wit, a Netherlands-trained judge from the Netherlands Antilles, a legal system based on Roman-Dutch law. Note that the Netherlands Antilles is not a contracting party to the court nor a member of CARICOM. The CCJ Agreement does not impose any requirement that the bench be comprised of judges from different legal systems.

[166] See Chapter 2 for a discussion of the importance of linguistic diversity on the ICJ and ICC and the efforts made by states to ensure that different languages are represented on the courts.

[167] Council of Europe Parliamentary Assembly, Recommendation 1646 (2009), *Nomination of candidates and election of judges to the European Court of Human Rights*, op.cit., para 4.4.

[168] Brandeis Institute for International Judges, *International Justice: past, present and future* (Brandeis University, 2009): <http://www.brandeis.edu/ethics/pdfs/internationaljustice/biij/BIIJ 2009.pdf> (Accessed 28 April 2010).

[169] ACJHR Protocol, Article 6.

be useful in the ICJ context, but it is possible these developments may influence other courts in the future as international law develops as a discipline.

At the outer edges of the debate on diversity are nascent discussions on ethnic diversity and the representation of minorities. The Committee on Legal Affairs and Human Rights of the Council of Europe Parliamentary Assembly has said that: 'Given the Court's mandate for the protection of the rights of all, the Assembly may wish to consider introducing other representation criteria (eg belonging to a visible minority) in the future'.[170] Such requirements may find a foothold in human rights courts and then be applied more widely.

Although many of the developments on diversity and representation are at an early stage, they demonstrate that there is increasing interest in the skills and attributes that are required to make up an effective international court. There is also more acceptance of the idea that legitimacy and diversity are closely connected.

F. Conclusion

Reforms to the processes for selecting the international judiciary, like those for the international court system itself, have been ad hoc, shaped by and responding to the particular functions and context of each court. This is particularly evident in relation to the two courts that are the subject of this study. The ICJ occupies a unique position as the principal judicial body of the United Nations. It depends upon the consent of parties to its jurisdiction over any particular case and by its nature must deal with issues which are inherently political and concerned with inter-governmental relations. These factors place real constraints on potential reforms. The ICC, in contrast, was established relatively recently, with much wider involvement and participation of practitioners, academics, NGOs and interest groups in the debate about its composition and selection process. Its specialized and less explicitly political criminal jurisdiction also focused greater attention on the professional experience and qualities needed on the bench. This context opened space in the debate on judicial selection for considerations of transparency and merit-based processes which are likely to be evident in future discussion about possible reforms. On the other hand, the fact that the ICC is a young court may make states hesitant to accept further limitations on their control over judicial appointments. Given the ICC's remit, there is significant interest in seeing how it functions in practice, and a period of confidence-building and the development of an ICC 'culture' and approach may be required before further reforms are contemplated.

[170] Parliamentary Assembly of the Council of Europe, Committee on Legal Affairs and Human Rights, 'Report: Nomination of candidates and election of judges to the European Court of Human Rights', op. cit., para 39.

Innovations in the ICC selection process, such as the gender balance requirements, are also a reflection of the fact that it is generally much easier to introduce forward-looking and more radical provisions at the point when a court is created than to institute such changes in established courts. Because the international court system is relatively new, and many courts have been created in the last two or three decades, novel developments in judicial selection are generally found in these younger courts. The result is that the lack of uniformity of practice, which has been identified throughout this work as a feature of the international judicial selection system, is likely to become more marked over time as new courts are created with selection systems which reflect contemporary concerns and may diverge quite notably from those of established courts. The creation of the first fully independent judicial appointments commission in the Caribbean Court of Justice is an example of this trend.

Nonetheless, despite this increasing diversity in the mechanisms, rules and practices of selecting international judges, there appears to be an emerging consensus in the various reform agendas as to the common challenges currently faced by those selection processes. In particular, the lack of openness, the excess of politicization, and the need for greater regard for issues of merit, diversity and representation have been key drivers of many recent changes or proposals for change. Although interviewees generally identified these problems as being of equal relevance in the ICJ and ICC, and most supported the reforms that have occurred in other courts, there was significant scepticism about the scope for root and branch reform in relation to either court, but most particularly the ICJ. It was generally thought unlikely that changes would be made in the near future to the formal nomination provisions set out in the ICJ Statute or the Rome Statute and most felt that it would be more realistic to look towards 'light-touch' reform. This conclusion was driven by the view that states prefer an unstructured process that allows room for political influence, and 'are very reluctant to being told how they should choose their candidates'.[171]

The degree of acceptance, and sometimes resignation, expressed by interviewees about the power of the status quo may, however, underestimate the longer-term influence of the newer courts. Moreover, the establishment of newer courts has tended to be marked by greater involvement of civil society and NGOs who have argued for transparency, fair processes and systems which ensure representation of certain sections of society such as women.[172] If this trend continues, and the gap between the processes of the older and newer courts widens, it is possible that the established courts will appear increasingly outmoded and may ultimately be compelled to introduce reforms if they are to retain credibility and legitimacy.

[171] T3, 16.

[172] See J. Limbach et al, *Judicial Independence: Law and Practice of Appointments to the European Court of Human Rights*, op. cit., 28.

6

Conclusions

The findings from this study present a mixed picture. On a number of issues there was a degree of consensus amongst those interviewed. In other areas, there were some sharp divergences of views, both in terms of factual understanding about the way the judicial selection processes currently function and about how they ought to work. Such disparate opinions are in themselves revealing of the lack of transparency and common standards in the processes we examined. However, out of these various perspectives a number of recurrent themes emerged. Some of these relate specifically to the ICJ and the ICC; others shed light on wider issues in the selection processes of the international courts more generally.

A. Summary of findings on the ICC and ICJ

For many states, representation on the ICJ or ICC is regarded as an opportunity to protect state interests, gain prestige and influence the jurisprudence of the international courts. Our findings show that whether or not individual states are successful in obtaining a seat depends to a considerable extent upon prevailing political and economic power relations and on bilateral agreements between states and regional blocks. Evidence of politicization is apparent at both the nomination and election stages. For both courts, nomination practices are fragmented, lacking in transparency, and highly varied. At one end of the spectrum, a few candidates emerge following a transparent and formal consultative process that focuses on merit; at the other end, it is not unusual for individuals to be selected as a result of overtly political considerations or even nepotism. Whatever form of nomination process is adopted, all nominated candidates must work their way through a highly politicized election process.

The interview data presents an indisputable picture of elections which are often barely distinguishable from elections to the political institutions of the international organizations. It is apparent that efforts to insulate ICC elections from politicized electoral practices have largely failed, so that selection to both the ICJ and ICC is seen as being part of a broader landscape of political elections, often with very limited regard for the judicial nature of the posts. Vote-trading, campaigning, and regional politicking invariably play a greater part in candidates' chance of being elected than considerations of individual merit. Equally significant for any candidate's prospects of success is the political influence of his or her state in its regional group or its membership of the UN P5 grouping.

The importance of political and economic factors is such that states with less leverage will inevitably find that their candidates are disadvantaged. The point was put in a pithy comment from one unsuccessful ICC candidate: 'I don't think I lost because I am bad and had I won, it would not have been because I am good.'[1]

Yet although the interview evidence indicates that merit is often a secondary factor in the selection processes, this does not mean that successful candidates necessarily lack quality. A wide range of views are held as to the effects of politicization on the outcome of judicial elections for the ICJ and the ICC. Some feel that the system generally leads to the appointment of good judges, whether because of or despite the system. Others, however, are less sanguine, believing that it sometimes results in good candidates being overlooked and, on occasion, even produces manifestly unqualified judges.

One indirect effect of the importance of the 'electability' of candidates is to limit successful nominations to those individuals who are thought to have the right sort of international profile and are known in the right networks or circles. This is particularly the case for the ICJ, where a disproportionately high number of successful candidates emerge from an international network of UN bodies, including the Security Council and the International Law Commission. The effect is that the pool of judicial candidates is smaller than might otherwise be the case. This, in turn, has a direct impact on the composition of the two courts.

Both the ICJ and the ICC are subject to statutory requirements on the minimum qualifications for individual judges and on the composition of the bench as a whole. In form, at least, these requirements appear to be strikingly different. The ICJ has minimal criteria for the selection of individual judges and the rules governing the composition of the bench are largely based on practices and conventions that have emerged over the past six decades. By contrast, the ICC has detailed criteria for individual selection and overall bench requirements, focusing on the need to ensure a balanced composition of expertise in subject areas, regional geographical representation and gender. Unlike the ICJ, the ICC is not subject to any convention guaranteeing certain states a seat on the court. These differences are the consequences of variations in the political and historical contexts of the courts: the ICJ operates in the entrenched, political environment that is the UN, whereas the ICC operates, at least in formal terms, in a non-UN environment.

Despite the differences, the composition rules of neither court seem to command universal or even wide respect, and persuasive doubts have been expressed as to whether the ICC approach has led to any overall improvement in the make-up

[1] T32, 14.

of the bench. What is less clear is how the ideal make-up of the courts should be achieved. Geographical representation remains the lodestar for both courts and a key indicator for perceptions of legitimacy and authority among states. Given the extent to which powerful states are advantaged by the current selection processes, with their emphasis on campaigning and vote-trading, geographical representation rules play an important role in redressing the political imbalance in the system. Without rules which ensure some degree of representation for less politically powerful regions it is likely that the dominance of the 'great powers' on the courts would be even more marked. To some extent, the sub-regional representation conventions that have evolved within some regional groups could be seen in turn to ensure additional balance at the regional level. Vital though it is, however, geographical representation will always, to some extent, be in tension with merit-based selection. Whether or not it overrides other considerations depends on the value placed on merit-based selection criteria and qualifications.

The evidence indicates that a number of factors other than geographical representation are taken into account in nomination and election decisions: the need to ensure a place for different legal systems, for linguistic diversity, for specialized legal expertise, and for equitable gender representation. Some favour formal rules for prioritizing these characteristics, others feel that quotas or rigid formulae risk undermining selection decisions. This division of opinion is particularly evident in relation to gender balance in the courts, which has only recently found its way onto the agenda. While there is almost universal lip service paid to the need for a mix of women and men on the bench, the minimum gender requirements for the ICC, which have achieved this outcome, remain controversial. Lack of judicial experience on the two courts, particularly the ICC, is also a developing source of tension. For the ICC in particular, many would like to see more judges selected with national or international judicial experience, and concerns have been expressed that diplomats and civil servants, as well as academics, may not always have the professional experience to create the settled international jurisprudence that could enhance legitimacy and effectiveness.

B. The broader relevance of the findings—trends and reforms

Many of these concerns are not unique to the ICJ and ICC. Issues of politicization, lack of transparency and the balance between geographical and other selection criteria have relevance across all the international courts. The specifics inevitably differ from court to court, but our research reveals recurring general themes.

One way to try to make sense of this evidence is to relate it to the debates and context of judiciaries at national level. Here, after all, we can draw on a much more developed body of principles and rules, established conventions and academic literature on the role of the courts and the judicial appointments processes.

Many of the debates about politicization and representation in the international judiciary and much of the language used and solutions proposed in the interviews have direct resonance with those at national level.

Nor is the relationship between the national and international selection processes of purely academic interest. In practice it is clear that there is increasing interaction between the two levels of court, with judges moving from one to the other, lawyers practising in both, and academics engaging in comparative study of the two justice systems. The judgments of international courts are also of growing relevance at the national level. If this trend continues, it is likely that there will be pressure towards greater cross-influences between national and international level judicial selection procedures. Each might draw inspiration from the other, developing procedures as deemed politically appropriate. The emergence of a 'global community' of judges is likely to enhance this tendency.[2] In the light of this trend, the movement towards more independent, transparent, diverse, and merit-based selection procedures in many national courts should be seen as significant in establishing certain judicial selection norms that may increasingly filter through into the international nomination process.[3] This could eventually result in harmonization of national and international nomination procedures or at least the harmonization of international nomination procedures in a particular state, taking into account the needs of the two processes in each state.[4]

While closer links between international and national courts and selection processes look likely, it is more difficult to discern from the findings the probable direction of other trends in the years ahead, given that two apparently contradictory patterns can be identified. On the one hand, there is evidence of greater political involvement in some selection processes, with more emphasis on campaigning, vote-trading and backroom 'deal-making' between states, strengthening the role of the more powerful states and the interests they represent.[5] On the other hand, the findings suggest increasing pressure on the P5 convention and moves towards greater professionalization, with the introduction of more rule-based, open and formalized practices. Given the very dynamic and diverse nature of the international court system, it may take some time and further study to gain a clearer picture of how these different trends will play out. What is more apparent from

[2] This may also have the benefit of promoting the recognition and application of the decisions of international courts in national courts. It would provide a kind of vertical integration to complement the horizontal integration of international judges over recent years. For a more general discussion of these issues see A-M. Slaughter, 'A Global Community of Courts' *Harvard International Law Journal* 44(1) (2003) 191.

[3] As an intermediate step, there may also be a role for greater consultation with national senior judicial selection bodies.

[4] See the Slovenian legislation and the Finnish proposals referred to in Chapter 3, n 4.

[5] M. Wood, 'The Selection of Candidates for International Judicial Office: Recent Practice' in Tafsir Malick Ndiaye and Rüdiger Wolfrum (eds), *Law of the Sea, Environmental Law and Settlement of Disputes: Liber Amicorum Judge Thomas A. Mensah* (The Hague: Martinus Nijhoff Publishers, 2007) 357–68, 357.

our research is that there is room within the current selection processes of the ICJ and ICC, at least, for procedures to encourage greater independence and transparency and the promotion of approaches that emphasize merit.

Any proposal for reform in relation to judicial appointments should start with the caveat that the role of the procedures and practices in determining the nature and quality of the courts should not be overstated. 'An entity is only as good as the individuals that are nominated and elected. We can have the best procedure and criteria, but that doesn't guarantee you a great court.'[6] The purpose of this research project was not to assess the merits of the judges elected to the ICJ and ICC or elsewhere. But our findings do indicate real concerns that weaknesses in the selection processes may sometimes lead to a failure to select the very best possible candidates from the broadest pool of qualified individuals. These fears, whether fully justified or not, are likely to damage the legitimacy and effectiveness of the courts. The general lack of transparency in the processes at both national and international levels only serves to make criticisms of this kind more likely.

If the quality of the courts is a product of the quality of those individuals who stand as judges, then whether high-quality candidates are willing and able to put themselves forward, and whether they are selected if they do so, depends on a range of factors. Some of these lie outside the scope of this study, such as the reputation and prestige of the courts in different legal and political cultures, and the pay and conditions of judicial office. But there is little doubt that the selection procedures, the individual selection criteria and the collective composition rules are vital factors in shaping the courts and therefore the concerns about the selection processes revealed in this study are significant. Questions have been raised which indirectly affect the competence, legitimacy and independence of the courts, and the prospects for the future development of the international rule of law.

In thinking about how to address some of the concerns raised in this research, one of our governing principles had to be respect for the diversity of the international courts—in relation to the types of judicial selection processes and also the composition of the courts themselves. Just as it is clear that there is no 'ideal international judge' so there is no 'ideal court'. Each court needs a different type of judge, and equally each court requires a wide range of members on its bench, whatever its particular function. The fact that there are such divergent views about the relative merits of different judicial backgrounds and characteristics suggests that it is not always easy to predict, on the basis of prior experience, who will prove to be an excellent judge once on the bench. The presence of judges with backgrounds in academia, politics, national judiciaries, and other international courts is likely to enhance and enrich the understanding and decision-making of the courts. Similarly, a gender balance as well as cultural and legal diversity

[6] T4, 19.

amongst the judges will potentially deepen the quality of judicial deliberations as well as strengthening the legitimacy of the courts.

The need to allow for this diversity in judicial composition as well as to take account of the different functional and historical contexts of each court means that a variety of selection processes will always be necessary and appropriate. There cannot be a one-size-fits-all approach to judicial selection. There are, however, some important general principles which are applicable to all courts. International conventions and minimum standards on judicial independence clearly articulate that selection processes must be based on merit and must be independent and impartial, as well as being seen to be so. In 2004, the Study Group of the International Law Association on the Practice and Procedure of International Courts and Tribunals produced the Burgh House Principles on the Independence of the International Judiciary which distilled some of these principles:

> 2.1 In accordance with the governing instruments, judges shall be chosen from among persons of high moral character, integrity and conscientiousness, who posses the appropriate professional qualifications, competence and experience required for the court concerned.
>
> 2.2 While procedures for nomination, election and appointment should consider fair representation of different geographic regions and the principal legal systems, as appropriate, as well as of female and male judges, appropriate personal and professional qualifications must be the overriding consideration in the nomination, election and appointment of judges.
>
> 2.3. Procedures for the nomination, election and appointment of judges should be transparent and provide appropriate safeguards against nominations, elections and appointments motivated by improper considerations.
>
> 2.4. Information regarding the nomination, election and appointment process and information about candidates for judicial office should be made public, in due time and in an effective manner, by the international organization or other body responsible for the nomination, election and appointment process.[7]

Our findings suggest that these principles command support, and even beyond these very general propositions, a range of 'second-tier' principles can be identified which can be applied within broadly similar selection models, such as the nomination and election systems used by the ICJ and ICC. Inevitably, the more specific these are, the more controversial they become and the less of a consensus they command. Nevertheless, some more detailed changes seem to us to be justified by the research findings. In particular, there is a need for reforms which ensure

[7] The Study Group of the International Law Association on the Practice and Procedure of International Courts and Tribunals, in association with the Project on International Courts and Tribunals, *The Burgh House Principles on the Independence of the International Judiciary*; available at: <http://www.ucl.ac.uk/laws/cict/docs/burgh_final_21204.pdf> (accessed 2 December 2008). See also P. Sands, C. McLachlan and R. Mackenzie, 'The Burgh House Principles on the Independence of the International Judiciary' *The Law and Practice of International Courts and Tribunals* 4 (2005) 247–60.

greater transparency at the nomination stage, including better and more open information about candidates and potential candidates through mechanisms such as guidelines on advertising posts, the use of model curricula vitae and interview panels. These should be coupled with efforts to expand the selection pool through proactive efforts to seek out highly qualified candidates who might not be as visible as those in the traditional networks. At the same time, the development of more formalized and specific selection criteria should be considered, setting out the competencies required for different posts. Developments in newer courts and reforms in older courts such as the ECtHR, as well as reforms at national court level, show that these sorts of changes are both possible and effective.

Such reforms are not intended to alter the intrinsic nature of the system nor threaten the diversity of the international judicial selection processes. The aim instead is to enhance the rigour, fairness and transparency of the systems so that unjustified or politically motivated decision-making is less likely to occur and, if it does, has more chance of being scrutinized and challenged. This study has shown that it is difficult enough to reach a consensus about the sort of experiences, qualities and characteristics that should be prioritized in a merit-based judicial selection process. Merit is a slippery and open-ended concept and there is room for reasonable people to reach different conclusions on what it means and how it should be evidenced. But the chances of selecting the very best and—perhaps more pertinently for the international courts—*only* the very best, recedes as more powerful political considerations come into play.

That said, just as we recognize that the selection processes make up only one part of the whole picture of how the international courts are constructed, we do not wish to overstate the dangers of political influences in a judicial selection process. The system of international courts and tribunals remains in the early stages of development. Few are more overtly political that the US Supreme Court, yet it has undoubtedly produced many first-rate judges. It is perhaps less the presence of politics per se in the international judicial selection processes which is a cause for concern than the particular nature of that politicization. It is both endemic and, in contrast to the US Supreme Court, almost completely lacking in public scrutiny or political accountability. This potentially toxic combination threatens the long-term stability, effectiveness and authority of international courts. In practice, states will not contemplate giving up control over elections; nor, arguably, should powerful judicial decision-makers be selected through processes which are wholly disconnected from elected governments. Nevertheless, we would argue that urgent steps need to be taken to limit the growing and pervasive role of extraneous political factors in order to ensure that politics does not overwhelm the prospects for selecting the very best judges for the international courts.

APPENDIX 1
Research Methodology

A. Background

The two courts chosen to be the focus of the study, the International Court of Justice (ICJ) and the International Criminal Court (ICC), were selected primarily because they are broadly representative of the two different models of international judicial nomination and election procedures. As the older institution, the International Court of Justice applies rules and procedures based on those of its predecessor, the Permanent Court of International Justice. These provide only minimum individual selection criteria and requirements for the overall composition of the bench, while the guidance for the conduct of elections is purely advisory. In contrast, the International Criminal Court represents a newer and more formalized judicial selection model. It applies a complex procedure for the nomination and election of judges and formal rules which are designed to ensure a balance in the composition of the court, based on geographical representation, gender and legal expertise.

The literature search and background paper prepared at the beginning of the project indicated that there was little academic writing on this subject and scant information available in the public domain. This project is therefore one of the first attempts to gather detailed information on the nomination and election processes for international judges. The key to this subject appeared to be finding out what happens in practice, rather than assessing formal legal rules, so the project team focused the research on gathering baseline empirical qualitative and quantitative data.

The empirical research involved three main phases: (1) a questionnaire on national nomination processes which was distributed to a wide range of international judicial, legal, and governmental actors; (2) interviews with staff members (based in New York) of the Permanent Missions to the United Nations of a range of countries to elicit information on lobbying and election procedures; and (3) nine country case studies in different regions of the world to conduct interviews with key actors at the national level to gather more in-depth information about how candidates are selected for the ICJ and ICC.

The project was guided by an advisory committee, comprised of pre-eminent experts on international law, chaired by Lord Woolf, former Lord Chief Justice of England and Wales. The advisory committee was consulted on an ongoing basis as to the focus, structure and conduct of the research. However, it was clear that all responsibility for the research would rest with the project team.

An important methodological decision had to be taken early in the project as to whether the project should review the election of individual candidates. In conjunction with the advisory committee, it was decided that in light of the project objectives it would not be appropriate or desirable to scrutinize individual cases. Rather, the project should focus, as the first extensive empirical study in this field, on the broader processes and issues raised by the nomination and election of international judges. It was determined that the data on nominations and elections would be gathered through the use of survey questionnaires and interviews.

B. Questionnaires

In late 2006, a questionnaire consisting of twenty-three multiple and free text questions was prepared to obtain factual information on the national nomination processes for judges of the ICC and ICJ and, where possible, information on election procedures. As recommended by the project advisory committee, a consultant survey instrument analyst was engaged to review the draft questionnaire.

In January and February 2007, the questionnaire was widely distributed in both hard copy and electronic formats. The target respondents were:

- relevant staff members of the Permanent Missions to the United Nations in New York, including legal advisers and election officers;
- academics;
- Members of the Permanent Court of Arbitration national groups (a selection of PCA national groups members from a range of countries was made, from the list available on the PCA website based on geography, language, legal culture and previous nominations);
- Ministry of Foreign Affairs and Ministry of Justice Legal Advisers (again selected on the basis of geography, language, legal culture and previous nominations);
- contacts from the Fifth Session of the Assembly of States Parties to the Rome Statute of the International Criminal Court in The Hague in November 2006; and
- other relevant individuals identified through contacts of the project team.

The questionnaire was also distributed on an ad hoc basis to interviewees and other persons, and posted on the internet (accessible by the use of a password that was emailed to recipients). Forty-six responses were initially received, spread over the different groups. Respondents were asked to recommend further contacts so as to expand the 'snowball' sample of interviewees.

C. Interviews in New York

In early 2007, interview invitations were sent to 182 staff from the Permanent Missions in New York. This list was based on the frequency of previous nominations and successful campaigns, previous cases before the ICJ and regional, sub-regional and linguistic spread. In March 2007, interviews were conducted with nineteen staff from Permanent Missions to the United Nations from seventeen countries and a number of United Nations staff members. The Permanent Mission staff interviewed ranged from Permanent Representatives to Third Secretaries and, where possible, included the legal advisers and the election officers for those missions that have these posts.

The interviews broadly followed a question guide that focused on aspects of judicial appointments of most concern and relevance to Permanent Mission staff: the lobbying and election procedures. Recommendations were sought as to potential interviewees in their particular countries, with a view to gathering information for the selection of countries in which to base case studies. Less structured contacts of this nature were also made at the Fifth and Sixth Sessions of the Assembly of States Parties to the Rome Statute of the International Criminal Court in The Hague in 2006 and New York in 2007.

D. Case studies

Methodology for selection of case study countries

To gather further detailed information on the national processes for the nomination of candidates to the ICJ and ICC, it was decided that between six and ten country-based case studies would be conducted. The objective was not to gather detailed information on individual countries with a view to producing separate studies on those countries' nominations processes; rather, it was to gather contextualized information across countries representing different geographical regions, legal cultures, levels of economic development, languages and political systems, and to study the process of judicial nominations and the interactions of the key local actors in discrete national contexts. It was also anticipated that each national context would have its own relationship with the regional and international levels. The intention was to gather data that would serve to highlight key issues generally arising in the nomination of candidates to the ICJ and ICC, with sufficient regard to variations across different regions, legal cultures and other factors. This data would then be used in the discussion of key thematic issues.

The selection of the countries to form the case studies in July 2007 was a particularly important decision for the project. In order to make the selection, the project team considered the data gathered in the preliminary research and consulted with the advisory committee. Then, based on this information and guidance, a list of criteria for the selection of countries was determined (not in order of importance):

1) Countries from all UN regional groups, and where funding allows, sub-regional groups;
2) One or two Permanent Members of the Security Council;
3) Countries that represent a range of legal systems and legal cultures;
4) Countries that represent different linguistic groupings (at least francophone, anglophone and hispanophone countries);
5) Developed and developing countries;
6) Countries with a previous record of nominations and perhaps also a record of successful campaigns to either ICJ or ICC or, ideally, both;
7) Countries with different national judicial appointment processes (ranging from strong executive involvement, judicial appointment commissions, parliamentary involvement, etc), which may or may not be applied to international judicial nominations and different international judicial nomination procedures (ie in those

countries where there is no Permanent Court of Arbitration national group to make ICJ nominations);
8) Countries of interest in light of recent elections to the ICJ and the ICC.

A key variable was the need for states selected for the case study to have some experience of making nominations and conducting campaigns for the ICJ and/or the ICC. In the light of this, a table was prepared setting out the number of nominations and successful elections by every country for the ICJ and ICC. Countries were then ranked by UN regional group in accordance with the frequency with which they had nominated candidates. Based on this information, a preliminary list of approximately twenty potential countries was produced in accordance with the criteria set out above. Where possible, the project team sought to ensure that overall, the list met the stated criteria to provide a balanced group of countries with a reasonably high overall level of previous nominations to the ICJ and ICC.

The preliminary list was then reduced to a 'long list' of approximately fifteen countries, to which two further countries were added on the advice of the advisory committee. This was done primarily through reconsidering the above criteria in addition to practical aspects, namely, the project budget, staff capacity, prospects for obtaining a sufficient number of interviews. The list was separated into a 'likely' list of eleven countries and a 'reserve' list of six countries.

Additional research was then completed on the seventeen countries to gather information on the previous nominations made by each country, current international judges and International Law Commission members, the national procedures for international nominations (if known), the processes for judicial appointments to the highest courts at the national level, potential interviewees, and likely cost. It also sought to identify key government and non-government contacts in each country who could be approached for advice as to the feasibility and conduct of the case study. For the 'likely' countries, these individuals were contacted and the majority provided input on potential interviewees and the likelihood of obtaining interviews. Based on this information, the 'long list' was reduced to a final list of nine countries.

Case study methodology

Prior to each case study, invitation letters were sent to potential interviewees that included an interview question guide, setting out in detail the proposed interview questions and aspects relating to recording and confidentiality. The interviews focused on nomination processes and, where relevant, they also covered lobbying and election procedures. They were not specifically focused on particular nominations; however, questions were posed relating to individual nominations to obtain information on general nomination processes. They also covered nominations to courts other than the ICJ and ICC at the regional and international levels and sought to elicit comparisons with national judicial nomination processes.

In each case study country, invitation letters were sent to a range of government representatives, Permanent Court of Arbitration national group members, Bar Association representatives, senior judges, academics and NGO representatives. The objective was to interview people both within and outside of the relevant processes, including former candidates and judges. Potential interviewees were determined based on a review of

United Nations documents, Permanent Court of Arbitration documents, documents from organizations such as the International Law Association and the Institut du Droit International, and internet-based research. Potential interviewees were also identified through the project team's contacts and by personal recommendations of other interviewees. In many cases, a 'snowball' effect developed, with interviewees recommending other potential interviewees and so on. We sought to ensure the inclusion of those people who would bring a range of perspectives and personal or institutional interests; for example, we wanted to interview both successful and unsuccessful judicial candidates.

As a result of the sensitivity of the data being sought, interviews were conducted on a confidential basis, to ensure that the most detailed information could be gathered without interviewees being concerned that they could be identified. The interview invitation stated that any statements made in an interview would not be attributed to the interviewee in resulting project publications, except with prior agreement. Interviewees were also informed that in the final project outputs, every effort would be made to draft the text to avoid identification of the interviewee or any individuals referred to. Furthermore, the interviewee's name would not appear in the list of interviewees unless otherwise agreed. To ensure the highest level of confidentiality, it was subsequently decided that even a partial list of interviewees would not be included in this publication.

Interviewees were informed that the interview would be recorded and verbal consent for tape-recording was obtained at the outset of the interview. The vast majority of interviewees agreed to be tape-recorded and masked transcripts were made of those interviews for internal use by the project team.

The interviews were conducted on a semi-structured 'funnel' format, with the interview commencing with more general issues before focusing on more detailed questions, according to the role and knowledge of the interviewee. The interview guide was not followed strictly and interviews developed organically in a conversational style. The majority of interviews were of around one hour in duration, with some significantly longer.

Where possible, the project team sought to verify and 'triangulate' data gathered through other interviews. This was done by raising questions with interviewees which would verify information provided by other interviewees, and also by undertaking external research so as to reveal any baseline assumptions and to verify factual information provided.

During the period October 2007 to May 2008, nine country-specific case studies were conducted, mainly by in-country visits, supplemented by telephone interviews. Each case study was of approximately three to five days in duration, depending on the number of positive interview responses received. In each country, approximately eight to ten interviews were conducted. The majority were conducted in English but some were also conducted in Spanish through an interpreter, or directly in French.

Analysis and presentation of data

In total, 106 interviews of approximately one hour's duration were conducted, which yielded some 82 interview transcripts and 50 file notes.

Data analysis was undertaken on a thematic basis, working from the written transcripts, file notes and other research materials. Further background documentary research was undertaken to supplement the base data gathered in the literature search completed at the start of the project. In the light of the absence of an existing body of academic work on these processes, it was considered appropriate to use direct quotes from the interviews, where possible, with relatively little deconstruction. We considered that the language itself used by the interviewees revealed key assumptions and issues. It is through these direct quotes that the political and personal context of these processes became apparent to us, so we have sought to use them wherever possible, and have made only limited grammatical amendments to them. Where quotations are used in the text of this book, or where specific observations made by interviewees are referred to, citations are given in the footnotes to the relevant interview transcripts (T) or file notes (F).

A draft discussion paper was prepared in July–September 2008 setting out the project findings in relation to a limited number of key issues. This paper formed the basis of discussions at an expert seminar, convened in New York in September 2008, to bring together members of the Permanent Missions, academics, lawyers, judges and other commentators to seek their comments on the preliminary outputs. The comments gathered during this one-day seminar shaped the form of the final project findings.

APPENDIX 2

The Jurisdiction and the Judicial Selection Procedures of the ICJ and ICC

A. The jurisdiction of the International Court of Justice

As the principal judicial organ of the UN, the ICJ has a global remit. It has two main areas of jurisdictional competence:

- To decide, in accordance with international law,[1] international disputes submitted to it by parties, and all matters provided for under the UN Charter or under international conventions or treaties (known as the 'contentious jurisdiction');[2]
- To render advisory opinions on legal questions submitted to it by the organs of the UN and other authorized agencies[3] (known as the 'advisory jurisdiction'[4]).

The contentious jurisdiction of the court is not compulsory and operates only with the consent of the parties. There are three main bases on which consent can be provided. First, by making a declaration under what is known as the 'Optional Clause':

The states parties to the present Statute may at any time declare that they recognize as compulsory ipso facto and without special agreement, in relation to any other state accepting the same obligation, the jurisdiction of the Court in all legal disputes concerning:

a. the interpretation of a treaty;
b. any question of international law;
c. the existence of any fact which, if established, would constitute a breach of an international obligation;
d. the nature or extent of the reparation to be made for the breach of an international obligation.[5]

At present, sixty-six states have made declarations recognizing the jurisdiction of the court to be compulsory.[6]

[1] ICJ Statute, Article 38(1) (all references in sections A and B of this Appendix are to the ICJ Statute unless otherwise stated). The court also has power to decide a case *ex aequo et bono* if the parties so agree: Article 38(2).

[2] Article 36(1).

[3] UN Charter, Article 96. For the Organs and Agencies of the United Nations Authorized to Request Advisory Opinions, see: <http://www.icj-cij.org/jurisdiction/index.php?p1=5&p2=2&p3=1> (Accessed 18 March 2010).

[4] Part IV.

[5] Article 36(2).

[6] Information on the declarations and any relevant reservations made by these states is available on the ICJ website: <http://www.icj-cij.org/jurisdiction/index.php?p1=5&p2=1&p3=3> (Accessed 18 March 2010).

Second, where the relevant states are parties to a treaty or convention that confers jurisdiction on the court, this is taken to represent consent by the parties.[7] Third, states may agree at any time to submit a matter to the court by notification of a 'special agreement'.[8]

Only states can be parties in cases before the court,[9] although international organizations may be asked to submit information relevant to a case to the court or may present such information on their own initiative.[10] Where a constitutive instrument or convention concluded under the auspices of a particular international organization are to be interpreted, the court must inform the organization and provide copies of the written proceedings.[11] States may be requested by the court to submit information in relation to requests for advisory opinions.[12]

The decisions of the court are binding only between the parties to the particular dispute.[13] Under Article 94 of the UN Charter, states undertake to comply with decisions of the court and may request the Security Council to 'make recommendations or decide upon measures to be taken to give effect to the judgment' as it deems necessary. Any such decisions of the Security Council would be subject to the veto of the five permanent members.

B. The nomination and election of ICJ judges

Composition requirements

The Statute of the Court provides that the ICJ is composed of fifteen independent judges (referred to by the Statute as the 'members of the Court')[14] elected, without regard to nationality, by the General Assembly and the Security Council.[15]

Article 2 provides that the judges must be of high moral character and either:

- possess the qualifications required in their respective countries for appointment to the highest judicial offices; *or*
- be jurisconsults of recognized competence in international law.

The judges elected to the ICJ must each be of a different nationality.[16] Article 9 of the Statute recommends that states elect a body of judges that is representative of the main forms of civilization and the principal legal systems of the world.

Nomination procedures

The national groups in the Permanent Court of Arbitration (PCA) nominate candidates for election to the ICJ.[17] National groups consist of the four individuals that states parties are entitled to nominate under the 1899 and 1907 Hague Conventions for the Pacific

[7] For the relevant treaties and conventions, see <http://www.icj-cij.org/jurisdiction/index.php?p1=5&p2=1&p3=4> (Accessed 18 March 2010).

[8] By special agreement under Article 40(1).

[9] Article 34(1), see also Article 35. [10] Article 34(2). [11] Article 34(3).

[12] Article 66(2). [13] Article 59. [14] Articles 2 and 3. [15] Articles 2 and 4(1).

[16] Article 3. [17] Article 4(1).

Settlement of International Disputes to be placed on a roster of arbitrators maintained by the PCA International Bureau.[18]

If a UN member state is not represented on the PCA, candidates are nominated by that state through national groups set up on the same basis as the national groups of the PCA.[19]

More than three months before the date of the election and no more than one month after a vacancy has arisen,[20] the Secretary-General of the UN must send a written request to the members of the PCA of the parties to the ICJ Statute and the national groups established under Article 4(2) to nominate potential candidates by a specified date.[21] The Security Council sets the date for the election.[22]

National groups may nominate up to four candidates,[23] of which a maximum of two may be of the same nationality as the national group.[24] The Statute also provides that '[i]n no case may the number of candidates nominated by a group be more than double the number of seats to be filled'[25] which would apply in casual elections, where there may be only one seat available.

Before nominations are returned, 'each national group is recommended to consult with its highest court of justice, its legal faculties and schools of law, and its national academies and national sections of international academies devoted to the study of law'.[26]

The nominations are submitted to the Secretary-General of the UN who produces an alphabetical list of the individuals nominated,[27] which also includes a list of the national group(s) that have nominated those candidates. Except as provided in Article 12(2) (which is discussed in the next section), no other person is eligible for election.[28] The Secretary-General of the UN then submits the list of candidates to the General Assembly and the Security Council.[29] The curricula vitae of candidates are circulated prior to elections.[30]

Election procedures

The judges of the ICJ are elected by the General Assembly and the Security Council from the list of persons nominated by the national groups in the PCA.[31] The General Assembly and the Security Council are to elect judges to the court 'independently of one another'.[32]

[18] PCA members must be of known competency in international law and have a high moral reputation (1899 Hague Convention, Article 23; 1907 Hague Convention, Article 44). More than one state may select the same individual to act as a PCA member. PCA members serve six-year renewable terms. The list is transmitted periodically by the PCA International Bureau to the parties to the 1899 and 1907 Hague Conventions (1899 Hague Convention, Article 23; 1907 Hague Convention, Article 44) and is available at <http://www.pca-cpa.org/showpage.asp?pag_id=1041> (Accessed 18 March 2010).

[19] Article 4(2).

[20] Articles 5 and 14.

[21] Article 5(1).

[22] Article 14.

[23] Article 5(2).

[24] Article 5(2).

[25] Article 5(2).

[26] Article 6.

[27] Article 7(1).

[28] Article 7(1).

[29] Article 7(2).

[30] See, for example, United Nations General Assembly and United Nations Security Council, *Curricula Vitae of Candidates Nominated by National Groups: Note by the Secretary-General*, UN Doc. A/63/188-S/2008/504.

[31] Article 4(1). See also regarding general procedure: United Nations General Assembly, *Rules of Procedure of the General Assembly*, UN Doc. A/520/Rev.15, Rules 150 and 151 and United Nations Security Council, *Provisional Rules of Procedure of the Security Council*, UN Doc. S/96/Rev.7, Rules 40 and 61.

[32] Article 8.

If a state is not a member of the UN but a party to the ICJ Statute, it may participate in judicial elections on the conditions laid down by the General Assembly, on the recommendation of the Security Council.[33]

Article 9 seeks to encourage states to have some regard to diversity of representation on the bench in casting their votes, hence '[a]t every election, the electors shall bear in mind not only that the persons to be elected should individually possess the qualifications required, but also that in the body as a whole the representation of the main forms of civilization and of the principal legal systems of the world should be assured'.

It has been noted that, in practice, the ICJ consists of five judges from the five permanent members of the Security Council and ten additional judges from the different geographical regions of the world.[34] The court follows the principle of 'equitable geographical distribution' that distributes the fifteen seats of the court in accordance with the five UN General Assembly geographical groups, which in turn follow the distribution of membership of the Security Council. As a result, Africa has three seats, GRULAC two seats, Asia three seats, WEOG five seats and Eastern Europe two seats. As judges from the five permanent members of the Security Council are always elected to the court, in what is informally referred to as the 'P5 convention', the seats available to non-P5 members of WEOG and Asia are reduced respectively to two and Eastern Europe to one.[35]

At the election, each state has the same number of votes as the number of vacancies on the court. A candidate is elected when he or she obtains an absolute majority of votes in both the General Assembly and the Security Council.[36] If more than one national of a particular state obtains the absolute majority of the General Assembly and the Security Council, the oldest candidate is taken to be elected.[37]

Traditionally in the General Assembly and in the Security Council, '[t]he consistent practice of the United Nations has been to interpret the words "absolute majority" as meaning a majority of all electors, whether or not they vote or are allowed to vote. The electors in the General Assembly will be all 192 Member States. Accordingly, 97 votes constitutes an absolute majority in the Assembly for those elections...In the Security Council, eight votes constitutes an absolute majority and no distinction is made between permanent and non-permanent members of the Council (Article 10, paragraph 2, ICJ Statute)'.[38]

[33] Article 4(3); Article 93(2), UN Charter and United Nations General Assembly, *Conditions Under Which, a State that is a Party to the Statute of the International Court of Justice, but not a Member of the United Nations, May Participate in Elections of Members of the Court,* GA Res. 264 (III) (8 October 1948).

[34] Philippe Sands, Ruth Mackenzie, and Yuval Shany (eds), *Manual on International Courts and Tribunals* (London: Butterworths, 1999) para 1.5.

[35] S. Rosenne, *Rosenne's The World Court: What It Is and How It Works*, Legal Aspects of International Organization Series No. 41, edited by Terry D. Gill (6th revised edn, Leiden: Martinus Nijhoff, 2003) 44–9 and <http://www.icj-cij.org/court/index.php?p1=1&p2=2> (Accessed 18 March 2010).

[36] Article 10(1). [37] Article 10(3).

[38] United Nations General Assembly and Security Council, *Election of five members of the International Court of Justice. Memorandum by the Secretary-General*, UN Doc. A/63/186-S/2008/502 (30 July 2008), paras 8–9. This document also sets down the procedural rules in relation to independent General Assembly and Security Council voting and general voting procedure.

If seats remain to be filled, a second and, if necessary, a third round of elections may be held.[39] If seats are vacant after the third round, Article 12 provides for a six-member 'joint conference', that may be established at any time on the request of either the General Assembly or the Security Council. Three of the joint conference members are appointed by the General Assembly and three by the Security Council. The joint conference selects, by an absolute majority, one name for each vacant seat, and then submits the names to the General Assembly and Security Council for their 'respective acceptance'. If the joint conference unanimously agrees on a person who was not nominated but who fulfils the individual requirements to be a judge of the ICJ, that person may be included on the list.[40]

Under Article 12(3), if the joint conference is of the opinion that it will not be able to fill the vacant seats, the judges already elected must fill the vacant seats by selection from those candidates who received votes in the General Assembly or Security Council. The voting requirements under Article 12(3) are not defined in the Statute.

Term of judicial office, re-election and vacancies

Judges are elected to the ICJ for a term of nine years and may be re-elected.[41] The term of office runs from 6 February of the year in which the vacancy arises, unless the judge has been elected to fill a vacancy for a judge whose term has not yet expired, in which case, it will run from the date of election.[42]

As discussed above, to ensure the continuity in the court, the ICJ Statute provides for staggered elections so that no more than five ordinary vacancies arise every three years. Therefore, immediately after the first elections, lots were drawn by the Secretary-General of the UN, selecting five judges for an initial term of three years and five judges for an initial term of six years.[43]

When the term of a judge has expired, the judge continues to undertake his or her duties until the vacancy is filled, and, when he or she is replaced, the judge completes any ongoing cases.[44]

When a judge resigns, his or her resignation is addressed to the President of the Court who then conveys it to the Secretary-General of the UN. On this notification, the seat becomes vacant.[45] When a judge is dismissed by the unanimous decision of the bench for failure to meet the required conditions, his or her seat becomes vacant upon notification of the Secretary-General of the UN by the Registrar of the Court.[46]

A judge elected to replace a judge whose term has not expired serves only the remainder of his or her predecessor's term[47] but is then eligible for re-election.

Ad hoc judges

If a party to a case before the court does not have a judge of its nationality on the bench, it may appoint an ad hoc judge to sit on the case.[48] Ad hoc judges must meet

[39] Article 11. [40] Article 12(2). [41] Article 13(1).
[42] Rules of Court, Article 2, 1 July 1978, ICJ Acts and Documents concerning the Organization of the Court, No. 5 (1990). [43] Article 13(1) and (2).
[44] Article 13(3). [45] Article 13(4). [46] Article 18. [47] Article 15.
[48] Article 31(2) and (3).

the same service requirements as the permanent judges and they participate in the deliberations of the court on an equal basis with other judges.[49] An ad hoc judge need not be of the nationality of his or her appointing state, but should preferably be chosen from amongst those candidates previously nominated for election to the ICJ.[50] Ad hoc judges may also be appointed to ad hoc chambers under Article 26 of the Statute.[51]

C. The jurisdiction of the International Criminal Court

The ICC has jurisdiction over individuals in relation to 'the most serious crimes of concern to the international community as a whole'; in particular, crimes of genocide, crimes against humanity, and war crimes, including grave violations of the 1949 Geneva Conventions and other serious violations of the laws of war.[52] The Statute also provides for jurisdiction over the crime of aggression once the definition of that crime and the conditions for the exercise of that jurisdiction are agreed.[53]

The ICC only has jurisdiction over crimes that took place after the entry into force of the Rome Statute for that state.[54] When a state ratifies the Rome Statute, it automatically accepts the jurisdiction of the court under Article 5 and no further consent is required.[55] A state can otherwise accept the jurisdiction of the court.[56]

The court can only exercise jurisdiction when a 'situation in which one or more of such crimes appears to have been committed' has been submitted to the prosecutor by a state party[57] or by the Security Council acting under Chapter VII of the Charter of the United Nations[58] or an investigation has been initiated by the prosecutor.[59]

The court has jurisdiction over crimes that have occurred in the territory of a state party or state that has otherwise accepted the jurisdiction of the court; or where the accused is a national of a state party or state that has otherwise accepted the jurisdiction of the court;[60] or where the Security Council has referred a matter to the prosecutor, regardless of the location or nationality of the accused.[61]

The principle of complementarity, however, means that, even if these requirements are met, a case is not admissible if the state that has jurisdiction over the crime investigates or prosecutes it, unless that state is unwilling or unable genuinely to do so.[62] A case will also be inadmissible if the crime is not of sufficient gravity to justify further action by the court.[63]

[50] ICJ Rules, Article 31(2) and (3) and Article 35(1). [49] Article 31(6).
[51] S. Schwebel, 'Ad Hoc Chambers of the International Court of Justice' *American Journal of International Law* 81(4) (1987) 831–54.
[52] Rome Statute, Article 5(1) (all references in sections C and D of this Appendix are to the Rome Statute unless otherwise stated). [53] Article 5(2).
[54] Article 11(1) and (2). [55] Article 12(1).
[56] Article 12(3). This can include accepting the jurisdiction of the court from the period from 1 July 2002: Article 11(2). [57] Article 13(a).
[58] Article 13(b). [59] Article 13(c). [60] Article 12(2), [61] Article 12(2).
[62] Article 17(1)(a), (b) and (c). [63] Article 17(1)(d).

D. The nomination and election of ICC judges

Composition requirements

The Rome Statute provides that the ICC consists of eighteen judges,[64] subject to the powers of the ASP, on the initiative of the Presidency of the Court, to increase the number of judges.[65] The judges are elected by the states parties of the Rome Statute during a meeting of the ASP.[66]

Judges elected to the ICC must:

- be of high moral character, impartiality and integrity;[67]
- possess the qualifications required in their respective states for appointment to the highest judicial offices;[68] *and*
- have established competence in:
    - criminal law and procedure and the necessary relevant experience in criminal proceedings as a judge, prosecutor, advocate or similar;[69] *or* (List A)
    - relevant areas of international law (such as international humanitarian law and human rights law) and extensive experience in a professional legal capacity that is relevant to the work of the ICC;[70] *and* (List B)
- have an excellent knowledge of and be fluent in at least one of the working languages of the court.[71]

Each judge of the court must be of a different nationality.[72]

Further, the quotas set down by Article 36(5) ensure diversity in the professional backgrounds and expertise of judges on the bench, by requiring that at least nine judges from List A and at least five judges from List B be elected in the first elections, and that these numbers be maintained.

The Rome Statute also requires that states, when electing judges, 'take into account' the need for the representation of the principal legal systems of the world, equitable geographical representation and fair gender representation,[73] and the need for judges with particular legal expertise on specific issues, for example, violence against women or children.[74] These provisions are not mandatory, although resolutions of the ASP seek to give them effect, an issue discussed further, below.

Nomination procedures

Nominations of candidates can be made by any state party to the Rome Statute by either of two procedures:

1) the procedure for nominations to the highest judicial offices of that state;[75] *or*

[64] Article 36(1). [65] Article 36(2).

[66] Article 36(6)(a). See also Rule 85 of the Rules of Procedure of the Assembly of States Parties (Part II(C) of the Assembly of States Parties to the Rome Statute of the International Criminal Court, First Session, New York, 3–10 September 2002, *Official Records*, ICC-ASP/1/3) which refers to the procedure under Articles 36 and 37.

[67] Article 36(3)(a). [68] Article 36(3)(a). [69] Article 36(3)(b)(i).
[70] Article 36(3)(b)(ii). [71] Article 36(3)(c). [72] Article 36(7).
[73] Article 36(8)(a). [74] Article 36(8)(b). [75] Article 36(4)(a)(i).

2) the procedure set down in the Statute of the ICJ for nominations to the ICJ (ie nominations by the national groups of the PCA).[76]

Each state party may nominate one candidate for election to the court. The candidate need not be a national of the nominating state, but must be a national of a state party.[77] Nominations must be accompanied by a statement that sets out how the candidate fulfils the criteria in Article 36(3).[78]

The Statute provides for the possibility of the ASP establishing an 'Advisory Committee on nominations', with its composition and mandate to be determined by the ASP.[79] No such committee has yet been established.

The Statute does not further specify the procedures for the nomination of candidates. Nomination procedures were later agreed between the states parties in relation to the first elections in the form of the *Procedure for the nomination and election of judges, the Prosecutor and Deputy Prosecutors of the International Criminal Court*, adopted by resolution of the ASP on 9 September 2002.[80] This resolution was superseded on 10 September 2004 by the *Procedure for the Nomination and Election of Judges of the International Criminal Court*[81] (ASP Resolution 6) reproduced in Appendix 3 below.

ASP Resolution 6 provides that the Secretariat of the ASP shall circulate invitations to states parties to submit nominations, which shall include the text of Article 36 paragraphs (3), (4) and (8), the Resolution and information on the application of all minimum voting requirements.[82] The nomination period opens twenty-six weeks before the elections for a period of twelve weeks.[83] States parties communicate their nominations to the Secretariat of the ASP.[84]

The Resolution also elaborates on the required contents of the statements accompanying nominations. It requires that states parties include:

- information in necessary detail as to how the candidate meets the requirements of Article 36(3)(a)–(c) (as required by Article 36(4)(a));[85]
- an indication of whether the candidate is proposed under List A or List B as required by Article 36(5);[86]
- information relating to Article 36(8)(a)(i)–(iii);[87]
- an indication of whether the candidate has any expertise referred to in Article 36(8)(b);[88] *and*
- an indication of the nationality of the candidate, in the case a candidate has nationality of two or more states.[89]

[76] Article 36(4)(a)(ii). [77] Article 36(4)(b). [78] Article 36(4)(a).
[79] Article 36(4)(c).
[80] Assembly of States Parties, *Procedure for the Nomination and Election of Judges, the Prosecutor and Deputy Prosecutors of the International Criminal Court*, ICC-ASP/1/Res.2 and Assembly of States Parties, *Procedure for the Nomination and Election of Judges of the International Criminal Court*, ICC-ASP/1/Res.3.
[81] Assembly of States Parties, *Procedure for the Nomination and Election of Judges of the International Criminal Court*, ICC-ASP/3/Res.6 ('ASP Resolution 6' in the following notes).
[82] ASP Resolution 6, paras 1 and 2. Note that paras 1 and 2 of ASP Resolution 2 only required the text of Articles 36 (3) and (8) and did not require the inclusion on information regarding minimum voting requirements.
[83] ASP Resolution 6, para 3. The nomination period for the first elections was set by the Bureau of the ASP (ASP Resolution 2, para 3), see para 11 of that Resolution.
[84] ASP Resolution 6, para 5. [85] ibid, para 6(a). [86] ibid, para 6(b).
[87] ibid, para 6(c). [88] ibid, para 6(d). [89] ibid, para 6(e).

The Resolution requires that the supporting statement, the curriculum vitae of each candidate and other supporting documentation are posted on the website of the court (<http://www.icc-cpi.int>)[90] as soon as possible after their receipt by the Secretariat of the ASP.[91] Non-governmental organizations, such as the Lawyers Committee on Human Rights (now Human Rights First) and the Coalition for the International Criminal Court have undertaken interviews with candidates in past elections and published the transcripts of the interviews on the internet with tables comparing the qualifications and experience of candidates.[92]

A list of candidates in alphabetical order, with the accompanying documents, is then prepared by the Secretariat of the ASP and circulated through diplomatic channels to the states parties.[93]

Six weeks after the opening of the nomination period, the President of the ASP informs states parties of the number of nominations received in relation to each minimum voting requirement.[94] The Resolution requires that the regional and gender voting requirements be matched by at least double the number of candidates who meet those requirements, that the number of candidates exceeds the number of vacant seats and that the number of candidates meeting the requirements for List A and B be at least equivalent to the voting requirement for each of those categories.[95] If these requirements are not met, the nomination period can be extended, as permitted by the Resolution.

Election procedures

The date of the election is fixed by the Bureau of the ASP.[96] The names of the candidates are organized into two separate lists:[97]

1) List A—candidates with expertise in criminal law and procedure;[98] and
2) List B—candidates with expertise in international law.[99]

In relation to the first elections, the Statute mandates that at least nine judges be elected from List A and at least five judges from List B, and that subsequent elections be organized so as to maintain the same proportion of judges on the bench.[100] As a result, paragraph 18 of ASP Resolution 6 provides that '[n]o more than 13 candidates from list A and no more than 9 candidates from list B shall be considered elected, taking into account the number of judges remaining in office'. The Resolution also imposes minimum gender voting requirements that are discussed further, below.

[90] Before the first elections, the curricula vitae of candidates were placed on the UN website at: <http://www.un.org/law/icc/elections/judges/judges_nominations.htm>. Before the second and third elections, such information was posted on the website of the ASP (a page on the ICC website) at <http://www.icc-cpi.int/asp/election_2007.html> (Accessed 26 April 2009). See also information on the 2009 elections at <http://www.icc-cpi.int/Menus/ASP/Elections/Judges/Previous+Election+of+judges.htm> (Accessed 18 March 2010).

[91] ASP Resolution 6, para 8, see also Thordis Ingadottir, 'Nomination and Election of Judges' in Thordis Ingadottir (ed), *The International Criminal Court: Recommendations on Policy and Practice: Financing, Victims, Judges, and Immunities* (Ardsley, NY: Transnational Publishers Inc., 2003) 173.

[92] See <http://www.humanrightsfirst.org/international_justice/icc/election/elections.htm> and <http://www.iccnow.org/?mod=electionjudges> (Accessed 18 March 2010).

[93] ASP Resolution 6, para 9.

[94] ibid, para 10.

[95] ibid, paras 10 and 11.

[96] ibid, para 13.

[97] ibid, Article 36(5) and para 14.

[98] Pursuant to Article 36(3)(b)(i).

[99] Pursuant to Article 36(3)(b)(ii).

[100] Article 36(5).

Article 36(8)(a) requires that states parties, in electing judges to the ICC, take into account the need for the representation of the principal legal systems of the world, equitable geographical representation and fair representation of female and male judges. Article 36(8)(b) requires that states parties also take into account the need to include judges with particular legal expertise, including in relation to the issues of violence against women and children.[101]

The judges are elected by secret ballot during a meeting of the ASP. The candidates that obtain the highest number of votes and a two-thirds majority of the states parties present and voting are elected.[102] The quorum is an absolute majority of states parties.[103] Successive ballots may be held if there are seats that remain vacant.[104]

A system of minimum voting requirements is set down by ASP Resolution 6. A ballot paper is only valid if it meets the relevant minimum voting requirements.[105] After adjustment in accordance with the number of judges meeting the criteria remaining on the bench and whether the minimum thresholds have been met in terms of the number of candidates nominated,[106] states parties must vote for at least nine judges from List A, that is, candidates with 'competence in criminal law and procedure, and the necessary relevant experience, whether as judge, prosecutor, advocate or in other similar capacity, in criminal proceedings';[107] at least five judges from List B, that is, candidates with 'established competence in relevant areas of international law such as international humanitarian law and the law of human rights, and extensive experience in a professional legal capacity which is of relevance to the judicial work of the Court';[108] (at present) at least three judges from the Western Europe and Other States group ('WEOG'), Africa, Latin America and Caribbean States group (GRULAC) and two each from Eastern Europe and Asia;[109] and at least six judges of each gender.[110]

The minimum voting requirements are to be adjusted between ballots (if there are multiple voting rounds) until they cannot be met. When one voting requirement can no longer be met, all regional and gender voting requirements no longer apply. Furthermore, once the fourth ballot has been undertaken, all regional and voting requirements no longer apply. The voting requirements regarding List A and B shall be applied until they are fulfilled.[111]

Term of judicial office, re-election and vacancies

Judges hold office for a term of nine years and cannot be re-elected.[112] Judges are organized into four divisions: the Presidency, an Appeals Division, a Trial Division and a Pre-Trial Division.[113]

[101] See also ASP Resolution 6, para 19.
[102] ibid, Article 36(6)(a) and para16.
[103] ibid, Article 112(7)(a) and paras 15 and 16.
[104] Article 36(6)(b).
[105] ASP Resolution 6, para 22.
[106] ibid, para 20(a)–(c).
[107] ibid, Article 36(3)(b)(i) and para 20(a). See also the requirements set down in the Statute itself: Article 36(5), noted above.
[108] ibid, Article 36(3)(b)(ii) and ibid, para 20(a). See also the requirements set down in the Statute itself: Article 36(5).
[109] ibid, para 20(b). This leaves five seats as 'floating seats' that can be allocated to candidates from any region. Note that the number of seats formally allocated to a region can increase when states parties from the region surpass 16: ibid, para 20(b).
[110] ibid, para 20(c).
[111] Paragraph 21, in fulfilment of Article 36(5).
[112] Article 36(9)(a).
[113] Article 34.

To ensure the continuity of the court, the Rome Statute provides for staggered elections so that no more than six ordinary vacancies arise every three years. Therefore, at the first elections, six judges were selected by lot to serve for a term of three years and a further six judges for a term of six years, with the remaining six serving for a term of nine years.[114] The six judges who served a term of three years were eligible for re-election at the second elections.[115] Judges assigned to the Trial or Appeals Chamber remain in office to complete any trial or appeal the hearing of which started before the expiry of their term.[116]

In the case of any vacancy on the bench, the Article 36 nomination and election procedure is to be followed.[117] Judges elected to fill a vacancy will serve the remainder of the predecessor's term. If the remainder is three years or less, the judge will be eligible for re-election for a full term.[118]

Judges of the ICC serve on a full-time basis, although this may be adjusted by the Presidency in accordance with the workload of the court.[119] The judges comprising the Presidency must serve on a full-time basis.[120]

[114] Article 36(9)(b). [115] Article 36(9)(c). [116] Article 36(10).

[117] ASP Resolution 6, Article 37(1); Part C. See also the rules regarding the application of List A and List B, regional and gender minimum voting requirements to the nomination of candidates to fill judicial vacancies: (ASP Resolution 6, para 27). [118] Rome Statute, Article 37(2).

[119] Article 35. [120] Article 35(2).

APPENDIX 3

International Criminal Court Assembly of States Parties: Resolution ICC-ASP/3/Res.6

Resolution ICC-ASP/3/Res.6

Adopted at the 6th plenary meeting, on 10 September 2004, by consensus

ICC-ASP/3/Res.6
Procedure for the nomination and election of judges of the International Criminal Court

The Assembly of States Parties,

Bearing in mind the provisions, of the Rome Statute of the International Criminal Court,

Mindful of the Rules of Procedure of the Assembly of States Parties,

Convinced of the need to fully implement the provisions of article 36 of the Rome Statute,

Noting that in its resolution ICC-ASP/l/Res.3 the Assembly of States Parties agreed that it would review the procedure for the election of judges on the occasion of future elections with a view to making any improvements as may be necessary,

Approves the following procedure for the nomination and election of judges of the International Criminal Court, replacing resolution ICC-ASP/1/Res.3 and parts A, B and C of resolution ICC-ASP/l/Res.2.

A. Nomination of candidates for judges

1. The Secretariat of the Assembly of States Parties shall circulate through the diplomatic channel the invitations for nominations of judges of the International Criminal Court.
2. The invitations for nominations of judges will include the text of article 36, paragraphs 3, 4 and 8, of the Statute, the present resolution as well as specific information regarding the application of all minimum voting requirements in the elections.
3. The nomination period shall open 26 weeks before the elections and shall last 12 weeks.

4. Nominations submitted before or after the nomination period shall not be considered.
5. States Parties to the Statute shall communicate nominations for the election of judges of the International Criminal Court through the diplomatic channel to the Secretariat of the Assembly of States Parties.
6. Every nomination should be accompanied by a statement:
   (a) Specifying in the necessary detail how the candidate fulfils each of the requirements in article 36, paragraph 3(a), (b) and (c), of the Statute, in accordance with article 36, paragraph 4(a), of the Statute;
   (b) Indicating whether the candidate is being nominated for inclusion in list A or list B for the purposes of article 36, paragraph 5, of the Statute;
   (c) Containing information relating to article 36, paragraph 8(a)(i) to (iii), of the Statute;
   (d) Indicating whether the candidate has any expertise under article 36, paragraph 8(b), of the Statute;
   (e) Indicating under which nationality the candidate is being nominated for the purposes of article 36, paragraph 7, of the Statute, where a candidate is a national of two or more States.
7. States that have started the process of ratification, acceptance or approval of or accession to the Statute may nominate candidates for the elections of judges of the International Criminal Court. Such nominations shall remain provisional and shall not be included in the list of candidates unless the State concerned has deposited its instrument of ratification, acceptance, approval or accession with the Secretary-General of the United Nations before the end of the nomination period and provided that that State is a party to the Statute in accordance with article 126, paragraph 2, of the Statute on the date of the election.
8. The Secretariat of the Assembly of States Parties shall place the nominations of candidates for judges, the accompanying statements referred to in article 36 of the Statute and other supporting documentation on the Internet web site of the International Criminal Court, in any of the official languages of the Court, as soon as possible after receiving them.
9. The Secretariat of the Assembly of States Parties shall prepare a list in English alphabetical order of all persons thus nominated, with accompanying documents, and shall circulate it through the diplomatic channel.
10. Six weeks after the opening of the nomination period, the President of the Assembly of States Parties shall inform all States Parties through diplomatic channels and through specific information on the web site of the International Criminal Court on the number of candidates nominated with respect to each minimum voting requirement.
11. The President of the Assembly of States Parties shall extend the nomination period for two weeks, but no more than three times, if at the end of the nomination period any regional or gender minimum voting requirement[1] is not matched with at least twice the number of candidates fulfilling that requirement.

[1] To be calculated in accordance with paragraph 20(b), second sentence, and paragraph 20(c), second sentence, only.

12. The President of the Assembly of States Parties shall extend the nomination period for two weeks at a time, if at the end of the nomination period the number of candidates remains less than the number of seats, or the number of candidates from list A or B remains less than the respective minimum voting requirement.

B. Election of judges

13. The Bureau of the Assembly of States Parties shall fix the date of the election.
14. The Secretariat of the Assembly of States Parties shall prepare, in accordance with article 36, paragraph 5, of the Statute, two lists of candidates in English alphabetical order.
15. The election of judges shall be a matter of substance, and subject to the requirements of article 112, paragraph 7(a), of the Statute.
16. The persons elected to the Court shall be the 6 candidates who obtain the highest number of votes and a two-thirds majority of States Parties present and voting, provided that an absolute majority of the Slates Parties constitutes the quorum for voting.
17. When two or more candidates of the same nationality obtain the required majority, the candidate who receives the higher number of votes shall be considered elected.
18. No more than 13 candidates from list A and no more than 9 candidates from list B shall be considered elected, taking into account the number of judges remaining in office.
19. States Parties shall, in the election of judges, take into account the need for the representation of the principal legal systems of the world, equitable geographical representation and a fair representation of female and male judges. They shall take into account the need to include judges with legal expertise on specific issues, including, but not limited to, violence against women and children.
20. During any given ballot, each State Party shall vote for no more candidates than seats to be filled, whereby it shall observe the minimum voting requirements regarding lists A and B, regional groups and gender. At the outset of each ballot, each minimum voting requirement shall be determined or discontinued in accordance with paragraphs 21 and 22.
    (a) Each State Party shall vote for a minimum number of candidates from lists A and B. For list A, this number shall be 9 minus the number of judges from list A remaining in office or elected in previous ballots. For list B, this number shall be 5 minus the number of judges from list B remaining in office or elected in previous ballots.
    (b) Each Party shall vote for a minimum number of candidates from each regional group. This number shall be 2 minus the number of judges from that regional group remaining in office or elected in previous ballots.

    If the number of States Parties of any given regional group is higher than 16 at that moment, the minimum voting requirement for that group shall be adjusted by adding 1.

    If the number of candidates from a regional group is not at least double the respective minimum voting requirement, the minimum voting requirement shall be half the number of candidates from that regional group (rounded up to the nearest whole number where applicable). If there is only one candidate from a regional group, there shall be no minimum voting requirement for that group.

(c) Each State Party shall vote for a minimum number of candidates of each gender. This number shall be 6 minus the number of judges of that gender remaining in office or elected in previous ballots. However, if the number of candidates of one gender is 10 or less, the minimum voting requirement for that gender shall be adjusted in accordance with the following formula:

Number of candidates	*Minimum requirement shall not exceed:*
10	6
9	6
8	5
7	5
6	4
5	3
4	2
3	1
2	1
1	0

21. Each minimum voting requirement shall be adjusted until that requirement can no longer be met, whereupon the use of that requirement shall be discontinued. If an adjusted voting requirement can be met individually, but not jointly, the use of all regional and gender voting requirements shall be discontinued. If, following four ballots, there still remain seats to be filled, these minimum voting requirements shall be discontinued. The minimum voting requirements regarding lists A and B shall be applied until they are fulfilled.
22. Only ballot papers observing the minimum voting requirements shall be valid. If a State Party fulfils the minimum requirements using less than the maximum number of votes allowed for that ballot, it may abstain from voting for the remaining candidates.
23. Once regional and gender voting requirements are discontinued and the minimum voting requirements regarding lists A and B are fulfilled, each further ballot shall be restricted to the most successful candidates of the previous ballot. Before each ballot, the candidate (or, in the event of a tie, the candidates) having obtained the lowest number of votes in the previous ballot shall thus be excluded, provided that the number of candidates remains at least twice the number of seats to be filled.
24. The President of the Assembly of States Parties shall be responsible for the election procedure, including the determination, adjustment or discontinuation of the minimum voting requirements.
25. Ballot papers shall be organized in a manner facilitating such an election process. The minimum voting requirements, the adjusted requirements and the discontinuation of any requirements shall be clearly indicated on the ballot papers. Before the

day of the election, the President shall distribute to all States Parties copies of the instructions and samples of the ballot papers. On the day of the election, clear instructions and sufficient time shall be given for each ballot. In each ballot, before the voting process is concluded, the President shall repeat the instructions and the minimum requirements to allow each delegation to verify that its vote meets those requirements.

26. The Assembly of States Parties shall review the procedure for the election of judges on the occasion of future elections with a view to making such improvements as may be necessary.

C. Judicial vacancies

27. In the event of a judicial vacancy in accordance with article 37 of the Rome Statute, the procedures for the nomination and election of judges shall apply mutatis mutandis, subject to the following provisions:
    (a) Within one month of the occurrence of the judicial vacancy, the Bureau of the Assembly of States Parties shall fix the venue and date of the election, which should not be later than 20 weeks after the occurrence of the vacancy.
    (b) The nomination period shall open 12 weeks before the elections and shall last 6 weeks.
    (c) If the judicial vacancy reduces the number of judges from list A to below 9 or the number of judges from list B to below 5, only candidates from the underrepresented list can be nominated.
    (d) If at the time of the election a regional or gender minimum voting requirement is not fulfilled, only candidates that can satisfy any of the underrepresented regional minimum voting requirements as well as the underrepresented gender minimum voting requirement can be nominated.
    (e) A judge elected to fill a vacancy shall serve for the remainder of the predecessor's term and, if that period is three years or less, shall be eligible for re-election for a full term under article 36 of the Statute.

Annex I
Illustrative tables of minimum voting requirements

The following tables are included for illustration purposes only.

Table 1. Minimum voting requirements for list A

If the number of judges from list A remaining in office or elected in previous ballots is:	*. . . then the minimum voting requirement for list A is:*
9 or more	fulfilled
8	1
7	2
6	3
5	4
4	5
3	6
2	7
1	8
0	9

Table 2. Minimum voting requirements for list B

If the number of judges from list B remaining in office or elected in previous ballots is:	*. . . then the minimum voting requirement for list B:*
5 or more	fulfilled
4	1
3	2
2	3
1	4
0	5

Table 3. Regional minimum voting requirements

If the number of judges from a given region remaining in office or elected in previous ballots is:	*... then the minimum voting requirement for this region is:*
3 or more	fulfilled
2	1
1	2
0	3

(Further adjustments might be necessary in accordance with para. 21(b) of the resolution.)

Table 4. Gender minimum voting requirements

If the number of judges from one gender remaining in office or elected in previous ballots is:	*... then the minimum voting requirement for the gender is:*
6 or more	fulfilled
5	1
4	2
3	3
2	4
1	5
0	6

(Further adjustments might be necessary in accordance with para. 21(c) of the resolution.)

Annex II
Sample Ballot Paper: Election of 6 Judges of the ICC

This sample ballot paper is included for illustration purposes only.

	VOTE FOR A MAXIMUM OF 6 CANDIDATES			
REGIONAL GROUPS	LIST A VOTE FOR AT LEAST X FROM LIST A		LIST B VOTE FOR AT LEAST X FROM LIST B	
	GENDER DISTRIBUTION: VOTE FOR AT LEAST X MALES AND X FEMALES			
	MALE	FEMALE	MALE	FEMALE
AFRICA VOTE FOR AT LEAST X CANDIDATES FROM THIS REGION	☐ Name (Country) ☐ Name (Country)	☐ Name (Country)	☐ Name (Country)	☐ Name (Country) ☐ Name (Country)
ASIA VOTE FOR AT LEAST X CANDIDATES FROM THIS REGION	☐ Name (Country) ☐ Name (Country)	☐ Name (Country)	☐ Name (Country)	
EASTERN EUROPE VOTE FOR AT LEAST X CANDIDATES FROM THIS REGION	☐ Name (Country)	☐ Name (Country)	☐ Name (Country) ☐ Name (Country)	☐ Name (Country)
LATIN AMERICA/ CARIBBEAN VOTE FOR AT LEAST X CANDIDATES FROM THIS REGION	☐ Name (Country)	☐ Name (Country) ☐ Name (Country)	☐ Name (Country) ☐ Name (Country)	☐ Name (Country)
WESTERN EUROPE AND OTHER VOTE FOR AT LEAST X	☐ Name (Country) ☐ Name (Country)	☐ Name (Country) ☐ Name (Country)	☐ Name (Country) ☐ Name (Country)	☐ Name (Country)

Bibliography

ABILA Committee on Intergovernmental Settlement of Disputes, 'Reforming the United Nations: What About the International Court of Justice?' *Chinese Journal of International Law* 5(1) (2006) 39–65.

Abi-Saab, Georges, 'Ensuring the Best Bench: Ways of Selecting Judges: Presentation by Professor Georges Abi-Saab' in Connie Peck and Roy S. Lee (eds), *Increasing the Effectiveness of the International Court of Justice: Proceedings of the ICJ/UNITAR Colloquium to Celebrate the 50th Anniversary of the Court* (The Hague: Kluwer Law International, 1997) 166–88.

Aceves, William J., 'Critical Jurisprudence and International Legal Scholarship: A Study of Equitable Distribution' *Columbia Journal of Transnational Law* 39(2) (2001) 299–393.

Alter, Karen, 'Who are the "Masters of the Treaty"?: European Governments and the European Court of Justice' *International Organization* 52(1) (1998) 121–47.

—— 'Agents or Trustees? International Courts in their Political Context' *European Journal of International Relations* 14(1) (2008) 33–63.

Ambos, Kai, '"Witness proofing" before the International Criminal Court: a reply to Karemaker, Taylor, and Pittman' *Leiden Journal of International Law* 21(4) (2008) 911–16.

Amerasinghe, Chittharanjan F., 'Judges of the International Court of Justice—Election and Qualifications' *Leiden Journal of International Law* 14(2) (2001) 335–48.

Amnesty International, 'International Criminal Court: Checklist to Ensure the Nomination of the Highest Qualified Candidates for Judges', AI Index: IOR 40/023/2002, available at: <http://www.amnesty.org/en/library/info/IOR40/023/2002/en> (accessed 3 August 2006).

—— 'International Criminal Court: Amnesty International's Urgent Appeal to Countries That Have Ratified the Rome Statute Creating the International Criminal Court to Address the Disturbing Lack of Nominations of Female Candidates for Judges', AI Index: IOR 40/034/2002 (published online 30 September 2002), available at: <http://www.amnesty.org/en/library/info/IOR40/034/2002/en> (accessed 3 August 2006).

—— 'African Court on Human and Peoples' Rights: Checklist to Ensure the Nomination of the Highest Qualified Candidates for Judges', AI Index: IOR 63/001/2004 (published online 16 February 2004), available at: <http://www.amnesty.org/en/library/info/IOR63/001/2004> (accessed 3 August 2006).

Anand, R. P., 'Role of International Adjudication' in Leo Gross (ed), *The Future of the International Court of Justice*, vol. I (Dobbs Ferry, NY: Oceana Publications, 1976) 1–21.

Aznar-Gómez, Mariano J., 'Chapter I. Organization of the Court: Article 2' in Andreas Zimmerman et al (eds), *The Statute of the International Court of Justice: A Commentary* (Oxford: Oxford University Press, 2006) 205–18.

Aznar-Gómez, Mariano J., 'Chapter I. Organization of the Court: Article 3' in Andreas Zimmerman et al (eds), *The Statute of the International Court of Justice: A Commentary* (Oxford: Oxford University Press, 2006) 219–24.

Baroness Hale of Richmond, 'The Appointment and Removal of Judges: Independence and Diversity', International Association of Women Judges 8th Biennial Conference, 3–7 May 2006, Sydney, Australia, available at: <http://www.iawj.org/what/Session3 Hale.doc> (accessed 20 November 2008).

Bartram, Darin R., and David B. Rivkin Jr, 'The ICC's First False Step' *Wall Street Journal* 17 February 2003.

Batongué, Alain B., 'Campagne: Le Cameroun en ordre de bataille pour Maurice Kamto' (published online 11 September 2008), available at: <http://www.toutcameroun.com/politique.php?subaction=showfull&id=1221129453&archive=&start_from=&ucat=1> (accessed 22 September 2008).

Baxter, R. R., 'The Procedures Employed in Connection with the United States Nominations for the International Court in 1960' *American Journal of International Law* 55(2) (1961) 445–6.

Bilder, Richard B., 'International Dispute Settlement and the Role of Adjudication' in Lori F. Damrosch (ed), *The International Court of Justice at a Crossroads* (Dobbs Ferry, New York: Transnational Publishers Inc., 1987) 155–82.

Blokker, Niels, and Sam Muller, 'The 1996 Elections to the International Court of Justice: New Tendencies in the Post-Cold War Era?' *International and Comparative Law Quarterly* 47(1) (January 1998) 211–23.

Brandeis Institute for International Judges, *International Justice: past, present and future*, (Brandeis University, 2009) 19–25, available at: <http://www.brandeis.edu/ethics/pdfs/internationaljustice/biij/BIIJ2009.pdf> (accessed 17 September 2009).

Broude, Tomer, '"Judges Shalt Thou Make Thee in All Thy Gates": Reforming Judicial Office in the WTO Dispute Settlement System' *Free University of Amsterdam Journal of International and Comparative Law* (*The Griffin's View*) 6(2) (2005) 30–58.

Brown Weiss, Edith, 'Judicial Independence and Impartiality: A Preliminary Inquiry' in Lori F. Damrosch (ed), *The International Court of Justice at a Crossroads* (Dobbs Ferry, New York: Transnational Publishers Inc., 1987) 123–54.

Brown, Chester, 'The Evolution and Application of Rules Concerning Independence of the "International Judiciary"' *The Law and Practice of International Courts and Tribunals* 2(1) (2003) 63–96.

Cameron, Hazel, 'Establishment of the European Union Civil Service Tribunal' *The Law and Practice of International Courts and Tribunals* 5(2) (2006) 273–83.

Caron, David D., 'War and International Adjudication: Reflections on the 1899 Peace Conference' *American Journal of International Law* 94(1) (2000) 4–30.

Chappell, Louise, 'The International Criminal Court: A New Arena for Transforming Gender Justice' in Shirin M. Rai and Georgina Waylen (eds), *Global Governance: Feminist Perspectives* (Basingstoke: Palgrave Macmillan, 2008) 160–84.

—— 'Women's Rights and Religious Opposition: The Politics of Gender at the International Criminal Court' in Yasmeen Abu-Laban (ed), *Gendering the Nation State: Canadian Comparative Perspectives* (Vancouver: University of British Columbia Press, 2008) 139–61.

Charlesworth, Hilary, and Christine Chinkin, *The Boundaries of International Law: A feminist analysis* (Manchester: Manchester University Press, 2000).

Coalition for an Effective African Court on Human and Peoples' Rights, 'Guidelines for Nomination of Judges to the African Court on Human and Peoples' Rights' (n.d.), available at: <http://www.africancourtcoalition.org/content_files/files/Publication1.pdf> (accessed 2 July 2006).

—— 'The Election of Judges to the African Court on Human and Peoples' Rights' document submitted to the Assembly of Heads of State and Government, the Executive Council and the Permanent Representatives Committee of the African Union Mid-term Summit in Khartoum, the Sudan, 16–25 January 2006' (n.d.), available at: <http://www.amtdatatechnologies.com/acc/UploadedDocuments/119200612747PM718.doc> (accessed 2 July 2006).

Coalition for the International Criminal Court, 'Questionnaire to ICC Judicial Candidates 2007 Elections: Saiga, FUMIKO, Ms.' (November 2007), available at: <http://www.iccnow.org/documents/CICC_Questionnaire_res_SAIGA.pdf> (accessed 25 November 2007).

Coalition for the International Criminal Court, 'CICC Recommended Criteria for States Parties to Nominate and Elect Judges to the ICC' (published online October 2008), available at: <http://www.iccnow.org/documents/CICC_Judicial_Nomination_Election_Criteria_FINAL.pdf> (accessed 3 October 2008).

Commission on Global Governance, *Our Global Neighbourhood: The Report of the Commission on Global Governance* (Oxford: Oxford University Press, 1995).

Copithorne, M. D., 'The Permanent Court of Arbitration and the Election of Members of the International Court of Justice' *Canadian Yearbook of International Law* 16 (1978) 315–27.

Damrosch, Lori F., 'Ensuring the Best Bench: Ways of Selecting Judges: Commentary by Professor Lori Fisler Damrosch' in Connie Peck and Roy S. Lee (eds), *Increasing the Effectiveness of the International Court of Justice: Proceedings of the ICJ/UNITAR Colloquium to Celebrate the 50th Anniversary of the Court* (The Hague: Kluwer Law International, 1997) 188–201.

—— 'The Election of Thomas Buergenthal to the International Court of Justice' *American Journal of International Law* 94(3) (2000) 579–82.

Defensor Santiago, Miriam, 'News Release: Miriam Addresses the UN General Assembly' (published online 5 November 2007), available at: <http://www.miriam.com.ph/2007/11/news-release-5-november-2007-miriam.html> (accessed 8 November 2007).

Dingle, Lesley, 'Conversations with Professor Sir Elihu Lauterpacht. Fifth Interview: The Nineties and new Millennium', 28 March 2008, available at: <http://www.dspace.cam.ac.uk/bitstream/1810/197070/2/Eli%20Lauterpacht%20interview%205%20transcript%20-%2028%20March%202008.doc> (accessed 20 November 2008).

Dugard, John, 'Chapter I. Organization of the Court: Article 13' in Andreas Zimmerman et al (eds), *The Statute of the International Court of Justice: A Commentary* (Oxford: Oxford University Press, 2006) 303–13.

—— 'Chapter I. Organization of the Court: Article 14' in Andreas Zimmerman et al (eds), *The Statute of the International Court of Justice: A Commentary* (Oxford: Oxford University Press, 2006) 315–19.

—— 'Chapter I. Organization of the Court: Article 15' in Andreas Zimmerman et al (eds), *The Statute of the International Court of Justice: A Commentary* (Oxford: Oxford University Press, 2006) 321–2.

Eagleton, Clyde, 'Choice of Judges for the International Court of Justice' *American Journal of International Law* 47(3) (1953) 462–4.

Eldar, Ofer, 'Vote-Trading in International Institutions' *European Journal of International Law* 19(1) (2008) 3–41.

Elias, Taslim Olawale, 'Report: Does the International Court of Justice, as it is Presently Shaped, Correspond to the Requirements which Follow from its Functions as the Central Juridical Body of the International Community?' in Hermann Mosler and Rudolf Bernhardt (eds), *Judicial Settlement of International Disputes: International Court of Justice, Other Courts and Tribunals, Arbitration and Conciliation; An International Symposium* (Berlin: Springer Verlag, 1974) 19–33.

Embassy of the Philippines to the Kingdom of Belgium and the Grand Duchy of Luxembourg and Mission of the Philippines to the European Communities, 'Exchange of Visits' (n.d.), available at: <http://www.philembassy.be/theembassy.htm> (accessed 21 April 2009).

Etter, Lauren, 'Call for ICC to Learn ICTY Election Lessons', 26 November 2004, available at: <http://www.globalpolicy.org/intljustice/icc/2004/1126icclessons.htm> (accessed 10 July 2006).

Eyffinger, Arthur, *The International Court of Justice: 1946–1996* (The Hague: Kluwer Law International, 1996).

—— *The 1899 Hague Peace Conference* (The Hague: Kluwer Law International, 2000).

Falzon, Neil, Matthias Goldmann, and Ketevan Khutsishvili (eds), *Nomination and Election of Judges to International Courts: A Comparative Study* (Brussels: The European Law Students' Association Legal Research Group, published online April 2002), available at: <http://www.elsa.ee/doc.php?1334> (accessed 7 July 2006).

Fassbender, Bardo, 'Chapter I. Organization of the Court: Article 9' in Andreas Zimmerman et al (eds), *The Statute of the International Court of Justice: A Commentary* (Oxford: Oxford University Press, 2006) 261–84.

—— 'Chapter I. Organization of the Court: Article 10' in Andreas Zimmerman et al (eds), *The Statute of the International Court of Justice: A Commentary* (Oxford: Oxford University Press, 2006) 285–94.

—— 'Chapter I. Organization of the Court: Article 11' in Andreas Zimmerman et al (eds), *The Statute of the International Court of Justice: A Commentary* (Oxford: Oxford University Press, 2006) 295–7.

—— 'Chapter I. Organization of the Court: Article 12' in Andreas Zimmerman et al (eds), *The Statute of the International Court of Justice: A Commentary* (Oxford: Oxford University Press, 2006) 299–302.

Fitzmaurice, Gerald, 'Enlargement of the Contentious Jurisdiction of the Court' in Leo Gross (ed), *The Future of the International Court of Justice*, vol. I (Dobbs Ferry, New York: Oceana Publications, 1976) 461–98.

Foreign and Commonwealth Office, 'Press Release—UK Candidate for International Criminal Court Judge Confirmed (02/10/2003)' (2 October 2003), available at: <http://www.fco.gov.uk/resources/en/press-release/2003/10/fco_npr_310702_iccjudgeukcand> (accessed 11 December 2008).

Franck, Thomas M., *Fairness in International Law and Institutions* (Oxford: Oxford University Press, 1995).

Galicia, Loui, 'Campaign for Santiago's ICJ nomination starts' (published online 23 August 2007), available at: <http://www.louigalicia.blogspot.com/2007/08/campaign-for-santiagos-icj-nomination.html> (accessed 27 April 2009).

Georget, Patricia, Vladimir Golitsyn, and Ralph Zacklin, 'Chapter I. Organization of the Court: Article 4' in Andreas Zimmerman et al (eds), *The Statute of the International Court of Justice: A Commentary* (Oxford: Oxford University Press, 2006) 225–39.

—— 'Chapter I. Organization of the Court: Article 5' in Andreas Zimmerman et al (eds), *The Statute of the International Court of Justice: A Commentary* (Oxford: Oxford University Press, 2006) 241–7.

—— 'Chapter I. Organization of the Court: Article 6' in Andreas Zimmerman et al, (eds), *The Statute of the International Court of Justice: A Commentary* (Oxford: Oxford University Press, 2006) 249–51.

—— 'Chapter I. Organization of the Court: Article 7' in Andreas Zimmerman et al, (eds), *The Statute of the International Court of Justice: A Commentary* (Oxford: Oxford University Press, 2006) 253–6.

—— 'Chapter I. Organization of the Court: Article 8' in Andreas Zimmerman et al (eds), *The Statute of the International Court of Justice: A Commentary* (Oxford: Oxford University Press, 2006) 257–60.

Godefridi, Drieu, 'On the Legitimacy of the International Criminal Court' *Wall Street Journal* 7 March 2003.

Goff, Phil, 'NZ Backing Sir Kenneth Keith for ICJ' (published online 26 August 2003), available at: <http://www.beehive.govt.nz/Print/PrintDocument.aspx?DocumentID=17649> (accessed 20 August 2006).

Golden, Jeffrey B., 'The World Court: The Qualifications of the Judges' *Columbia Journal of Law and Social Problems* 14(1) (1978) 1–46.

Gordon, Edward, 'Observations on the Independence and Impartiality of the Members of the International Court of Justice' *Connecticut Journal of International Law* 2(2) (1987), 397–426.

Government Communications Unit, 'Greater transparency in the nomination of judges to serve in international and EU courts: Press Release 451/2006 7 December 2006' (published online 7 December 2006), available at: <http://formin.finland.fi/public/default.aspx?contentId=84448&nodeId=15145> (accessed 22 June 2008).

Grice, Christine, 'Media Statement: Sir Kenneth Keith Candidature', 26 August 2003; on file with authors.

Gross, Leo, 'The International Court of Justice: Consideration of Requirements for Enhancing its Role in the International Legal Order' *American Journal of International Law* 65(2) (1971) 253–326.

—— 'Compulsory Jurisdiction Under the Optional Clause: History and Practice' in Lori F. Damrosch (ed), *The International Court of Justice at a Crossroads* (Dobbs Ferry, New York: Transnational Publishers Inc., 1987) 19–57.

Harland, Christopher, 'Special Report: International Court of Justice Elections: A Report on the First Fifty Years' *Canadian Yearbook of International Law* 34 (1996) 303–68.

Harvey, Claire, 'NZers of the year: Sir Kenneth Keith, international jurist' *The New Zealand Herald*, 17 December 2005, available at: <http://www.nzherald.co.nz/new-zealanders-of-the-year/news/article.cfm?c_id=1501017&objectid=10360346> (accessed 27 April 2009).

Helfer, Laurence R., and Anne-Marie Slaughter, 'Why States Create International Tribunals: A Response to Professors Posner and Yoo' *California Law Review* 93(3) (2005) 899–956.

Hensley, Thomas R., 'National Bias and the International Court of Justice' *Midwest Journal of Political Science* 12(4) (1968) 568–86.

Hogan, Willard N., 'The Ammoun Case and the Election of Judges to the International Court of Justice' *American Journal of International Law* 59(4) (1965) 908–12.

Hudson, Manley O., 'The Election of Members of the Permanent Court of International Justice' *American Journal of International Law* 24(4) (1930) 718–27.

—— *The Permanent Court of International Justice, 1920–1942: a treatise* (New York: The Macmillan Company, 1943).

Hughes, Valerie, 'The WTO Dispute Settlement System—from initiating proceedings to ensuring implementation: what needs improvement?' in Giorgio Sacerdoti, Alan Yanovich, and Jan Bohanes (eds), *The WTO at Ten: The Contribution of the Dispute Settlement System* (WTO/Cambridge University Press, 2006) 193–234.

Human Rights Watch, 'Nomination of Candidates for the 2009 ICC Judicial Election: Letter to Foreign Affairs Ministers of ICC States Parties' (published online 19 August 2008), available at: <http://www.hrw.org/en/news/2008/08/19/nomination-candidates-2009-icc-judicial-election> (accessed 3 September 2008).

Ingadottir, Thordis, 'Nomination and Election of Judges' in Thordis Ingadottir (ed), *The International Criminal Court: Recommendations on Policy and Practice: Financing, Victims, Judges, and Immunities* (Ardsley, New York: Transnational Publishers Inc., 2003) 145–82.

Institut de Droit International, 'Etudes des amendments à apporter au Statut de la Cour internationale de Justice: Rapport présenté par M. Max Huber' in *Annuaire de l'Institut de Droit International, Tome I,* Session d'Aix-en-Provence 1954, Vol. 45 (Bâle: Éditions juridiques et sociologiques S.A., 1954) 407–555.

International Court of Justice, 'History' (n.d.), available at: <http://www.icj-cij.org/court/index.php?p1=1&p2=1> (accessed 10 August 2006).

International Court of Justice, 'Members of the Court' (n.d.), available at: <http://www.icj-cij.org/court/index.php?p1=1&p2=2> (accessed 10 August 2006).

International Court of Justice, 'Press Release 2005/23: United Nations General Assembly and Security Council Proceed to the Election of Five Members of the Court', 8 November 2005, available at: <http://www.icj-cij.org/presscom/index.php?p1=6&p2=1&pr=638&search=%22armes%22> (accessed 20 November 2006).

International Criminal Court, 'Press Release: 24.04.2009: Passing of Judge Fumiko Saiga: ICC-CPI-20090424-PR407: IN MEMORIAM', 24 April 2009, available at: <http://www.icc-cpi.int/Menus/ICC/Press+and+Media/Press+Releases/Passing+of+Judge+Fumiko+Saiga.htm> (accessed 20 May 2009).

International Law Commission, '2006 Election of the International Law Commission', 25 April 2007, available at: <http://www.un.org/law/ilc/> (accessed 10 November 2008).

Jennings, Robert Y., 'The International Court of Justice after Fifty Years' *American Journal of International Law* 89(3) (1995) 493–505.

Jones, John R. W. D., 'Composition of the Court', in Antonio Cassese, Paola Gaeta, and John R. W. D. Jones (eds), *The Rome Statute of the International Criminal Court: A Commentary*, vol. I (New York: Oxford University Press, 2002) 235–67.

Keith, Kenneth, 'Member of the Permanent Court of Arbitration', in Tim L. H. McCormack and Cheryl Saunders (eds), *Sir Ninian Stephen: A Tribute* (Melbourne: Melbourne University Publishing, 2007) 155–75.

—— 'International Court of Justice: Reflections on the Electoral Process' *Chinese Journal of International Law* 9(1) (2010) 49–80.

Kenney, Sally, 'Breaking the Silence: Gender Mainstreaming and the Composition of the European Court of Justice' *Feminist Legal Studies* 10(3–4) (2002) 257–70.

Kinsai, Nformi Sonde, 'Cameroon: Gov't Campaigns for Prof. Kamto's Election Into ICJ' (published online 18 September 2008), available at: <http://www.allafrica.com/stories/200809180917.html> (accessed 25 September 2008).

Kirby, Michael, 'Neville Wran—A Lawyer Politician—Reflections of Law Reform and the High Court of Australia', Inaugural Neville Wran Lecture, Parliament of New South Wales, Thursday 13 November 2008 (published online 13 November 2008), available at: <http://www.nswbar.asn.au/circulars/november08/wran.pdf> (accessed 14 November 2008).

Kirs, Eszter, 'Talking with Géza Herczegh, former Hungarian Judge of the International Court of Justice' *Miskolc Journal of International Law* 1(2) (2004) 317–20.

Kuijer, Martin, 'Voting Behaviour and National Bias in the European Court of Human Rights and the International Court of Justice' *Leiden Journal of International Law* 10(1) (1997) 49–67.

Lachs, Manfred, 'A Few Thoughts on the Independence of Judges of the International Court of Justice' *Columbia Journal of Transnational Law* 25(3) (1987) 593–600.

—— 'Some Reflections on the Nationality of Judges of the International Court of Justice' *Pace Yearbook of International Law* 4 (1992) 49–68.

Lauterpacht, Elihu, 'The Composition of Tribunals' in *Aspects of the Administration of International Justice*, Hersch Lauterpacht Memorial Lectures (No. 9) (Cambridge: Grotius Publications Limited, 1991) 77–98.

—— 'The Role of *Ad Hoc* Judges: Presentation by Professor Elihu Lauterpacht' in Connie Peck and Roy S. Lee (eds), *Increasing the Effectiveness of the International Court of Justice: Proceedings of the ICJ/UNITAR Colloquium to Celebrate the 50th Anniversary of the Court* (The Hague: Kluwer Law International, 1997) 371–8.

—— 'The International Lawyer as Judge' in Chanaka Wickremasinghe, *The International Lawyer as Practitioner* (London: British Institute of International and Comparative Law, 2000) 125–44.

Lauterpacht, Hersch, 'The Revision of the Statute of the International Court of Justice' *The Law and Practice of International Courts and Tribunals* 1(1) (2002) 55–128.

—— *International Law: Being the Collected Papers of Hersch Lauterpacht*, vol. V, *Disputes, War and Neutrality, Parts IX–XIV*, edited by Elihu Lauterpacht (Cambridge: Cambridge University Press, 2004).

Lavelle, Roberto, 'Nationality as a Factor in the Election of the Members of the International Court of Justice, with Particular Reference to Occasional Elections' *Revue belge de droit international* 29(2) (1996) 625–32.

Lawyers Committee for Human Rights, *LCHR's Chart Showing Gender and Regional Balance in Elections to International Courts and Tribunals*, (n.d. [c. 2003]), available at: <http://www.humanrightsfirst.org/international_justice/icc/election/judges_gender_region_040303.pdf> (accessed 23 November 2007).

Lee, Edward G., and Edward McWhinney, 'The 1987 Elections to the International Court of Justice' *Canadian Yearbook of International Law* 25 (1987) 379–88.

Lee, Matthew Russell, 'At UN, Election of ICJ Judges is Archaic, Somali and French Electioneering', 6 November 2008, available at: <http://www.innercitypress.com/gasc1icj110608.html> (accessed 18 December 2008).

Lee, Roy S., 'Introduction' in Roy S. Lee (ed), *The International Criminal Court: The Making of the Rome Statute: Issues, Negotiations, Results* (The Hague: Kluwer Law International, 1999) 1–39.

Lee-Brago, Pia, 'Miriam stands a good chance of winning ICJ seat—sources' *The Philippine Star* (published online 26 October 2008), available at: <http://www.philstar.com/Article.aspx?articleid=410172> (accessed 10 November 2008).

Leigh, Monroe, and Stephen D. Ramsey, 'Confidence in the Court: It Need Not Be a "Hollow Chamber" ', in Lori F. Damrosch (ed), *The International Court of Justice at a Crossroads* (Dobbs Ferry, New York: Transnational Publishers Inc., 1987) 106–22.

Lim Ubac, Michael, 'Santiago Blames "Power Game" ' *Philippine Daily Inquirer*, 8 November 2008, available at: <http://globalnation.inquirer.net/news/breakingnews/view/ 20081108–171051/Sant> (accessed 12 November 2008).

Limbach, Jutta et al, *Judicial Independence: Law and Practice of Appointments to the European Court of Human Rights* (London: INTERIGHTS, May 2003).

Linehan, Jan, 'Women and Public International Litigation: Background Paper Prepared for the Project on International Courts and Tribunals' (2001), available at: <http://www.pict-pcti.org/publications/PICT_articles/Women1.pdf> (accessed 20 August 2006).

Lord Hoffman, 'The Universality of Human Rights', Judicial Studies Board Annual Lecture, 19 March 2009, available at: <http://www.jsboard.co.uk/downloads/Hoffmann_2009_JSB_Annual_Lecture_Universality_of_Human_Rights.doc> (accessed 20 March 2009).

Mackenzie, Ruth and Philippe Sands, 'International Courts and Tribunals and the Independence of the International Judge' *Harvard International Law Journal* 44(1) (Winter 2003) 271–85.

—— 'Judicial Selection for International Courts: Towards Common Principles and Practices' in Kate Malleson and Peter H. Russell (eds), *Appointing Judges in an Age of Judicial Power: Critical Perspectives from Around the World* (Toronto: University of Toronto Press, 2006) 213–37.

McLachlin, Beverley, 'Why We Need Women Judges', International Association of Women Judges 8th Biennial Conference, 3–7 May 2006, Sydney, Australia, available at: <http://www.iawj.org/what/Session4BMcLachlin.doc> (accessed 20 November 2008).

McWhinney, Edward, 'Law, Politics and "Regionalism" in the Nomination and Election of World Court Judges' *Syracuse Journal of International Law and Commerce* 31(1) (1986) 1–28.

—— *The International Court of Justice and the Western Tradition of International Law* (Dordrecht: Martinus Nijhoff, 1987).

—— 'The Contemporary International Court as Independent, and as Representative Tribunal' in Edward McWhinney, *Judicial Settlement of International Disputes: Jurisdiction, Justiciability, and Judical Law-making on the Contemporary International Court* (Dordrecht: Kluwer, 1991) 123–53.

—— 'The International Court of Justice and International Law-making: The Judicial Activism/Self-Restraint Antinomy' *Chinese Journal of International Law* 5(1) (2006) 3–13.

McWhinney, Edward, and Serge April, 'The 1990 Triennial Elections to the International Court of Justice and the 1989 Casual Election' *Canadian Yearbook of International Law* 28 (1990) 403–16.

Malleson, Kate, 'Assessing the Performance of the South African Judicial Service Commission' *South African Law Journal* 116(1) (1999) 36–49.

—— 'Creating a Judicial Appointments Commission: Which Model Works Best?' *Public Law* (Spring 2004) 102–21.

—— 'Rethinking the Merit Principle in Judicial Selection' *Journal of Law and Society* 33(1) (2006) 126–40.

—— 'Parliamentary scrutiny of Supreme Court nominees: A view from the UK' *Osgoode Hall Law Journal* 44(3) (Fall 2006) 557–64.

—— 'Promoting Judicial Independence in the International Courts: Lessons from the Caribbean' *International and Comparative Law Quarterly* 58(3) (July 2009) 671–97.

Malleson, Kate, and Peter H. Russell (eds), *Appointing Judges in an Age of Judicial Power: Critical Perspectives from Around the World* (Toronto: University of Toronto Press, 2006).

Marín-Bosch, Miguel, *Votes in the UN General Assembly*, Nijhoff Law Specials, vol. 35 (The Hague: Kluwer Law International, 1998).

Marston, Geoffrey, 'The London Committee and the Statute of the International Court of Justice' in Vaughan Lowe and Malgosia Fitzmaurice (eds), *Fifty Years of the International Court of Justice: Essays in Honour of Sir Robert Jennings* (Cambridge: Cambridge University Press, 1996) 40–60.

Ministry of Foreign Affairs of Japan, 'Press Release: Election of Ms. Fumiko Saiga, Ambassador in Charge of Human Rights and Member of the Committee on the Elimination of All Forms of Discrimination against Women (CEDAW), as Judge of the International Criminal Court (ICC)' (published online 1 December 2007), available at: <http://www.mofa.go.jp/announce/announce/2007/12/1176491_840.html> (accessed 25 September 2008).

—— 'Press Release: Nomination of Ms. Fumiko Saiga, Judge of the International Criminal Court (ICC)' (published online 23 May 2008), available at: <http://www.mofa.go.jp/announce/announce/2008/5/1180269_1010.html> (accessed 25 September 2008).

Moore, John Bassett, *History and Digest of the International Arbitrations to Which the United States Has Been a Party*, vol. 1 (Washington, Government Printing Office, 1898).

Mowbray, Alastair, 'The Consideration of Gender in the Process of Appointing Judges to the European Court of Human Rights' *Human Rights Law Review* 8(3) (2008) 549–59.

Mundis, Daryl A., 'The Election of *Ad Litem* Judges and Other Recent Developments at the International Criminal Tribunals' *Leiden Journal of International Law* 14(4) (2001) 851–66.

O'Boyle, Michael, 'On Reforming the Operation of the European Court of Human Rights' *European Human Rights Law Review* 1 (2008) 1–11.

Odinkalu, Chidi Anselm, 'How the Judges of the African Court Emerged,' 31 January 2006, available at: <http://allafrica.com/stories/200601310508.html> (accessed 12 July 2006).

Orrego Vicuña, Francisco and Christopher Pinto, 'Peaceful Settlement of Disputes. Prospects for the 21st Century: Revised Report Prepared for the Centennial of the First International Peace Conference, 1999' in Frits Kalshoven (ed), *The Centennial of the First International Peace Conference* (The Hague: Kluwer Law International, 2000) 261–416.

Parliamentary Assembly of the Council of Europe, Committee on Legal Affairs and Human Rights, 'Report: Nomination of candidates and election of judges to the European Court of Human Rights', 1 December 2008, Doc. 11767, available at: <http://www.assembly.coe.int/Main.asp?link=/Documents/WorkingDocs/Doc08/EDOC11767.htm> (accessed 18 September 2009).

Pasqualucci, Jo M., 'Sonia Picardo, First Woman Judge on the Inter-American Court of Human Rights' *Human Rights Quarterly* 17(4) (1995) 794–806.

Pauwelyn, Joost, 'La sélection des juges à l'OMC, et peut-être celle d'un Chinois, mérite plus d'attention', *Le Temps, Economie & Finance* 16 November 2007, available at: <http://www.letemps.ch/Page/Uuid/d4952ece-ac44-11dd-bf59-ad3d6140ad87%7C2> (accessed 22 April 2009).

Peters, Winston, 'Sir Kenneth Keith ICJ election welcomed—Peters' (published online 8 November 2005), available at: <http://www.beehive.govt.nz/node/24329> (accessed 27 April 2009).

Plender, Richard, 'Rules of Procedure in the International Court and the European Court' *European Journal of International Law* 2(2) (1991) 1–30.

Posner, Eric A., 'The International Court of Justice: Voting and Usage Statistics' *American Society of International Law Proceedings* 99 (2005) 130–32.

—— 'The Decline of the International Court of Justice' in Stefan Voigt, Max Albert, and Dieter Schmidtchen (eds), *International Conflict Resolution* (Tübingen: Mohr Siebeck, 2006) 111–42.

—— and Michael F.P. de Figueiredo, 'Is the International Court of Justice Biased?' *Journal of Legal Studies* 34(2) (2005) 599–630.

—— and John C. Yoo, 'Judicial Independence in International Tribunals' *California Law Review* 93(1) (2005) 1–74.

—— 'Reply to Helfer and Slaughter' *California Law Review* 93(3) (2005) 957–74.

Pozen, David E., 'The Irony of Judicial Elections' *Colombia Law Review* 108(2) (2008) 265–330.

Prott, Lyndel, *The Latent Power of Culture and the International Judge* (Abingdon: Professional Books, 1979).

Reisman, W. Michael, 'Redesigning the United Nations' *Singapore Journal of International and Comparative Law* 1(1) (1997) 1–27.

Republic of the Philippines Department of Foreign Affairs, 'Press Release: Senator Santiago Puts Up Good Fight in Bid for Seat in ICJ', PR-643-08 (published online 7 November 2008), available at: <http://dfa.gov.ph/?p=1310> (accessed 24 April 2009).

Resnik, Judith, 'Judicial Selection and Democratic Theory: Demand, Supply, and Life Tenure' *Cardozo Law Review* 26(2) (2005) 579–658.

Reut-Nicolussi, Eduard, 'The Reform of the Permanent Court of International Justice', *Transactions of the Grotius Society, Problems of Peace and War, Papers Read before the Society in the Year 1939*, 25 (1939) 135–49.

Robinson, Davis R., 'The Role of Politics in the Election and the Work of Judges of the International Court of Justice' *American Society of International Law Proceedings* 97 (2003) 277–82.

Romano, Cesare P. R., 'The Judges and Prosecutors of Internationalized Criminal Courts and Tribunals' in Cesare P. R. Romano, André Nollkaemper, and Jann K. Kleffner (eds), *Internationalized Criminal Courts and Tribunals: Sierra Leone, East Timor, Kosovo, and Cambodia*, International Courts and Tribunals Series (Oxford: Oxford University Press, 2004) 235–70.

Romero, Paolo, 'GMA to Campaign for Miriam in ICJ Bid During New York Visit' (published online 23 June 2008), available at: <http://www.philstar.com/Article.aspx?articleid=69101> (accessed 21 August 2008).

Rosenne, Shabtai, 'The Composition of the Court' in Leo Gross (ed), *The Future of the International Court of Justice*, vol. I (Dobbs Ferry, New York: Oceana Publications, 1976) 377–441.

—— 'Elections of Members of the International Court of Justice: Late Nominations and Withdrawals of Candidacies' *American Journal of International Law* 70(3) (1976) 543–9.

—— 'The 1981 Occasional Elections to Fill Two Vacancies on the International Court of Justice' *American Journal of International Law* 75(2) (1981) 349–61.

—— 'Election of Five Members of the International Court of Justice in 1981' *American Journal of International Law* 76(2) (1982) 364–70.

—— 'The Election of March 1982 to Fill One Vacancy in the International Court of Justice' *American Journal of International Law* 76(4) (1982) 863–6.

—— 'Establishing the International Tribunal for the Law of the Sea' *American Journal of International Law* 89(4) (1995) 806–14.

—— (ed), *The Hague Peace Conferences of 1899 and 1907 and International Arbitration: Reports and Documents* (The Hague: T.M.C. Asser, 2001).

—— *Rosenne's The World Court: What It Is and How It Works*, Legal Aspects of International Organization Series No. 41, edited by Terry D. Gill (6th revised edn, Leiden: Martinus Nijhoff, 2003).

—— *The Law and Practice of the International Court, 1920–2005*, vol. I: *The Court and the United Nations* (4th edn, The Hague: Martinus Nijhoff, 2006).

Rozenburg, Joshua, 'Choosing Lawyers Who Will Judge the World' *Daily Telegraph* 6 February 2003, available at: <http://www.telegraph.co.uk/news/uknews/1421206/Choosing-lawyers-who-will-judge-the-world.html> (accessed 1 December 2006).

—— 'Brief Encounters', *Daily Telegraph*, 4 January 2008, available at: <http://www.telegraph.co.uk/news/uknews/1574378/Brief-encounters.html> (accessed 15 December 2008).

Rudzinski, Aleksander W., 'Election Procedure in the United Nations' *American Journal of International Law* 53(1) (1959) 81–111.

Rufo, Aries C., 'RP Faces Tough Challenge in ICJ Campaign for Santiago' (published online 23 May 2008), available at: <http://www.abs-cbnnews.com/nation/05/23/08/rp-faces-tough-challenge-icj-campaign-santiago> (accessed 27 July 2008).

Rwelamira, Medard R., 'Composition and Administration of the Court' in Roy S. Lee (ed), *The International Criminal Court: The Making of the Rome Statute: Issues, Negotiations, Results* (The Hague: Kluwer Law International/UNITAR, 1999) 153–73.

Sands, Philippe, 'Global Governance and the International Judiciary: Choosing Our Judges' *Current Legal Problems* 56 (2003) 481–504.

—— Ruth Mackenzie, and Yuval Shany (eds), *Manual on International Courts and Tribunals* (London: Butterworths, 1999).

—— Campbell McLachlan, and Ruth Mackenzie, 'The Burgh House Principles on the Independence of the International Judiciary' *The Law and Practice of International Courts and Tribunals* 4(2) (2005) 247–60.

Schachter, Oscar, 'The Invisible College of International Lawyers' *Northwestern University Law Review* 72(2) (1977) 217–26.

Scharf, Michael P., 'The Politics of Establishing an International Criminal Court' *Duke Journal of Comparative and International Law* 6(1) (1995) 167–74.

Schermers, Henry G., 'Election of Judges to the European Court of Human Rights' European Law Review 23(6) (1998) 568–78.

Schiff, Benjamin N., *Building the International Criminal Court* (Cambridge: Cambridge University Press, 2008).

Schwebel, Stephen M., 'Ad Hoc Chambers of the International Court of Justice' *American Journal of International Law* 81(4) (1987) 831–54.

—— 'Relations Between the International Court of Justice and the United Nations', in *Le Droit international au service de la paix, de la justice et du développement: Mélanges Michel Virally* (Paris: A. Pedone, October 1991) 431–43.

—— 'National Judges and Judges Ad Hoc of the International Court of Justice' *International and Comparative Law Quarterly* 48(4) (1999) 889–900.

Scott, James Brown, 'The Election of Judges for the Permanent Court of International Justice' *American Journal of International Law* 15(4) (1921) 556–8.

Senate of the Philippines 14th Congress, 'Press Release: July 30, 2007: Transcript of Interview with Senator Miriam Defensor Santiago' (published online 30 July 2007), available at: <http://www.senate.gov.ph/press_release/2007/0730_santiago1.asp> (accessed 28 October 2008).

Simamba, Bilika H., 'Appointment and Term of Office of Judges of International Courts: Innovations from Africa?' *Commonwealth Law Bulletin* 34(3) (2008) 515–25.

Simma, Bruno (ed), *The Charter of the United Nations: A Commentary*, 2 vols (2nd edn, New York: Oxford University Press, 2002).

Simons, Marlise, 'An American with Opinions Steps Down Vocally at War Crimes Court' *New York Times* 24 January 2002.

Simpson, J. L., 'The 1960 Elections to the International Court of Justice' *British Yearbook of International Law* 37 (1961) 527–35.

Sinclair, Ian, *The International Law Commission*, Hersch Lauterpacht Memorial Lectures (No. 7) (Cambridge: Grotius Publications Limited, 1987).

Skubiszewski, Krzysztof, 'The Role of *Ad Hoc* Judges: Commentary by Professor Krzysztof Skubiszewski' in Connie Peck and Roy S. Lee (eds), *Increasing the Effectiveness of the International Court of Justice: Proceedings of the ICJ/UNITAR Colloquium to Celebrate the 50th Anniversary of the Court* (The Hague: Kluwer Law International, 1997) 378–84.

Slaughter, Anne-Marie, 'A Global Community of Courts' *Harvard International Law Journal* 44(1) (2003), 191.

Smith, Adam M., '"Judicial Nationalism" in International Law: National Identity and Judicial Autonomy at the ICJ' *Texas International Law Journal* 40(2) (2005) 197–232.

Spees, Pam, 'Women's Advocacy in the Creation of the International Criminal Court: Changing the Landscapes of Justice and Power' *Signs* 28(4) (Summer, 2003) 1233–54.

Spiermann, Ole, *International Legal Argument in the Permanent Court of International Justice: The Rise of the International Judiciary,* Cambridge Studies in International and Comparative Law Series No. 34 (Cambridge: Cambridge University Press, 2005).

Starke, J. D., 'Rules and Procedure Governing Election of Judges of International Court of Justice' *Australian Law Journal* 52(4) (1978) 230–32.

—— 'Nomination by the Australian National Group of Candidates for Election to the International Court of Justice' *Australian Law Journal* 52(7) (1978) 396–7.

—— 'Nominations by the Australian National Group of Candidates for Election to the International Court of Justice' *Australian Law Journal* 53(3) (1979) 115–16.

Steains, Cate, 'Gender Issues', Roy S. Lee (ed), *The International Criminal Court: The Making of the Rome Statute: Issues, Negotiations, Results* (The Hague: Kluwer Law International, 1999) 357–90.

Stephen, Chris, 'Women Judges Dominate World's New War Crimes Court' *Guardian* 9 February 2003, available at: <http://www.guardian.co.uk/world/2003/feb/09/warcrimes> (accessed 12 November 2008).

Study Group of the International Law Association on the Practice and Procedure of International Courts and Tribunals and the Project on International Courts and Tribunals, *The Burgh House Principles on the Independence of the International Judiciary* (n.d.), available at: <http://www.ucl.ac.uk/laws/cict/docs/burgh_final_21204.pdf> (accessed 2 December 2008).

Sturgess, Gary and Philip Chubb, *Judging the World: Law and Politics in the World's Leading Courts* (Sydney: Butterworths, 1988).

Suh, Il Ro, 'Voting Behavior of National Judges in International Courts' *American Journal of International Law* 63(2) (1969) 224–36.

Sutherland, Peter et al, *Future of the WTO: Addressing Institutional Challenges in the New Millennium*, Report by the Consultative Board to the Director-General Supachai Panitchpakdi (Geneva: World Trade Organization, 2004).

Sy, Marvin, 'Arroyo nominates Miriam to International Court of Justice' *Philippine Star* (published online 31 July 2007), available at: <http://www.philstar.com/Article.aspx?articleId=9559> (accessed 20 October 2007).

Ten Brinke, Daniel, and Hans-Michale Deml (eds), *Judges in the Service of the State? Procedures, Criteria and Political Influence on National Selection of Judges for the Highest Judicial Offices and their Possible Influence on the International Criminal Court* (Aachen: Shaker Verlag, 2002).

Terris, Daniel, Cesare P. R. Romano, and Leigh Swigart, *The International Judge: An Introduction to the Men and Women Who Decide the World's Cases,* International Courts and Tribunals Series (Oxford: Oxford University Press, 2007).

Thirlway, Hugh, 'The Drafting of ICJ Decisions: Some Personal Recollections and Observations' *Chinese Journal of International Law* 5(1) (2006) 15–28.

Tomuschat, Christian, 'National Representation of Judges and Legitimacy of International Jurisdictions: Lessons from ICJ to ECJ?' in Ingolf Pernice, Juliane Kokott, and Cheryl Saunders (eds), *The Future of the European Judicial System in a Comparative Perspective* (Baden-Baden: Nomos, 2006) 183–90.

Tridimas, Takis, 'The European Court of Justice and the Draft Constitution: A Supreme Court for the Union?' in Takis Tridimas and Paolisa Nebbia (eds), *European Union Law for the Twenty-First Century: Rethinking the New Legal Order* (Oxford: Hart Publishing, 2004) 113–141.

Tunnah, Helen, 'NZ Knight Elected Judge of the World's Top Court', *New Zealand Herald*, 9 November 2005, available at: <http://www.nzherald.co.nz/nz/news/article.cfm?c_id=1&objectid=10354326> (accessed 27 April 2009).

Valencia-Ospina, Eduardo, 'Editorial Comment' Law and Practice of International Courts and Tribunals 1(1) (2002) 1–12.

Van Den Hout, Tjaco T., 'The Permanent Court of Arbitration: Responding to a Century of Globalization', *International Law FORUM Du Droit International*, 2(4) (2000) 235–41.

Voeten, Erik, 'The Politics of International Judicial Appointments: Evidence from the European Court of Human Rights' *International Organization* 61(4) (2007) 669–701.

—— 'The Politics of International Judicial Appointments' *Chicago Journal of International Law* 9(2) (Winter 2009) 387–406.

Wald, Patricia M., 'The International Criminal Tribunal for the Former Yugoslavia Comes of Age: Some Observations on Day-To-Day Dilemmas of an International Court' *Journal of Law & Policy* 5 (2001) 87–123.

Waldock, Humphrey, 'The International Court of Justice as Seen from Bar and Bench' *British Yearbook of International Law* 54 (1983) 1–5.

'Wanted: Better Judgment, Fewer Crowd-Pleasers and Lickspittles' *The Economist* 20 November 2008.

Wen-qi, Zhu, and Sureta Chana, 'Article 36: Qualifications, Nomination and Election of Judges', in Otto Triffterer (ed), *Commentary on the Rome Statute of the International Criminal Court: Observers' Notes, Article by Article* (2nd revised edn, Oxford: Hart Publishing, 2008) 941–8.

Women's Initiatives for Gender Justice, *Profile of Judicial Candidates: Election November 2007* (November 2007), available at: <http://www.iccwomen.org/news/docs/Judges dossier2007.pdf> (accessed 5 December 2007).

—— *Profile of Judicial Candidates: Election—JANUARY 2009* (10 November 2008), available at: <http://www.iccwomen.org/news/docs/Profile_of_Judicial_Candidates-Web_Final.pdf> (accessed 5 December 2008).

Wood, Michael, 'The Selection of Candidates for International Judicial Office: Recent Practice' in Tafsir Malick Ndiaye and Rüdiger Wolfrum (eds), *Law of the Sea, Environmental Law and Settlement of Disputes: Liber Amicorum Judge Thomas A. Mensah* (The Hague: Martinus Nijhoff Publishers, 2007) 357–68.

World Trade Organization, 'Press Release—WTO appoints four new Appellate Body members', 27 November 2007, available at: <http://www.wto.int/english/news_e/pres07_e/pr501_e.htm> (accessed 12 November 2008).

Yankov, Alexander, 'The International Tribunal for the Law of the Sea and the Comprehensive Dispute Settlement System of the Law of the Sea' in P. Chandrasekhara Rao and Rahmatullah Khan (eds), *The International Tribunal for the Law of the Sea: Law and Practice* (The Hague: Kluwer Law International, 2001) 33–47.

Index

The manufacturer's authorised representative in the EU for product safety is Oxford University Press España S.A. of El Parque Empresarial San Fernando de Henares, Avenida de Castilla, 2 - 28830 Madrid (www.oup.es/en or product.safety@oup.com). OUP España S.A. also acts as importer into Spain of products made by the manufacturer.
Printed and bound by CPI Group (UK) Ltd, Croydon, CR0 4YY
14/09/2026
02216308-0010